BREWER ST
LIBRARY
TUSCALOOSA CENTER

W9-BYY-391

H
91
.G37

Gastil, Raymond D.

Social humanities

DISCARDED

DATE			

© THE BAKER & TAYLOR CO.

BREWER STATE JR. COLLEGE
LIBRARY
TUSCALOOSA CENTER

SOCIAL
HUMANITIES

Toward an
Integrative Discipline
of Science and Values

BREWER STATE JR. COLLEGE
LIBRARY
TUSCALOOSA CENTER

Raymond D. Gastil

SOCIAL
HUMANITIES

DISCARDED

Jossey-Bass Publishers
San Francisco • Washington • London • 1977

SOCIAL HUMANITIES
Toward an Integrative Discipline of Science and Values
by Raymond D. Gastil

Copyright © 1977 by: Jossey-Bass, Inc., Publishers
615 Montgomery Street
San Francisco, California 94111
&
Jossey-Bass Limited
44 Hatton Garden
London ECIN 8ER

Copyright under International, Pan American, and
Universal Copyright Conventions. All rights
reserved. No part of this book may be reproduced
in any form—except for brief quotation (not to
exceed 1,000 words) in a review or professional
work—without permission in writing from the publishers.

Library of Congress Catalogue Card Number LC 76-52580

International Standard Book Number ISBN 0-87589-318-X

Manufactured in the United States of America

JACKET DESIGN BY WILLI BAUM

FIRST EDITION

Code 7716

The Jossey-Bass
Behavioral Science Series

Preface

   The following analysis was engendered by personal experi-ence with trying to analyze problems in national and international policy on the basis of a background in social science. After spending several years studying and teaching in an academic environment, an experience that included degrees in area studies and social science as well as three years of teaching anthropology, I came to the Hudson Institute (a small, contract-research organization) in 1962 to apply my abilities to a variety of national defense and social problems. Almost immediately, I found that there were very few instances in which these years of study could be made relevant to the problems of the real world. Many social scientists in this environment act as though their specialities will solve the problems society faces—but generally they fool only themselves. Of course, social science tools, such as polling or experiment design, are useful in establishing the facts for policy analysis, but aside from such pure empiricism, the traditional social sciences produce little useful generalization.

   This fact bothered me, but in the rush of analysis it was for-gotten for the next few years. Yet I did notice that most studies at the institute were based on a common scheme of generalization that might be described as an institutionalized and historically informed common sense theory about what individuals and groups do under varying circumstances. Insofar as the theory derived from a social science, it was from market economics, which posits a rational man pursuing his interests through calculation and bargaining. As I will point out in Chapters Two and Three, I regard this common sense theory as largely correct. Yet it is important to know the limits and conditions of the theory, and we did not.

As time passed, I also noticed that the theoretical simplicity of the institute's work weakened its contribution in two respects. First, there was little accumulation; one study did not build on those that went before. Switching rapidly from subject to subject, we always started at the same point. This was a good way to produce quick results, but it seemed as though we should be growing intellectually, and we were not. Second, I noticed that the institute's work was disassociated from the vast mass of academic social science. One result was that institute analysts could seldom profit from social science when they needed help. On the other hand, when institute work was on the right track, it was hard for it to be translated in such a way as to contribute to the larger world of research.

During years of policy analysis at the Hudson Institute, it also became evident that the ostensible disputes of policy analysts were frequently smoke screens concealing much more fundamental differences, differences seldom discussed because few had either the evidence or argument to address these more fundamental levels, and because the consumers of analysis had no patience for such discourse. So on each side of each issue the opposing forces continued to marshal their facts and to go forth to do verbal battle. However, the resulting discussions were seldom decisive, for the real issues were only obscured by the facts. Differing assumptions about the nature of man, about the possibilities of human action, and about preferable hierarchies of values were the driving forces behind such debates as those over nuclear strategy, civil defense, the Vietnam War, the "War on Poverty," gambling laws, or the energy crisis. And after a while the futility of marshaling superficial facts, as though they would make a difference, became oppressive. I am not disparaging facts, for when the context of supporting assumptions is held constant, they are decisive. But today that context is seldom constant (and, as I point out in the appendix, this is related to other and more basic problems in our civilization).

Before coming to Hudson, I was well aware that there were two groups of people calling themselves social scientists. Those in one group mixed ideology and research so openly and thoroughly that their work, even that purporting to be empirical, could not be relied on. Those in the other, and much larger, group pursued a natural scientific ideal no matter what the subject matter, nor how often they failed. Their work may not have often been useful in Hudson analyses, but at least it could be looked on as a solid achievement and referred to with some confidence whenever connections between its findings and a practical issue could be drawn out. However, when on leaving Hudson I had an opportunity to deal more directly with social science, I noticed that the pressure of the 1960s to make social science more immediately useful and disillusion with the usefulness of the careful social science of the preceding generation had led to an alarming shift away from the acceptance of the natural scientific ideal. If this trend continued, the work of the next generation purporting to be social science would be generally suspect even in its empirical foundation. This descientizing of social science was surely not the way to make it serve policy.

The concept of social humanities, then, was developed to overcome the inadequacies in social science that I saw at Hudson, without destroying the scientific base of the social sciences themselves. It was also developed in an attempt to go beyond the superficiality of ad hoc analysis as developed at Hudson, while preserving the important strain of common sense that I had found there.

However, I should warn the reader that the concept of social humanities has come, in my mind, to have purposes that go quite beyond those that gave birth to it. On one level, as a contribution to policy discussion, this book strives to present a coherent methodology for relating knowledge to action, for searching out the probable course of human affairs, and for balancing values as we judge the desirability of that course. It presents a vision of a more comprehensive approach to the analysis of policy, of what is to be done, in individual and organizational life. But on another level, as a contribution to humane discourse, this book is an attempt to provide a framework within which we can make sense of the human world, relate in a comprehensible manner the plethora of bits and pieces of knowledge that each of us has, and start to overcome the meaningless of existence that paradoxically grows with the accumulation of knowledge over generations and with the aging of each generation. The problem of the dissolution of meaning and the responsibility of the intellectual to make an integrative response to this problem are considered in the appendix, but the reader should note that this issue concerns the book as a whole.

This book begins with a general argument for developing an area of analysis that I call the *social humanities*. It then moves, in Chapters Two through Four, to consider the fundamental assumptions of one "school" of explanation that might be developed within social humanities. Chapter Five considers the methodological issues of carrying through analysis in terms of this school and provides a number of examples. Chapters Six, Seven, and Eight provide more detailed examples of the application of this approach. Chapter Nine returns to the question of restoring meaning to individual life. Chapter Ten completes the argument by suggesting how social humanities might be institutionalized.

Although the present book summarizes a wide variety of previous influences, without the generous support and encouragement of the Battelle Memorial Institute over a period of years, this book would not have been written. The excellent support staff at Batelle's Seattle Research Center and the persistent interest of Everett Irish in social humanities should also be singled out. Professionally, I was greatly helped by the advice of Gordon Bermant, Gerald Dworkin, Peter Brown, and Lauren Wispe, former colleagues in Seattle, as well as by the detailed criticism of the manuscript by Nathan Glazer of Harvard University and Robert Jervis of the University of California, Los Angeles. Finally, a broader and deeper debt is owed to Pitirim Sorokin, Clyde Kluckhohn, Homer Barnett, Herman Kahn, and Alfred Kuhn—without them, also, this book would never have been written.

Seattle, Washington   RAYMOND D. GASTIL
March 1977

Contents

xiii

The Author

RAYMOND D. GASTIL grew up in Southern California, but received his education, including an A.B. in Social Relations, an A.M. in Middle Eastern Studies, and in 1958 a Ph.D. in an interdisciplinary program in Social Science, from Harvard University.

Gastil spent 1958–1959 at the Harvard Center for International Affairs as a research associate studying intercultural communication problems relevant to foreign aid programs. In the period 1959–1962 he taught anthropology and social science, including the study of the peoples of the Middle East and Central Asia, at the University of Oregon. While an employee member of the Hudson Institute from 1962–1969 Gastil conducted policy studies in a wide variety of fields, including national security, poverty, and population. During this period he contributed to *The Year 2000* (1967), co-authored *Can We Win in Vietnam?* (1968), and contributed two chapters to *Why ABM?* (1969).

At Battelle Seattle (1969–1976), and freed from contractual demands, Gastil pursued basic research on a number of problems. These included a study of variations by region in American society and culture and the related question of quality of civilization. This work culminated in the publication of *Cultural Regions of the*

United States (1975), and co-authorship of a manuscript on civilization in the Pacific Northwest. In Seattle Gastil also engaged in several studies for Hudson Institute, including an analysis of the social responsibility of business. Throughout his professional career, the concept of social humanities was emerging as a means to tie together the diverse approaches that are necessary to understand and evaluate the nature and possibilities of human life.

Currently, Gastil is a private consultant, working primarily on the improvement of the international Comparative Survey of Freedom, which he has developed during the last few years as an annual report for Freedom House.

Social Humanities is dedicated to my wife,
Jeannette, and to Leila and Raymond

SOCIAL HUMANITIES

Toward an Integrative Discipline of Science and Values

ONE

Social Humanities: Defining a Discipline

With the rise to eminence and influence of scientists in recent years, the distinction between scientific judgment and the judgment of scientists has been increasingly blurred.[1] In particular, the meaning and definition of the social sciences and of their auxiliary or applied disciplines have become confused. On the one hand, several value-centered undertakings, such as policy analysis and planning, have laid claim to status as sciences, while on the other hand, more and more social scientists have attacked the legitimacy or reasonableness of the goal of value-free social science. Scientific publicists further confuse the discussion by arguing for the discovery of a value-free, scientific basis for society in which applied science equals policy. The result has been to damage the effectiveness of both scientific and nonscientific efforts and to confuse the relationship of their activities in the minds of those who regularly cross a variety of scientific and nonscientific boundaries.

Social humanities is proposed in this chapter as a discipline, complementary to the social sciences, that will help to preserve and strengthen both scientific and nonscientific analysis. It is also hoped that as an integrative approach, social humanities will provide a framework for thinking about a wide range of personal and social problems in a disciplined manner.

The Challenge to Value-free Social Science

Science is the attempt to establish knowledge that is commonly agreed on by a community of knowledgable persons in terms of the results of rational and empirical tests. While conflicting explanations of common events are continually noted by outside laymen, conflicts exist generally in specified areas and on the basis of layer upon layer of consensus, the results of the resolved controversies of previous generations. For as Ziman (1968, pp. 1-29; see also Friedrichs, 1970, p. 206) points out, the goal of science is to achieve a publicly acknowledged consensus of those with rational, critical, and informed opinions. In most cases, its findings are generalizable and predictive, if only in the sense of productive taxonomic schemes. It is a mistake to confuse methodology with science or to see science only in those activities that approach the numerical and quantifiable (see Cicourel, 1964, especially p. 4). When the historian goes beyond his particularities to develop the bits and pieces of a theory of history, insofar as he uses rational and empirical methods, he is acting as a scientist, no matter how far his work may fall short of achieving scientific consensus.

Instead of going further into the thorny area of acceptable social science methodology within the scientific framework, in this chapter I will only assert the following: (1) Many social scientists strive to act in accordance with the basic norms of science that I have described and so are as "scientific" as anyone; (2) the more interesting general problems in social science are those where consensus seems furthest away; (3) social scientists are apt to care deeply about these general problems and are expected to have scientific knowledge about them; and (4) some social scientists, led by the tension between the second and third points, abandon both the restraints of rational-empirical argument and the search for consensus, without making clear that they no longer speak as scientists.

There are, of course, a variety of reasons why the social sciences lead to consistent deviations from the goal of objectivity. First, they are generally "loose" sciences, in the sense that the real world does not produce sufficiently replicable social situations for social laws to be meaningful. Social reality is too rich, and attempts to break it down take too much away (Garfinkel, 1967, pp. 2–3). Of course, physical reality is also rich. Perhaps the difference is that we can purify reality in the natural sciences for purposes of testing and application in a way we cannot in the social sciences. In particular, one can point to the prevailing lack of social units for the purpose of measurement or patterning. Another branch of this critique is the suggestion that human beings are inherently limited in the degree they can understand human nature and society, because human beings cannot stand outside their phenomena, nor can they study these phenomena without changing them. It may also be argued that it is impossible to understand a subject matter, such as man, to which the investigator is not intellectually superior. These limits are sometimes spelled out in arguments concerning the sociology of knowledge or the culturology of knowledge.

Perhaps the most succinct presentation of the inevitable limits of social science is provided by the philosopher Peter Winch (1958, pp. 50–92). He points out that human behavior is different in kind from prehuman behavior, because it is directed by the meanings attached to it. Winch points out that only social scientists have to be concerned whether their analytic categories correspond to the analytic categories of their subjects. Because of this concern, social sciences are the only sciences that are not arbitrarily improvable. For example, a social scientist has to be sensitive to how a person classifies himself in class terms. Even though a person objectively belongs to a different class than the one he identifies with, his subjective class identification may determine his action. Winch also explains that only in social science could a correct prediction be wrong in the event because the subject changed his mind. If a subject had a decision to make, he must have had a choice; if so, he can change his mind. (This issue will be discussed at greater length when we consider free will at the end of Chapter Two.)

Less serious than the judgment of the inevitable limits on the effectiveness of social science is the accusation that the selection of what to study is determined by values, for to a lesser extent this is true of the natural sciences as well. The worst result of such determination should be a certain jerkiness of growth and overall reduced progress. Although, as Blumer (1971; see also Manis, 1974) points out, the definition of social problems lies outside of science; if the resulting study of these problems is scientific, the results should lead to scientific advance, no matter how inefficient. Even though the choice of subject matter was generally not under scientific control, World War Two furthered scientific knowledge by giving scientists resources on a scale that was previously unknown.

These considerations lead us to the conclusion that if we properly define what is meant by *value-free*, the term can be shown to refer to a useful aspect of the aspiration of scientists as contrasted with non-scientists. To make the argument, it is necessary to distinguish the following five ways in which nonscientific concerns, including values, enter into basic scientific work:

1. Generally there are values placed by scientists on science, truth, or the pursuit of knowledge. These are the supportive values of science and scientists.
2. Scientists often develop commitments to particular scientific theories or hypotheses, and these theoretical values then determine the direction of their interests, further hypotheses, and methodological biases. These theories, in turn, are often related to the nonscientific cultures of the scientists.
3. Scientists are real people with ordinary emotions. The more they are involved with particular theories, the more their emotions will be involved with judging evidence for and against these theories. They are also emotionally involved in the success or failure of their friends and enemies (see Mitroff, 1974).
4. Scientists often choose to work in certain areas of science rather than others for extrascientific reasons. For example, the nuclear physicist may switch to biology, or the engineer to sociology, because of outside commitments. Scientists often work in an area because sponsors are interested in the area and this is where the money is.
5. Scientists may be influenced in their work by ideologies or purposes that both lie outside of science and determine to a major extent the conclusions of the work. For example, the communist may develop a special biology because it fits communist theory, or

a Christian fundamentalist may devise a special archaeology to sustain biblical statements. In other cases, scientists may be induced or forced to come to conclusions in line with the interests of sponsors.

Since scientists in all fields have admitted the influence of the first four classes of nonscientific concerns, evidently the claim for value-free science was not meant to apply to these concerns. The phrase *value-free science* means, then, that its practitioners strive to avoid the fifth type of interference with their work. This is the point that Mitroff (1974) overlooks in his attack on the assumption of scientific neutrality. By probing the attitudes of moon scientists, he proves only that the moon scientists are human beings. Mitroff fails to see his informants within their world of expectations, a world of much higher expectations of intellectual care and honesty than most of us can imagine. It is against these standards that Mitroff's informants discover failings in one another. Notice that in the midst of what can only be described as a tirade against the dishonesty of other scientists, one of Mitroff's informants says, "He wouldn't fudge data, but . . ." (p. 74).[2] In general, it remains the case that the standards of what is evidence and argument in science are very different than in general discourse, and the hesitancy with which most scientists are willing to come to a conclusion exasperates the broader community.

In particular, although there have been many lapses, most twentieth-century social scientists have striven to become scientists by emancipating their work from extrascientific ideological warping. Of course, the fifth type of interference with the scientific enterprise is not the only value interference that concerns scientists. Certain cultures, whether Marxist, capitalist, or Hinayana Buddhist, establish the context of thought for scientists who are their bearers. Science in the real world always reflects nonscientific cultural traits to some extent. The concept of deviance has often been pointed to as a prime example of this tendency, for it implicitly denigrates the nonconformist. At least until recently, most social scientists have acted as though deviance was obviously a problem that needed correction. Yet these divergences from a more careful science, insofar as they are divergences, can be seen as leading to commitments to inappropriate scientific theories (the second point in the list), and insofar as the individuals are scientists, they are always potentially correctable by adherence to the supporive values of science itself (the first point). Over time, the personal, emotional interests of scientists as individuals will cancel themselves out as the supportive values of science keep correcting the enterprise.

Applied science is explicitly directed by concerns or interests classified under the fourth and fifth points, extrascientific choice of subjects and of conclusions. However, just as in pure science, only if the interests or values involved affect the conclusions will they seriously interfere with the usefulness of the result. If the interests are of the fourth class, extrascientific choice of work may slow progress of a science by depriving part of it of parallel development, but this will not alter the basically scientific nature of the effort. Although it may not be to the advantage of society to concentrate efforts in certain areas to the exclusion of others, this is a matter of judgment that ultimately lies outside science.

More serious for the scientific status of social science is the continuing gap between its promise and its actuality. A few years ago Berelson and Steiner (1964) put together an "inventory of scientific findings" about individual and social behavior. It was an admirable attempt, yet for a citizen or decision maker it must have been as profoundly disappointing as it was for some social scientists (Ackoff and Emery, 1972, pp. 8–9). Perusals of more recent scientific texts will be similarly disappointing: For example, one can go through many chapters of the recent *Handbook of Social and Cultural Anthropology* (Honigmann, 1973) without finding anything of use to policy consideration. The elite public wants more social science than this and is willing to put money into research and application, yet the money is often ill spent. In the end, the findings often disappoint the givers, whether public or private. For the students and teachers of social science, the disappointment is just as real, for their motivation has often been to help man. In fact, most social scientists know little more than most educated persons that is useful concerning man or society, nor are most of their methods and theories especially useful ways to think about human problems in the absence of factual knowledge. Because social scientists as a group were perceived to have formulated or supported the programs in question, generations of psychological, sociological, and educational studies have been called into question by recent evaluative studies that show no difference in results among correctional programs or educational systems, and little benefit from ameliorative programs such as Head Start or Performance Contracting.[3] Evidently, progress in the social sciences is going to be very slow, and it may never reach the level of the natural sciences. Not being able to face this fact corrupts both science and those analysts who must willy-nilly go beyond science.

To increase the usefulness of social science, a variety of applied social sciences have been developed. Leaving aside those who use the term *applied* just to obtain financial support, applied social scientists have developed their efforts in three directions. First, there are some areas in which certain generalizations from social science can be applied. This would be especially true in areas that overlap with natural sciences, such as physiological psychology for understanding stress, endurance, or perception. More often, an applied social science leads a life of its own, separate from a scientific base. It is then a group of more or less useful methodologies and empirical traditions, such as polling and survey techniques, psychological warfare, or marketing analysis. Finally, applied social science may be primarily a popularization of unproved or unprovable social science theory.

We should not be surprised that the market has been filled with what Moynihan (1969, p. 191) referred to as the "sellers of snake oil." The society does need help, and this need will create those who strive to fill it. Many of these—systems analysts, operations analysts, religious prophets, propagandists, or revolutionaries—legitimately feel they can do something, while others are just playing what seems to be a rewarding game. More threatening is the fact that the market is filled with those who say they are social scientists, but who reject explicitly, or in fact, the modesty of science.

Miller (1971) has identified three responses of social scientists to the demand that they reject their pose of objectivity and deliberately gather data and present analyses in terms of particular ideologies and social-reform objectives. These are:

1. the abandonment of any pretense to objectivity, even as a goal,
2. ambivalence (pretending to be nonobjective while actually not abandoning the search for objective science), and
3. trying to pursue the objectives of both satisfying popular (at least

on university campuses) ideological claims and those of the scientific community.

Although the third alternative is most often tried, it most often fails; for while the form of work may remain scientific, the content pumped into it is progressively warped. Miller's example is the progressive change of Oscar Lewis' interpretation of the culture of poverty under the pressure of the 1960s.

The degree to which social scientists are coming to accept an antiscientific frame of mind while still claiming to be scientists threatens the gains of a previous generation of social scientists. For example, in the midst of a theoretical critique, anthropologist Valentine (1968, pp. 12–13) writes:

> *It is neither intellectually nor ethically acceptable to portray another way of life merely in terms of comparison, invidious or otherwise, with one's own cultural standards.... These foundations [of the culture of poverty] support the long-established rationalization of blaming poverty on the poor. Nothing could be further from the meaning, the spirit, or the ideological implications of the original concept of culture.*

In a few words, Valentine has thus dismissed the century-old attempt to carve out a scientific and anthropological meaning for culture (see Kroeber and Kluckhohn, 1952). He seems not to realize that the scientific concept of culture had no ideological implications, either of the right or the left. In anthropology, culture is preeminently a comparative concept, created because anthropologists noticed differences among groups that could be explained in no other way (Gastil, 1961). That a scientific concept may be used by nonscientists to blame a group is hardly surprising, just as understanding Freudian concepts may lead children to blame their parents for current ills. Another example is the recent popularity in academia of Gouldner's *The Coming Crisis in Western Sociology* (1970). Gouldner's approach is to combine Marxist sociology of knowledge with neo-Freudian psychoanalysis to explain why sociologists, especially of the functionalist school, describe society as they do. This is a perfectly legitimate and interesting undertaking, except that Gouldner then uses his analysis as a basis for attacking the validity of the sociological theories produced by the functionalists. This mistake, confusing an explanation of why someone thinks as he does with a critique of what he thinks, is one which the best Freudians have always carefully avoided. Gouldner concludes by prescribing a new "reflexive sociology" that comes, in his mind, to take the place of religion. While this sociology seems to be meant to help reform society, in the end Gouldner retreats and becomes essentially interested in the personal growth of sociologists.

Friedrichs' (1970) criticism of the objectivity of the social sciences is more in the tradition of the sociology of knowledge. However, he goes beyond the argument that no one is free of his social context and personal interests to argue that sociology is inevitably committed to change, because thinking about something implies changing it. The direction of the ideological commitment is seen in Friedrichs' endorsement of C. Wright Mills as the prophet of modern sociology: "He rarely engaged in pure analysis; he demanded that we judge each situation morally as well as objectively. . . . He felt a moral responsibility to set things right in the world" (p. 68).

The last few years have shown a reawakening of interest in what is now called *humanistic psychology.* The effort is to avoid the reductionism of the natural science model by seeing man as a whole and usually "at his best." In the hands of some scholars, such as Allport, this approach was still tied closely to the general tradition of psychology as a science—although Allport's interests went quite beyond science (see Allport, 1937). But in much of the recent writing, we find the regular use of quasi-scientific statements that are based neither on the scientific norms of search for consensus (in Ziman's [1970] terms) nor on rational-empirical evidence. Let us consider three statements culled from a collection of writings in humanistic psychology:

1. "The 'never-lost kernel' of man's existence is in this view 'his power to take some stand.' . . . In taking this stand, man makes use of and expresses his freedom. It is the moment of decision, in which man becomes truly human" (Buhler, 1967, p. 87).
2. "The compassion which we can direct toward other persons and

other nations is nothing less and nothing more than the compassion we feel toward ourselves" (Levine, 1967, p. 212).
3. "In order for growth and the development of one's potential to occur, the individual needs to face himself as he is at each moment" (Thomas, 1967, p. 227).

The foregoing statements are humanistic, yet devoid of recognizable methodology based on one or more of the humanistic disciplines. There seems to be a preference for hard-to-define terminology and high valuational content, yet this preference is obscured by a pretense of surety and science. The authors are building up a poetic, humane mythology that may reflect a useful way to apprehend the nature of man, or, more prosaically, that may be useful for subject or object in therapy. My intention is not to argue against the validity of this tradition, but to point out that it would be preferable if these authors could sort out what in their thinking is scientifically established, what is potentially open to scientific understanding, and what is simply beyond science.

The Humanities

As a counterpoise to science, academics are accustomed to refer to a broad catchall category of university courses as the *humanities*. If we examine what is generally grouped under this heading, it apparently includes all those intellectual undertakings in which the development of human consciousness or the transcendence of the human condition rather than substantive agreement on empirically provable fact is the objective. The concept may be given more content by considering the following subdivisions:

1. *Mathematics* has as its task the understanding of formal relations among elements in arbitrary schemes. The elements are generally discrete, quantitative units.
2. *Philosophy* is a discipline that attempts to critically and rationally examine the bases of all human knowledge and action. Branches of philosophy merge into mathematics, but we shall be particularly concerned with those branches that propose bases for critical judgment in areas such as ethics and aesthetics.

3. *Descriptive humanities* attempt to describe ideographically events and objects in the real world, often from particular value positions, and include history, the study of literature, and the appreciation of art.
4. *Creative humanities* have as their proper function the creation of alternative possibilities that test the capacity of man. Here are included artists of all kinds. All creators, including those of religious, ethical, political, and scientific systems, can also be analyzed from this perspective.

The term *humanities* in this book is used to refer primarily to those nonmathematical, scholarly activities that intentionally do not strive for scientific consensus. Mathematics is excluded because its concerns do not cover the value issues I wish to juxtapose with scientific knowledge. (In addition, although it is conventional wisdom to see undertakings such as mathematics as arbitrary, the quality of the specially disciplined arbitrariness of mathematics is very different from that of most other humanities.) Distinctions between the remaining humanities and the sciences are not, of course, always tightly drawn. In the descriptive humanities, many historians and ethnographers certainly operate along the margin of science, legitimately striving for as value-free a presentation of material as possible. It should also be noted that ethicists who restrict themselves to describing the ethics of others are functioning as social scientists.

For man as the observer of life, the humanities offer a variety of avenues to deeper understanding. The philosopher Johnstone (1954) says that science establishes the facts, while philosophy draws out the implications of these facts. According to Johnstone, philosophers should never get into an argument as to whether something is true substantively. They should rather start with the question, "If *x* is true, then what are the implications of this fact?"[4] It is only in terms of its implications that science has meaning for understanding life (and ultimately for establishing the directions of science itself).

However, in this book the humanities will be defined primarily as disciplines that create or affirm values and standards of behavior. Most important will be the study of ethics, for ethics offers the most evident intellectual guidance, once the facts of a situation are established. An intellectual leader needs to know what interests and values he would want to have or want others to have, could he convince them. It is his responsibility to go beyond the day-to-day thinking of the majority. For example, we cannot establish today's ethics on the basis of what the men of the future would have wanted us to do, because what they will want will be determined in large part by what we directly and indirectly teach them to want. They will ride on the shoulders of their history, and that fact underlines the seriousness of our responsibility today, for we are their ancestors. In accepting this responsibility, we must accept the freedom that stems from the fact that there are "ought" issues that cannot be solved universally and scientifically. This is because there are unavoidable disagreements on the appropriate methodology of solution and on the outcomes given the same methodology. For example, the philosopher John Rawls can never prove to the satisfaction of his peers that the veil of ignorance is a good way to mediate between the utilitarian maximum benefit to all and the strictly egalitarian division of available goods (see Chapter Four). Nor could we ever know what "strict equality" should imply when people obviously differ in so many ways, beginning with age. There is no best world, but there are many better worlds. From this perspective, humanistic indeterminism leads not so much to nihilism as to the expansion of man's possibilities.

The position for the humanities that this discussion implies is only tangentially related to cultural relativism, as the term is usually understood. There are surely universals in the structures and norms of societies. All societies, for example, have developed some form of funeral ceremonies, and there are only rare examples of societies that condone incest (see Van Gennep, 1960; Murdock, 1949; Kluckhohn, 1953). So we must assume that there are tendencies in human nature, as expressed in cultural traditions, that "cause" man to develop funereal customs and incest taboos. Since societies as well as organisms have come under selective pressure, and only a few have survived through recorded history or anthropology, we can say that the customs of surviving societies evidently had "survival value" (see Alland and McKay, 1973). But these observations are of moral interest only if our morals are simplistic and utilitarian. They say nothing about other humanistic values. Why is it morally wrong for a brother and sister to marry? We must search for an ethical argument, for to think that universality is a sufficient argument is to make that error of confusing science and the humanities, to which this discussion is addressed.

The humanities is an area in which we can agree that certain concerns exist, that certain values exist, but we cannot agree on what they are. We can agree on the superiority of Shakespeare's work to Jonson's, without achieving consensus on why and without agreeing on the superiority of either to Sophocles, or whether, indeed, a comparison of this kind makes any sense. We can agree that the question of euthanasia is a serious ethical or moral issue but will come to a variety of conclusions, and those who agree on conclusions may not agree on the bases of their agreement. Most humanists would object strenuously to Skinner's science-derived claim that cultures are only to be judged in terms of their survival value (Skinner, 1971, especially pp. 127–144), but they would not agree on the values cultures should then be judged by. Some humanists would emphasize "knowledge gained," others "happiness," and others "contribution to civilization"; but nearly all would agree that man's significance exists beyond mere biological survival and that his cultures must have significance beyond the degree of their own persistence. This belief— that there is "something more" to human existence than simple biological gratification—is the core belief of the humanities.

Contrasting Science with the Humanities

To summarize the argument to this point, science and humanistic judgment are both valuable kinds of intellectual activity, but no purpose is served by making their mixture in social science a positive virtue. Properly defined, the value-free striving of scientists is feasible, even in social science. This does not mean that scientists will not be influenced by the supportive values of science itself (such as the high value placed on knowledge), by the choices of areas of effort by scientists or their supporters, or by the theoretical biases that scientists always develop in the course of their work. But scientists do generally free themselves from extrascientific influences on the conclusions reached, and the success of our future civilization rests on the hope that they will continue to strive in this way to put knowledge above other values. For we, the public—and we are all public in regard to most sciences—have no way to control or evaluate a science that ceases to strive in this latter sense for objectivity.

Scientists are being asked to take humane values more into account, and certainly they should be responsive to such values, if not in the heart of their work. But this raises the question as to whether there are any values beyond science. Social scientists and philosophers such as Lundberg (1947), Skinner (1971), and Churchman (1961) turn the argument of the critical sociologists on its head by claiming that following essentially natural scientific methods solves all problems. It is true that scientific reality must play a large part in any potential understanding of values. Yet the Elbings are mistaken in concluding:

> *Insofar as the behavioral sciences can discover the probable consequences on human beings of various ethical attitudes, choices and acts, and insofar as we do define behavior as humanly, socially, morally valuable in terms of its probable consequences, then statements of such consequences yielded by the behavioral sciences . . . are tantamount to ethical value statements. [Elbing and Elbing, 1967, p. 208]*

In fact, these are not ethical value statements; for example, to know what will happen if one commits suicide adds information without judgment to unformed ethical value statements. Another way to make the point is to suggest that the range of scientific statements about ethics and the range of humanistic statements about ethics (with the discipline of ethics generally identified with the latter) overlap but are not identical.

We accept, then, the general position of philosophers that humanistic statements about human conduct are not derivable from scientific statements. The philosophical or humanistic terminology is not concerned with more or less as much as with better or worse. Humanists will generally agree that something beyond sheer biological or cultural survival must be used as the measurement of better or worse (see Skinner, 1971, especially pp. 127–144). But characteristically, they will not be able to agree on what. Theirs is not public knowledge in the sense of science, and it is more rational and intuitive than rational and empirical.

The Definition of Social Humanities

Social humanities is, then, an integrative discipline that requires that analyses by its practitioners take into account both the social sciences and the nonmathematical humanities. Unlike common sense analysis, which naturally includes both of these realms, the social humanities requires that both realms be understood on a sophisticated plane, so that the best available thought is available to the analysis. And it requires that the two realms not be mixed in analyses; for the scientific and humanistic elements must not be so entangled that they cannot be separately examined. The term *social humanities* is a hybrid that brings together the terms *social science* and *humanities*. Although the resulting term places *humanities* in the noun position, this does not indicate that priority is given to either of the originative terms. The reader should also be warned not to take the term *discipline* too seriously. But it is preferable to alternatives such as *approach* or *field of study*, because it suggests the need for the development of careful, academically respectable methodologies to replace the slackness that usually characterizes generalist work that goes beyond science.

Contrasting Social Humanities with Policy Science

The closest discipline to social humanities is the new field of "policy science," developed in the last decade through the medium of the journal *Policy Sciences*. Both the social humanist and the policy scientist are interested in pointing out the interrelations among what is, what considerations should be taken into account, and what can be most effective in achieving a desired result. However, by attaching the word *science* to the description of his activity, the policy scientist puts himself into a dilemma. On the one hand, insofar as he desires to continue to see himself as a scientist, he must emphasize applied social science rather than applied social humanities. He is not going to tell people what to do; he is only going to discuss the behavioral, action-and-reaction aspects of the problem. Yet since there is almost always a nonrandom audience for the information he develops, the charge of selling out one's knowledge and skills to particular interests has

validity even for the well meaning. On the other hand, were one to
develop the argument that certain choices should be preferred over
others because of the values or norms *of the analyst,* then the claim to
science would be forfeited, and the analyst could be accused of
attempting to impose his values on others surreptitiously. The
applied social humanist would avoid this dilemma by explicitly
entering both the scientific and humanistic realms.

The danger of the scientific constraint can be illustrated by reference to a recent paper by Harman (1972), which outlines his
thoughts on the next two decades. As an expert in educational policy,
Harman claims that there is a good case to be made for the view that
our society must accept a new "paradigm" of "humanistic capitalism," in which humanistic values (for example, worker satisfaction)
will be held more important than productivity. I believe that what
Harman wants to point out is that in terms of the scale of values he
projects for the next generation, the norms that govern business are
inappropriate. However, what Harman says is that:

1. We have a spiritual crisis (crime, revolution, mental illness, and so
   on), due to overemphasis on economic values that is forcing a new
   paradigm on society.
2. Present trends will lead to maladaptive totalitarian societies.
3. Humanistic capitalism presents an alternative that will resolve the
   crisis and be long lasting.
4. There is nothing we can do about anticipated changes in any
   event.

Harman's argument is encoded in terms of demonstrated knowledge.
His ostensible world is deterministic, in which we are *forced* to choose
among options that ironically make no difference. (We are reminded
of Marx and Calvin.) However, other evidence suggests that Harman
is not a determinist. Harman would simply like to convince us to
institutionalize humanistic capitalism *whether or not* the old paradigm could last for more centuries.[5]

Because Harman misunderstands his role, his argument is not
satisfactory. First, it is very hard to show the nature of an era, except
by comparison with other eras and in retrospect. There have been
assured statements of spiritual crises in every era (see the appendix for

our own version). Proving what causes a crisis is even more difficult, as is predicting where we are headed without a particular solution. What Harman could help us with is more discussion of the virtues and practicality of humanistic capitalism compared with other alternatives. The world needs well-developed options from which to choose, rather than pseudodeterminism.

Kaplan (1974) has recently suggested seven "planning principles." These are impartiality, individuality (individuals must benefit), maximin (improve the lower end of distributions), distributiveness (the more people that have a given thing, the better), continuity (change not a value), autonomy (government only does what it must), and urgency (emphasize present needs). This seems to me to represent fairly well the values of most planners, and so is in that sense descriptive science, but descriptive science is not Kaplan's purpose. He wishes to lay out these principles and, in the absence of dispute, to attain widespread consensus.

The social humanist would want to examine the implications and practicality of Kaplan's principles by the tests of science. He would want to know if the Egyptians might have ever built their pyramids, the Romans founded their empire, or the Americans landed men on the moon with such planning principles. He would want to know if it is reasonable to suppose that a democratic electoral process can actually apply the maximin principle to a society. If not, what kind of political process is implied? On the other hand, by the tests of the humanities, he would want to know the argument that asserts that it was a worthwhile human objective to build pyramids rather than reduce "the price of shoes" (in Kaplan's example). He would want, finally, to build alternative sets of principles and test them against both reality and humane argument. To proceed without this examination is to mislead the public.

The discussion suggests that a discipline of social humanities might help to develop and clarify the efforts of Kaplan and others. The discipline would incorporate the background of social science but go beyond into judgmental areas of policy and moral philosophy. The social humanist would raise the level of discussion in this borderland because of his adherence to developing rules of the new discipline based on standards of scholarship and argument derived from the traditional social sciences and humanities. While the discussion emphasizes the intermediary role between social science and the humanities, social humanities could also serve as the development of an intermediary discipline between all of science and the humanities. Issues at the conjunction of natural science and public policy fuse easily into those we are considering here, for the nature of society is determined in large part by the rise of its technology. Social and natural scientists and planners may want to assume the alternate role of social humanist. With this alternative, the scientist would be less likely to be frustrated by the irrelevance of his scientific role and to confuse his science with his values, while the social philosopher or planner would be less likely to call the explication of his personal values a science.

Perhaps closest to social humanities is policy analysis. Kahn and Wiener (1967, pp. 398–399) tell us that the policy analyst should:

1. clarify, define, and argue major issues,
2. design and consider alternative policies,
3. increase the ability to identify new patterns and problems and their significance,
4. generate and document conclusions and recommendations, and
5. educate decision makers in the first four points.

Significantly, this description of policy analysis is given in a volume dedicated to the study of the future. However, there is in the Kahn and Wiener outline a flavor of immediacy and very little of the humanist's task of creating new values and new patterns of life and meaning that are not in response to the problems and concerns of the day. Thus, while policy analysis would be a central feature of social humanities, it would only be a part.

Social humanities would improve even the best of current policy analyses and future studies by requiring that the assumptions and data that are used to support the conclusions of such works be seriously examined in scholarly studies. In performing this function, such studies would in turn increase the points of interaction between social science and studies beyond social science, interactions now almost wholly lacking. For example, analysts often fail to relate their work to theories of human behavior or social organization, except possibly to simple economics. Although social theories are discussed by Kahn and Wiener, the authors use them as metaphors or examples and avoid basing their discussions on assumptions of their validity. Were these questions asked, it might both help the nonscientific endeavor and spark new insights in social science. Similarly, the planner by his very assertions should raise the level of awareness of social scientists as to what problems science might most usefully attack. Thus, while the problem of poverty is not a scientific problem, poverty raises a variety of scientific questions that the social humanist might pursue and, through this inquiry, gradually answer from his own work as a social scientist or from work of full-time social scientists.

The actual methods of research or analysis of the proposed discipline will be borrowed from both science and the humanities, yet there will also develop some characteristic methodologies. In a recent discussion, Weinberg (1972) has suggested the distinction between science and "trans-science." Emphasizing the physical sciences, Weinberg distinguishes between what is definitely known now and what is not yet known or is inherently unknowable. The latter category includes those theoretically scientific questions that are simply unanswerable (for example, where samples required would be too large or, in "Aswan Dam" engineering questions, where building a full-scale model is unrealistic) and questions that involve values over which men will always differ (for example, the amount of money to be allocated to different sciences or the risk of reactor failure that is acceptable). For these questions, Weinberg advocates an adversary procedure. At first sight, this might be considered little different from the search for consensus that actually characterizes science; yet the difference is that the goal of the adversary procedure is a decision (often a compromise), rather than consensus or agreement.[6] In many cases, an actual adversary procedure would be impossible and would be replaced either with the intellectual creation of rational alternatives mentioned above or with the use of the comparative method.[7]

A basic tool of both the social sciences and the humanities is the comparative method. In the social sciences, communities or individuals or eras are compared in order to determine the limits of variation and response in man under varying conditions and to develop knowledge of the uniformities in individual or group behavior. In the humanities as we conceive them here, comparison serves the first function, albeit with somewhat different purposes, and it provides the material basis for the evaluation of the human desirability of alternative modes of behavior, life styles, and civilizational creations in terms of a variety of nonscientific but human criteria. Of course, the humanist does not arrange all of his information along one value dimension—too much simply cannot be compared. But the humanist must judge. The social humanist will be interested in both scientific and humanistic uses of the comparative method. In examining, for example, quality-of-life questions, he will want to know the possibilities for societies at different levels of economic or social development; he will want to know the extent of variation on each level; and he will want to make judgments, or at least consider judgments, as to the preferable choices among the available alternatives that are suggested by such comparisons.

This example suggests that there is also a third form of comparative studies that will be most appropriate for social humanities. In this case, we compare in order to borrow and improve the lives and accomplishment of one or all of the units compared. If we are interested, let us say, in improving the methods of campaign financing in this country, one way is to analyze the methods of financing in a variety of other countries. To some degree, each system will be found to work, yet each in its own way also impairs the functioning of the democratic system. Depending on what objective we value most highly, we will wish to investigate more fully those systems that offer advantages over the system in our country. Of course, many borrowings fail or have unwanted consequences. To succeed ultimately in developing improved alternatives for our society, we must study how American and other systems fit into their respective historical and social backgrounds. And the analysis must also consider what is known scientifically of the processes of borrowing and diffusion.

At least four areas of analysis might be included in social humanities. The first is consideration of the *meaning of life*. Most people on campus and in professional life are now little moved by traditional religion; they are secularists, and yet they have the same religious and philosophical interests and yearnings as their intellectual ancestors. The public contributions of Marcus Aurelius or Jefferson were sustained by faith in the best thinking of their time. Today there is little of comparable value to sustain our leaders. Recurrent bouts of national fascination with drug experiences, mysticism, astrology, and authoritarian group-awareness movements may stem in part from the abandonment of concern with ultimate questions by the traditional disciplines and by the best minds of our time (see Fair, 1974). It would be appropriate for the proposed discipline to devote its energies to expositions of the best alternatives that have been or can be generated in this area. No matter how pessimistic we might be about the outcome of such a search, the intellectual community cannot evade the responsibility of making the attempt.

The second area of analysis is the consideration of the *quality of life* on both individual and societal levels. Closely connected with questions of meaning, study in this area would be devoted to the idea of progress in terms of variations in life quality—past, present, and future. For example, those who assume that the meaning of life is summed up in a definition of maximum, individual happiness must inquire how this has been obtained or how it might be obtained. More generally, social humanists would inquire about the short- and long-term benefits of different, high-quality natural and human environments. They would be concerned with the best achievable kinds of life for people at different levels of mental and physical ability and at different levels of material plenty and technological achievement.

In the third area of analysis, the social humanities would consider *scientific issues* in the general domain of the academic social sciences, although with fewer academic boundaries. The social humanist would be interested in exploring the extent of plasticity of men and society, and the most adequate means of balancing requirements for force and accommodation in interpersonal or intersocietal relationships. He would explore the possibilities of comparative national history and comparative social indices. How does American history compare with other histories? How are we different as a nation, or how are some of our subgroups different from others? In this area, he would also attempt to improve the scientific base for forecasts of the future, especially those that relate to environmental, technological, or administrative change.

In the fourth area the social humanist would be interested in *social or policy issues,* such as those relating to war, marriage, or race relations. In this area, the analyst would explore problems of resource allocation in society and point to areas of waste or injustice or danger.

Often such studies would result in crude cost-effectiveness analyses; at other times, cost as usually measured would be less important than the meaning of alternative policies for particular versions of what a high quality of life should be in our time. Policy studies in social humanities would have the particular flavor of the social humanist's involvement in the other areas of analysis.

A discipline dedicated to these objectives would gradually both legitimatize and render more amenable to scholarly criticism the area between science and the humanities. At the same time, it would strengthen the legitimacy of those who wish to study man and society scientifically, no matter how slow the progress of their efforts might seem. As a result, both the scientist and the social humanist would be able to face their public and their subjects less hypocritically.

Conclusion and Prospectus

The discussion suggests that there can and should be an institutionalized social humanities based on a linked understanding of the social sciences and humanities. It has suggested that within this framework there will be no one correct answer, for our scientific and humanistic understanding is, and is apt to remain, too indefinite for that. But in practice we cannot remain indefinite, but must rather strive to reach conclusions through the use of reasonable lines of scientific and humanistic argument. These lines of argument will eventually coalesce into what might be called *schools of interpretation*. Should social humanities succeed as an integrative discipline, most people would come eventually to relate themselves to one or another of these schools.

The following chapters are an attempt to develop for social humanities the outline of one school of interpretation that can be used to think about and guide experience. In this way, the discussion must be one-sided, for in order to become intelligible, the argument must be developed so that there emerges at the end the possibility of action instead of the chaos of inaction. In order to do this, we will present a scientific model for man (Chapter Two), a scientific model for society (Chapter Three), a humanistic framework for evaluation (Chapter Four), a methodology for combining these approaches

(Chapter Five), and a number of applications of the approach to specific issues in succeeding chapters.

Notes

1. This chapter is an amplification and revision of the article by Gastil (1974a).

2. Mitroff uses his apparently empirical study to lay a foundation for advocacy of a new form of "inquiring system." Unfortunately, his system, like others of this genre, asks us to do all things at once, and so to do nothing at all.

3. For references to evaluations of these programs and the problems of their evaluation, see Bennett and Lumsdaine (1975, pp. 120–126).

4. It is unwillingness to accept this limitation on science that has led authors such as Ungar (1976) to strive for a value-laden "science" that synthesizes objective and subjective, consensual and private knowledge. The result is broad and complex, but not communicable.

5. Jervis (1970) points out in a recent review that Skolnick (1969) indulges in the same misuse of social science to achieve a desired end. In this case, the goal is "massive social reform" and the alternative "garrison cities." Like Harman, Skolnick offers no serious defense of his position.

6. The "science court" concept (Task Force, 1976) has somewhat narrower objectives than Weinberg's. The purpose here is to use advocates to help establish the facts of the case. Its only difference from normal science is that the problems addressed are those defined by public-policy issues rather than those developed in the course of theoretical scientific investigation; therefore the problems are far less determinant. Bermant and Brown (1976) have examined the concept of "forensic social science," in which frankly adversarial positions are taken by social scientists on social issues.

7. Jervis (1976) discusses the problems in avoiding misperceptions of complex issues and some of the means to avoid the problems through adversary and other procedures within bureaucracies.

TWO

The Individual: A Model of Economic, Psychological, and Humanistic Aspects

The Inadequacy of the Traditional Social Sciences as Guides to Action

Common men in most times and places have tended to see differences in behavior, both among individuals and among groups, in biological terms. The most formal ancient codifications of this approach are found in the writings of the Greeks, for example, in Plato's *Republic*. On the other hand, Aristotle's concept of the natural succession of governments from democracy through tyranny and monarchy back to democracy was an essay in "dynamic sociology." Christian tradition placed primary emphasis upon the basic nature of universal man, although some currents within Christianity emphasized social factors, pointing to the degree to which human behavior must be molded for the success of the group. Leaders of these traditions developed laws for the relationship of people that were meant to reflect the natural order.

In more recent times, popular authorities have presented man alternately as basically evil or basically good. Life was seen as a con-

24

tinual struggle between a basic nature and the external forces of a particular culture or social situation. Rousseau felt that a biologically healthy man was crushed beneath pernicious cultural traditions. To Hobbes and Freud, man was fundamentally a cruel and lustful animal, which was only tamed by training. Freud believed that although particularly unfortunate cultural traditions had grown up in the course of civilization, repression was necessary in any event, and the tension between man and society was inevitable. Marx saw man evolving successive cultures according to historical laws. Although some social orders emphasized the selfish and acquisitive aspects of man, he was perfectable under attainable social forms. For Marx believed that given the right situation, cultures could evolve that would free man of much of the injustice that had resulted from the institutions that unavoidably developed in the course of social evolution.

After the rise of modern social science, one theoretical fashion followed another. In the nineteenth century, behavior differences were often explained scientifically in terms of race or personal inheritance. After 1930, social scientists pointed instead to cultural differences among groups, often thought to be expressed in and ingrained by differing child-rearing practices. This approach reached its climax in the work of the anthropologists Ruth Benedict and Margaret Mead. While race as the source of intellectual or emotional differences was now totally rejected among the educated elite, reference to genetic differences among individuals only receded somewhat in popularity. Ideological determination of behavior was also popular during this period, with ideologists, philosophers, and utopians suggesting how people might be trained to live according to quite different sets of rules and values.

Recent years have seen a succession of explanatory fads. In the 1960s, McLuhan represented what appears to have been an aberrant form of technological determinism. While in the 1950s sociologists and anthropologists emphasized those long-term cultural traditions of the poor that tended to keep them poor, by 1970 they were describing the characteristic patterns of behavior of poor groups as determined by their social position and material want. Today, some social scientists believe that one should not generalize about the behavior of representatives of groups or classes but should approach each individual as a fresh experience. A generation ago, Freudian assumptions of a natural human proclivity toward aggression were common; today, social scientists are more likely to emphasize training in violence as the cause of trouble. However, among some conservative social scientists it is again fashionable to see violence as biosocially determined and to point to analogies between the territorial instincts of animals and human warfare.

There has been persistent disappointment with the accomplishments of social science. In Chapter One it was pointed out that social science is disappointing because it has so little consensual or testable information to offer. In sociology, there is hardly the beginning of a cumulative tradition of knowledge (Freese, 1972). The findings that are most praised in the public images of the social sciences are often firmly rejected by leading academic social scientists. Freudian psychology, for example, has had a great deal of influence on literature and considerable influence on applied social sciences (for example, certain kinds of counseling and education), but is dismissed as pseudo-science by many academic psychologists. It is as though Darwinian evolution and Mendelian genetics were regarded as mistaken dead ends by leading biologists. We expect evidence to be much clearer and more useful in biology. Mendelian principles are reflected in plant and animal breeding and have resulted in easily demonstrated progress in those fields, while improvement in the condition of human beings through applying Freudian psychology cannot be documented—even after years of psychoanalysis (Oden, 1974).

Turning to another area of discourse, the problem of predicting the direction of long-term social change has been central to social science since its inception. But how does social science help us answer where the world is today and where it is going? In a recent review of social change theories, one authority contrasts evolutionary theory, equilibrium theory, conflict theory, and rise-and-fall theory as well as their most recent variations (Appelbaum, 1970). According to these theories, societies are either: continually evolving toward higher, more differentiated stages (evolution); passing through periods of growth, maturity, decline, and dissolution (rise-and-fall); responding to stress or new inputs by readjusting mechanisms that provide for system maintenance (equilibrium); or continuously and progressively struggling among conflicting interest groups (conflict). As descriptions of what has happened in history, each of these theories fits a certain class of facts. We can assume that each will, at some future time fit similar classes of facts, yet we are left with little guidance as to which theories will be the best guide to our particular future or what we can do to influence it. In another recent treatment of theories of social change, important change factors in the future are identified as follows: the economic structure, science and technology, demographics, value alterations in particular groups, ideologies, leadership (individual, group, and type), the nature of government and the expansion of its influence, education, mass media, and the external world (Allen, 1971, pp. 29–31). Of course, it is useful to know all these factors, but taken together they do little to improve prediction.

Needless to say, the problem of the unusableness of the social sciences is not confined to broad social questions. Social science offers the parent trying to bring up his children conflicting bits of information and advice. He is to provide a firm moral structure with which the child can develop and against which the child can constructively rebel during his passage into adulthood. However, the parent is also to allow the child maximum freedom from an early age so that he can develop his own values and priorities.

The unusableness of social science was first brought home to me when I left a comfortable position teaching social sciences at a university to spend several years as a research analyst in national security. When encountering questions of predicting the behavior of leaders and the general public in a variety of cultures in specific future crises, I found that research analysts were guided by little more than common sense and a reading of history. And I found that the psychology, anthropology, sociology, political science, and geographical expertise that I had acquired did not add significantly to what was already realized by the common sense analyst. Social scientists who persisted in thinking that their training was of special value appeared, in this environment, to be more often disruptive than helpful. Realization of this impotence of learning in the social sciences came as a shock to me, but my realization was not an uncommon one for non-social scientists. The repeated experience of the unusableness of social science accounts for much of the contempt with which social scientists are held in government and business circles.[1]

There is, however, a second reason for the unwillingness of

men of action to be guided by social scientists. Following the natural
science model, the social scientist searches for generalizations from
social experience and ultimately for causes that will explain that
experience. While he understands the probabilistic scatter of events,
his guiding assumption is that the subjects under study cannot act
independently of deterministic forces. The idea of social science is,
therefore, confounded by several paradoxes. First, if the behavior of
subjects is determined, then the behavior (thinking) of all social scientists is also determined by their antecedents and environment. Even
Marxist analysis itself is a product of bourgeois society. Second, social
science asserts a deterministic flow to events that contradicts the intuitive human sense of independent decision, and so goes against the
grain of the apparent experience of most persons. Third, why should
human beings take upon themselves the pain of acting if they are not
independent of predetermined or stochastic processes? We are willing
enough to consider the effects of mixing oxygen and hydrogen in certain proportions to be predetermined, but our sense of human
autonomy makes us less willing to accept, for example, the social
inevitabilities that stem from transforming a traditional marriage
into an open marriage.

These comments lead me to conclude that to be useful to the
social humanist, social science must be based on two assumptions.
The first is that we must accept the normal human assumption that
there is an important area of indetermination in many social and personal situations, such that we can hope to influence the outcomes by
our decisions. The second is to accept the fact that man's natural,
insider view of personal and social events gives him a common sense
understanding of social reality that is unavailable to the natural scientists in regard to their subject matter. Thus, while most knowledge
in the natural sciences is the result of hard-won advance, most of the
equivalent knowledge in social science is available intuitively
through careful thought and study. Social science can only add mar-
ginally to our knowledge of ourselves, although it can add a great deal
in biological or physical offshoots of the social sciences, such as
physiological psychology or parts of demography.

Given this latter position, analysis in social science must begin
with a common sense model of how people can be expected to act in a
situation and, on a higher level, how social systems should be

expected to function when operated by individuals.[2] On the basis of simple assumptions on these levels, we should then look at how we might account for the processes emphasized by different social-change theories. For after all, the factors that these theories emphasize, such as evolution, growth and decline, societal self-correcting mechanisms, and conflict, are not keys to theories of change as much as they are descriptions of what happens in certain types of situations given relatively invariant human beings. If social science starts here, perhaps it can add more to common sense prediction and our sense of history than it has previously. This chapter and the next are devoted to the enterprise of trying to provide this kind of social science framework.

The Rational Self-Interest Model

For there to be a social humanities, human beings must be seen as both machines and more than machines. In this section, I will attempt to sketch a working model of man the machine and lay the basis for going beyond that model. In the process, I will leave many issues undefined, for my object is to provide no more than an initial platform on which an analysis of human events in any environment can begin.

Mechanistically, the behavior of individuals may be predicted from a variety of factors, including their *biological* inheritance and the current state of that inheritance, the *biosocial* laws of social interaction among persons, the particular *cultural* inheritance or learning experiences of individuals, and the interaction of these with the *situational environment* in which they find themselves (Gastil, 1972). Separately, human beings are animals with extensive biological possibilities. They inevitably form groups and develop technologies, and the nature of these limit or channel these possibilities. Traditions or cultures, products of the histories of particular groups of men, further channel behavior. But particular individuals and particular events determine the selections among these possibilities that finally become the specific happenings of life. For example, all human beings have the capacity for symbolic thought and for making a wide variety of sounds (biological). Living together in more or less permanent groups, men inevitably develop languages (biosocial). The people living in one area develop Swahili and in another English (cultural). Finally, some learn to speak well and others poorly (situational or personal). If we are explaining a group behavior, individual personalities are part of the situation; if we are explaining individual behavior, then the personality of the individual studied is obviously not treated as a situational factor. Explicating what these factors will lead to in particular situations could begin from an analysis of any one of the four classes of factors. For our purposes, it is most useful to begin by explicating a model of a biosocial individual acting in a variety of typical situational contexts, and then to move on to consider the influence of particular biological and cultural factors, and finally to consider personality or other strictly idiographic specifications.

Kuhn (1974) has suggested that the biosocial individual can be simply visualized as a mechanical unit with three types of basic capabilities: intelligence, decision-making, and action.[3] Intelligence includes both available information and the capacity to perceive and think about that information. Thus, intelligence is used in the limited sense of data gathering and processing (what an IQ test measures plus sensory ability) and not in the popular sense, which includes abilities to come to decisions and act effectively. Decision-making is the ability to use the output of intelligence to make choices in terms of unit interests. Action is the ability to know what to do after decision-making in order to achieve unit interests. In this model, man may seem to be a self-motivated computer. An electronic computer's capabilities are, however, nearly all intellectual; its decision-making capability is very simple—it does what it is told—and its action output is a stereotyped reflection of either its intellectual processing or directed decisions. The outputs of man, on the other hand, are most critically determined by his internal evaluations, valences, or desires, and their nature or power may lead to results quite different from those of a computerized unit concentrating on the processing of information input on the intellectual level. While a human being might eat or drink or smoke himself to death, a computer would never be programmed in this way. A computer is a slave, and a dead slave is useless.

The central problem of social science is what a unit with the basic capabilities ascribed to mankind will be expected to do in a specified situation. And the simplest answer is that a human being will be expected to do what appears to him to be in his own interest, given the intelligence available to him and the immediate or deferred satisfactions or dissatisfactions that the available actions have provided in the past. In saying this, we operate on a very high level of generalization, for what determines a person's view of his own interest is indeterminate, and a great deal of social science has been developed to show how people come to have similar or different interests. We shall return to the issue. Right now, by considering interest to be the central core of explanation, we have a way of initiating the discussion.

Given that a person has a certain interest, how will he go about maximizing it? Let us imagine that I am hungry, and that for the time being hunger overrides other interests. My first attempt will be to obtain or produce food through my own actions, perhaps by finding an apple tree and picking an apple. But if I am in a city, this may be hard to do, so I may ask where apples may be obtained; that is, I use communication to increase my information. If I locate an apple in someone else's possession, I may communicate again to open a transaction, in which I offer to exchange what I value less at the moment (money) for what I value more (the apple). But the store owner may want more for the apple than I wish to give him. If we cannot reach a solution by bargaining, he may point out that bread is cheaper, and on that basis our transaction can be concluded.[4]

The most important point to understand about this person is that in isolation his productivity, that is, his capacity to satisfy his wants, is relatively low. Therefore, he repeatedly strives through communication and transaction to increase his productivity. Communication involves exchange of information, and the exchange must be in the interest of those involved or it will not occur. The cost to the participants is only the cost of communication. Unless the person is a communicator by profession, no significant exchange of values has taken place. Transaction involves values beyond communication costs. In a marriage, both partners desire certain goods and feel they can best acquire these goods through marriage. Yet they must also give up something to achieve their objectives. This fact was signified in many primitive or peasant societies by actual economic exchange at the time of marriage. In our society, it is generally assumed without this symbolization that both partners trade away some of their independence and responsibility in marriage and that each will perform for the other their respective traditional roles or some other roles initially agreed upon.[5]

Transactions may also involve the transfer of "bads," at least on the part of one partner. Generally a bad is only threatened, and therefore the good of not receiving the threatened bad is actually the coin of the transaction. If I am held up at gun point, the robber asks for my money in exchange for not shooting me. If my boss threatens to dismiss me unless I work more assiduously, I exchange harder work for his not carrying out the threat. Since most people do not directly gain from exacting bads, carrying out threats is in most cases a form of communication, a way to increase the value of future threats in future situations involving the victim or observers.

The ordinary stance of persons engaging in transactions is that of neutrality, the assumption behind economics that trading partners desire neither to help nor to hurt those they trade with. Both sides deal as best they can, and only deal if there is advantage to both. However, in actual human situations, persons may take a generous or a hostile stance. If I am generous in a transaction, this means that I wish for my partner to have what he wants to such an extent that I am willing to give up something for him to achieve his purposes. This may be because to some extent I identify my interests with his—the best example might be of a parent's transactions with his children. Of course, many apparently generous transactions are really investments that one hopes to collect on in the future with interest. This is the reason for bargain prices at store openings, but it may also be the reason I lend a book to a friend, or even that some parents give generous wedding presents.

More generally, why do we give gifts? The cultural explanation is that under certain circumstances both giver and recipient have learned to expect gifts. But this does not explain why gifts came to be a part of life in the first place, nor what persons lose who fail to give. In terms of our model, giving a gift symbolizes the ability of the giver to make the gift. As such, it is a way to communicate the dimensions of the giver's power, a communication that can at times become very competitive, as in the potlatch. There are, however, several caveats. First, in giving, the giver may also be interested in the delight and pleasure of the receiver—indeed, this is especially the case in giving to the young. Second, the giving benefits the giver only if it is culturally appropriate in terms of time, place, nature of the gift, donor, and donee. If not, it detracts from the status of both parties. Finally, under special conditions, such as the distance between the parties, not to give a gift in return (or otherwise to act in the prescribed pattern) may enhance power through the demonstration of the power not to express power. Neither president nor pope is expected to match the gifts they receive from ordinary people.

The ability of a man to achieve his goals through a combination of personal effort, communication, and transaction may be thought of as his *generalized power*. In most societies, a man with a great deal of money or great eloquence or control over force can achieve almost anything, while one with none of these can achieve very little. For this reason, it is in the interest of most people to expend a great deal of effort to increase or maintain a maximum degree of power. Education is an investment in power in the same sense as putting money in a bank at interest. (Of course, the education paying the highest interest rate may not be offered in a school.) But generalized power should be distinguished from power in a specific situation, for the coin of one's power may not be exchangeable into that of the situation. In particular, general power must be distinguished from bargaining power. For example, in the transactional situation a person's bargaining power is enhanced by poverty, for this places a limit on what can be obtained from him. Paupers are not kidnapped.

In a hostile transaction, one partner desires that the other does less well than would be in the apparent interest of the first partner. For example, I may deliberately refuse to befriend a person whose racial or personal characteristics I do not like, in spite of the fact I know that an investment in this particular friendship would be rewarding in the future. Hostile transactions may also be useful if the advantages of the current deal do not outweigh long-term disadvantages. Thus, I may deliberately offend a person I do not want to deal with in the future; in this way I may disinvest in an undesirable future.

Hostile transactions are often transactions in bads. When two people meet that have an intense dislike for one another, dislike is likely to be the basis of their communication and transaction. Each may try to hurt the other in spite of the fact that only losses can occur as a result. Of course, since our model presupposes that persons always act in what they consciously or unconsciously understand to be their own best interest, the foregoing statement should be rephrased as: an actor in a no-gain situation engages in hostile acts in order to avoid losses that would occur if he did not so act (in other words, he acts in what he regards as self-defense) or to inflict losses on another that will bring him (the actor) pleasure in a way not ordinarily encompassed in the average man's rationality (although rational in terms of the interest of the actor at the time).

Faced with a situation in which his interests are not completely satisfied, a man will choose the interactional tool that costs him the least effort (Kuhn, 1974; Zipf, 1949). Looked at in isolation, this ordinarily means that an individual must attempt to improve his intelligence capabilities, which in our outline include his perception and cognition, or his understanding. This is essential, for he must improve feedback from his previous actions in order to correct and improve returns from subsequent actions. In other words, he must learn. Similarly, in the interpersonal situation, the least-effort principle means that emphasis will be placed on enlisting the interests of others in the satisfaction of one's own interest or in learning from others how to improve one's own productivity. Thus, communication becomes the preferred interactional means of achieving interests and, if adequate, lays the background for transactions of maximum value to those involved.

Kuhn distinguishes two types of influence that a communicator may have. *Intellectual influence* is the ability to alter the information from which others make decisions. *Moral influence* is the ability to alter the scheme of interests or values from which they decide (Kuhn, 1974, pp. 148–149). The reader may note the similarity of this distinction to that between science and the humanities as developed in Chapter One. He should also be reminded that for communicators, transferring information or value advice is their livelihood, so for them transaction and communication are professionally indistinguishable.

Communication may also be seen as of positive value to all participants in interpersonal situations in which no one is professionally involved. Here communication may not only be cost-free, but a benefit in itself. This is particularly true of animal communication; here benefits are often seen in group rather than individual terms (Bermant, 1973, pp. 307-357). Many apparent transactions are, then, really smoke screens for mutually rewarding verbal play. If this is so, generosity occurs not because of desires to maintain transacting relations but rather to maintain such pseudo-communication. Many activities have multiple returns. The frequency of social parties, for example, is promoted by the fact that for the host they are simultaneously opportunities for direct consumption, investments in future parties to be given by others, and validations of current social position.

For the sake of simplicity, most of the foregoing discussion has been addressed to a two-person model of interaction. However, the simplest biosocial fact is the difference between interaction in groups of different sizes, a point illustrated for dyads and triads in the recent study by Rubin and Brown (1975, pp. 64-74). Carrying this point further will, of course, be the task of Chapter Three.

Biological, Biosocial, Cultural, and Situational Footnotes

The primary biosocial model described above is a systems model that assumes little specific knowledge about human beings or variations among human beings. However, except for theoretical economists, most social scientists and biologists have been concerned with analyzing this specific information. In biology, including the now popular sociobiology, the specific variations from general assumptions are to be found on three levels: the evolutionary tendencies, individually and collectively, of organisms analogous to man, and thus by inference predictive of human tendencies; the known biological capabilities and tendencies of human beings individually or in groups; and the variability of these individually and across groups (defined by race, sex, age, and so on). Insofar as they involve group behavior, these questions are also biosocial but in a form somewhat different from those expressed previously in our model.

To what degree do these biological and supplementary biosocial considerations modify the predictive content of the systems model? On the one hand, defining such modifications is part of the future work of social science and human biology; but on the other hand, we must take a general position here on the degree to which we shall consider them. In this regard I heartily endorse the claim, recently popularized by Wilson (1975) in biology, that human infants are much more predetermined than simple learning machines that, with experience, produce human personalities. In linguistics, Chomsky (1972) and his followers (for example, see Postal, 1970) have argued the same point more narrowly in regard to a built-in linguistic competence that makes all human languages similar in certain organizational respects. We are no doubt programmed by our structures, including that of the brain, to learn easily to think and act in some ways and only with great difficulty in others.

A large part of the literature of physiological and social psychology is devoted to discovering variance in human thinking and communication. It is particularly significant, for example, that listeners and readers always tend to believe that speakers and writers believe the positions they are presenting, even when there are ample and obvious signals that they do not (Jones and Harris, 1967). This fact is good for advertisers and used car salesmen, but it is a major hindrance to the dispassionate and many-sided discussion required by policy analysis or social humanities. Human flexibility is limited (although a full understanding of the limits could only be achieved on a superhuman level of consciousness). Our model assumes, then, that such traits as aggression and territoriality on the personal and social levels are found not only because of general system requirements, but because systems in evolution produced a human being for which these patterns came particularly easily (see Wilson, pp. 254–255, 565–568). In making these statements, I am not suggesting that great discoveries have been made, rather that recent thinking in social science has tended to sweep away some particularly irksome nondiscoveries of the previous generation.[6]

Of major significance for the evaluation of the self-interest theory advanced here is the degree to which there is a biosocially determined moral development of human beings. By employing in this chapter behaviorist learning assumptions within a general self-interest model, we have rejected the romantic notion that human beings are basically good and need only to be allowed to unfold. However, there is an intermediate model, based on the claim that there are definite moral stages through which all persons potentially pass in the course of development from early childhood and encouraging cognitive development through moral discussion will cause a greater percentage of persons to attain the higher stages. Stemming from the work of John Dewey and Jean Piaget, this point of view has most recently been developed by Kohlberg (1972) and Kohlberg and Mayer (1972). In Kohlberg's view, the motifs of the individual's explanation of why he should behave morally at successive stages are: reward and punishment, an instrumental (transactional) understanding of human relations, a desire to gain approval, emphasis on order and duty, a social contract model, and a universal principle with emphasis on life, equality, and dignity. Apparently, there is some evidence for such a natural evolution in moral discussion, and that this evolution can be encouraged. However, it is not clear that this is more than a linguistic phenomenon, with most behavior (and thus effective thinking) remaining on the early levels no matter what the verbal evolution (Santrock, 1975; Adelson, 1975). Nevertheless, moral behavior does occur that the self-interest model does not adequately explain. Whatever the course of cognitive moral development, most adults appear to be honest and truthful most of the time and do develop a fundamental sense of justice (compare Walster, Berschied, and Walster, 1973).

The role of biology in human behavior has also been affirmed by studies that show that intellectual differences among individuals are not only due to learning and environment. While environment no doubt accentuates genetic differences, individuals are obviously not identical genetically in any measurable characteristics (see Williams, 1969; Tyler, 1965; Tyler, 1974), and this certainly extends to intelligence (Jensen, 1969; Kagan and others, 1969; Loehlin, Lindzey, and Spuhler, 1975). The relation of the specific XYY genotype to deviance seems to have been documented in spite of continuing controversy (Witkin and others, 1976; Hook, 1973). Of course, the biological basis of difference comes as no great revelation to the average person. There are no doubt also differences among races (or other groupings that have existed in relative genetic isolation for long periods) along important emotional and intellectual dimensions. However, here the picture is much fuzzier, and the extent of overlap among races is so great as to make the practical meaning of these differences unclear to the social humanist. In spite of the overstatement of environmental advocates, it should be said that the revelation of the degree to which variations in environment and learning have led observers to mistakenly ascribe genetic differences to races has been an important advance by social science beyond common sense.

The significance of cultural variations was vastly overplayed by the passing generation of anthropologists. Recent research has increasingly stressed the uniformities of the human experience, a result that parallels the rediscovery of the limitations placed on human response by biology. As a fascinating aspect of anthropological revisionism, a recent paper demonstrates the remarkable uniformity among primitive and modern societies in their understanding of mental illness (Murphy, 1976). It is apparently not true that those labeled insane in one society have analogous personalities to those of the prophets or healers in another. These results should not be surprising, for the requirements of life are sufficiently similar everywhere that only a limited amount of irrationality in day-to-day life will be accepted by any functioning group.

Cultural differences, however, remain an important part of our explanatory package, because group differences in behavior that were once thought to be racial (including classbound biological differences) have been shown in the last century to be largely cultural. The common sense understanding of tribal man was refuted. However, in saying this, we must also point to the fact that our misunderstanding of the behavior of a person from another society is usually not simply because we do not understand his culture. More often it is a mixture of misunderstanding his culture and misunderstanding his situation. Thus, poor people do develop cultures of poverty, which, for example, emphasize instant gratification rather than long-term goals. But the objective situation of many poor—including the elderly poor—makes postponing gratification for distant rewards an irrational choice (Ferman, 1965). If we thought enough about the objective situation of others, we might be able to predict their behavior adequately in terms of our basic model without the help of cultural footnotes.

Even within a country such as the United States, every family, religious group, ethnic group, and region teaches its members directly and indirectly, and the communicational inputs, values, and structuring of appropriate actions that are taught vary among these collectives. The Utah Mormon grows up in a different world from the

Southern mountaineer, and both are as different from a New York Jew as from each other. Some of the difference is stylistic, merely interesting, but much affects behaviors of more general interest in areas of the family, crime, or education. To ignore or misunderstand these cultural differences is to misunderstand the United States (Gastil, 1975b).

Less can be said about the role of situational variation in behavior, for our model posits an interaction of general laws with specific situations. Yet the more the situation is known, the less help one can expect to obtain from understanding the general model. The model is a way of beginning understanding, of getting into a subject, but not for completing analyses in specific instances. The reason is simply that all general statements in human affairs can only be statistical statements of the form: Given A and B, there is a reasonable probability that C will follow. But the more we know of A, B, and C, the more we can dispense with the model for estimating the likelihood of C following in this case. Since any important event includes many multiple chains of causation, the particularities along these chains will soon overwhelm the generalities we can ascribe to them from a distance. As the sociologist Nisbet (1969) concludes, "We turn to history and only to history if what we are seeking are the actual causes, sources, and conditions of overt changes of patterns and structures in society (p. 302; see also Hexter, 1971). Thus we can speak almost, but not quite, of a situational determination of events quite separately from the rest of the theory we have summarized.

The Biological Basis of Personality and Normality

In terms of our systems model, the personality of an individual may be considered to consist of a set of essentially durable, learned and unlearned states of his basic capabilities, which is for the individual what culture is for the group (Kuhn, 1974; Ackoff and Emery, 1972).[7] As a first approximation, we can imagine that experiences of pleasure and pain are the source of the learned states, although in human beings the rewards and punishment of life may be success or failure or even more purely abstract states of satisfaction and dissatisfaction (Nuttin and Greenwald, 1968). Operating through this mechanism, inputs through the intellectual receptors keep most personalities reasonably adjusted to reality. Theoretically, a person will only act or think in ways that give him pleasure and will avoid those actions and thoughts that have been painful in the past. Yet, neither asleep nor awake do we always follow this rule. Apparently, evolutionary demands of survival developed an organism in which signals of danger and fear may in crises override the short-sighted self-interest of always rewarding oneself with pleasurable thoughts or actions. Certainly, indulging in frightening nightmares confounds any simple assumptions of self-interest.

This leads us to realize that in developing this model of biosocial or interactional man, we have ignored many psychological questions. We need, then, additional complementary, provisional assumptions for the basic model. First, we assume that biologically man is provided with complex capabilities and sensibilities to feel pleasure and pain but that he has few organized, innate patterns of behavior that we may call instincts. Nevertheless, the interaction of capabilities, sensibilities, and nearly universal experiences during maturation make what appear to be, and to a large extent are, unavoidable drives or desires. Positive valences toward such things as food, drink, sex, and companionship are matched by negative valences in regard to various sources of pain, disgust, anxiety, and hatred. Clearly built into the organism are the capacities that come to be organized as responses, such as love, hate, fear, and curiosity, and their patterns of appropriate activity are built up by learning processes that include, but probably go beyond, the stimulus-response learning described by the behaviorists. In part, these patterns are universals; in part, characteristic of particular peoples; in part, idiosyncratic.

Since man was produced by the selective pressures of evolution, characteristics reflecting these selective pressures must be central to his description. Our model emphasizes, then, the "normal" person, or a person whose interests by and large reflect evolutionarily selected interests, as these are shaped in most individuals by maturation and learning. (Of course, I realize the great difficulty in establishing normality empirically. See Horton, 1971.) The *normal person* attempts to maximize both self-preservation and species preservation (reproductive activity and care of family). By extension, a normal person also has interests that develop in a fairly straightforward way out of these biological interests. Thus, his sexuality goes beyond action directly related to childbearing, his nurturing behavior goes beyond caring for his own children, his self-preservative interests come to include an interest in preservation of the group.

Abnormality in biosocial terms may be defined as those personal interests or abilities that clash with the biological imperatives and their extensions. Of course, abnormal interests must also result from the development of the individual or the group to which he is affiliated. Some may occur because the person is biologically different —for example, an individual may not be able to feel pain and is thus encouraged to develop an ultimately fatal interest in boxing. But often an abnormality that is not primarily biological results from a low probability development in the intellectual or decision-making systems, the thinking and valuing systems, of the individual. For example, a natural tendency to develop a sense of superiority may help mobilize a person to enhance personal survival and the conquest of mates. Yet if inadequate negative feedback allows this natural tendency to lead to a claim of divinity, in many societies this will imperil both the person's survival and reproductive possibilities. If so, then somewhere his learning, his information, or his processing of both has been inadequate. If he persists in the face of death to claim divinity, it is clear not only that his use of information is abnormal, but that his interests are also. For he prefers death to renouncing the claim to godhood. If to avoid punishment he flapped his arms in a futile attempt to fly from the scene, we might also say that his action capabilities were aberrant.

By saying that an interest is biosocially abnormal, as scientists we obviously do not mean to imply that it is wrong, but only that in calculating the interests of men, we do not understand how evolution would have selected such a tendency. As later discussion suggests, however, only in edging away from normality in the direction of abnormality does man achieve a life that is distinctively human.

Learning and Emotional Expression

We must, then, try to incorporate in our model two conflicting, partial models of man. First is the Freudian model that emphasizes the overriding influence throughout life of basic biological urges or of these urges as shaped in early life. To deny these urges is to seriously threaten the organization of the personality. In this model, emotions and desires not expressed become repressed, and health is restored by release. This is the assumption that lay behind Aristotle's concept of tragedy as catharsis.

Recognition of the continued role of primal forces in personality reminds us that the interest model is only predictive to the extent that the organism is in rational control of itself; the model never provides the whole explanation. In all human beings, emotions are present that frequently interfere with the pursuit of interests of any kind. For lower animals with poor intellectual capabilities, these emotions may have been selective, but for man they often are not. It may be biologically useful to surrender to sensuality under certain conditions, but the overpowering rages or immobilizing fears that often affect human beings are seldom useful. Even the tone of life is often hard for an individual to control in terms of his apparent interests. There is certainly no personal interest or survival value in a black mood. These are mysteries of biology and motivation that are unexplained but should not for that reason be left outside of our model.

The second partial model is that of the learning theorists, who see stimulus-response patterns, or cognitive patterns, built up through life, so that experiencing habitually achieved pleasure and avoiding habitually painful situations become the most satisfactory life. According to the first partial model, there will be an essentially fixed expression of aggressive or sexual impulses, which, if denied in one form, will break out in another. According to the second partial model, the more aggression or sexual behavior occurs (and to a lesser extent, the more it is rewarded), the more the individual will indulge to the point of physical capacity. Evidence can be found for both models, but I believe it is more useful to focus on the habits of thought or action produced by the reinforcement of behavior than on basic biological drives and the extent of their frustration.

On the biological base, learning leads to the development and differentiation of intellectual, decision-making, and action capabilities. Critical to all of these is the intellectual capability that must pick up and process feedback from previous information-evaluation-action cycles. However, since in actual life all three basic capabilities develop in tandem, their separation is essentially an analytical device.

In particular, interests grow out of the evaluation of the interaction of previous interests with the world. If a man comes to love his books more than his wife and saves them from a fire while she stands at the window screaming for help, it is apparently because his books have been more rewarding in the past. This suggests that interests are produced and shaped by experiences and that successful communications and transactions teach the individual what to want or value in subsequent communications and transactions, just as they teach how to improve the handling of input and output. In Vickers' (1968a) terms, every system continually matches an internal pattern of ideal expectations against actual inputs and continually strives to adjust either its ideals or its outputs to improve the match. Of course, failure to match may lead to so much stress that an individual achieves a pseudo-match by altering the perceived inputs as well. The concept of feedback thus allows us to incorporate and move beyond the stimulus-response approach that ignores purpose (Powers, 1973).

Evidence for the Reward-and-Punishment Model

This should lead us to expect, for example, that a major function of the criminal justice system is to deter crime. Certainly this became a major justification for the system as it evolved (along with incapacitation, retributive justice, and rehabilitation). It is commonly believed that the threat of punishment deters criminal behavior, and in spite of a great deal of conflicting data, social science generally confirms this belief. The first, and I would judge most important, source of supporting data is the many case studies, especially of professional criminals, that show that those contemplating crime often are highly informed about the justice system, the probabilities of capture, and the length of sentencing. For example, a professional burglar may make it a practice never to carry a gun, because to be caught with a gun guarantees a higher sentence (see King, 1972). The second form of evidence is the statistical, sociological literature that shows that the surety of arrest or punishment deters crime more effectively than severity (Logan, 1975; Tullock, 1974; Ehrlich, 1973). The fact that deterrence is least well documented (at least on a short-term basis) for homicide suggests that homicide is an area in which the effects of cultural variations (illustrated, for example, by the difference between Northern and Southern regional cultures in the United States) are more predictive of the decisions of individuals than a bio-social and situational understanding of the model's normal person (Gastil, 1971a; Loftin and Hill, 1974).

The best evidence for the importance of the learning-feedback model in understanding human behavior has been the fact that the reward and punishment theorists have been able to successfully transfer their approach from the animal laboratories to a new field of practical application to human behavior—behavior therapy (Logan and Wagner, 1965; Rimm and Masters, 1974). Employing a common sense approach, this therapy has been shown to alleviate a number of psychological impediments. The idea is simply to reward a desired behavior (such as standing up before a group at a public meeting) or to punish an undesirable one (such as smoking). Of course, we are using the terms *reward* and *punishment* in a most general sense, for what the therapist really attempts is to place a patient in a situation in which the feedback is controlled in the desired direction. In this manner, an individual is retrained to expect that undesirable acts or experiences have unpleasant side effects and desirable ones have pleasant side effects. The reward may be as abstract as imagining a pleasant situation in conjunction with a desired act. In some cases, the change in behavior is effected through the use of a model that acts in the desired way and is rewarded; this is then imitated by the patient. In aversion therapy, the same techniques are used in reverse, so that negative feedback results from the actions or experiences. Notice that what is happening is a restructuring of the individual's learning traditions through causing an unlearning of the expectations that had been set up more casually by previous feedback experiences.

Two notes, however, should be added. First, behavior therapy is probably not transferable beyond the level of particular individuals or families without the horrifying dangers of *Brave New World*. We can accept the idea of an individual requesting aversion therapy to get over alcoholism but not that of a society requesting that each of its individuals be given aversion therapy to get over petty crime. For one thing, there would no longer be genuine individual choice. But in the final analysis, all behavior therapy raises serious humanistic questions. To the systems analysts of this genre, in which Skinner surely belongs, human beings are primarily trainable machines and they are so treated. Much of behavior therapy has been applied to sexual inadequacy, and the resulting training in sexual mastery by the therapist has surely also had the by-product of changing the individual's attitude toward himself, that is, to regard his body as a pleasure machine. Thus, it may be that Rogers' *Client-Centered Therapy* (1951) is less efficacious, but it may have the humanistic value of being more respectful. The mechanistic attitude of behavior therapists seems to be associated with a low regard for the value of an individual's autonomy or free will, as are other features of the basic model we have adopted to this point. In describing rational-emotive therapy, the most cognitive of the behavior therapies, two authorities write:

> *Criminals are not* bad *or* evil *in the sense that they are deserving of punishment or damnation (although Ellis is not suggesting that society should not protect itself from their misdeeds), nor are Jonas Salk and Martin Luther King to be considered* good *people (although society is wise to reward the works of such individuals).* [Rimm and Masters, 1974, p. 419]

I find this a dismal neutrality, but an expectable result of the positive feedback of successful attempts at simplistic scientific explanation and therapy.

On Free Will

In the beginning of his collection of readings on determinism, a contemporary philosopher points out that while the determinists believe that acceptance of their views will make eutopia possible through eliminating the smug vanity and vengefulness spawned by human delusions, they fail to realize the fact that determinism also implies the elimination of the "entire notion of the human agent" (Dworkin, 1970, p. 10). To my mind, it is failure to realize the emotional and moral importance of this fact that makes the establishment of a position on the question of free will and determinism a key requirement for the development of the field of social humanities.

The recent philosophical discussion of determinism and free will might be best described as an intellectual game, in which each camp counters the other in an endless dialogue (Dworkin, 1970; Pears, 1963; Hampshire, 1965). While there are many positions, for our purposes they may be summarized as two. The first or *determinist position* is fundamentally reductionist. Decisions result from chance or programmed intrastimulation in the brain, which is made up of organic cells, which, in turn, are made up of chemical compounds. Under certain conditions, the intricate structure of the nervous system stores, retrieves, and relates information by means that are dependent upon biochemical or biophysical laws. Since we certainly do not think chemical compounds have free will, and we seldom ascribe free will to single cells, there is no reason to ascribe free will to higher levels of nervous organization just because we do not yet understand how they work. Perhaps most educated determinists do not actually make this analysis. Their analysis is simply this: Science has shown many events to be predictable if their antecedents are known. Scientific knowledge is continually explaining what previously was not explicable. Successful explanation has progressed beyond inanimate matter to explain much animal behavior and some simple areas of human behavior. While all events will never be predictable because of the complexity of the interactions of antecedent causes, one can only assume that there is potentially an infinite extrapolation of our ability to peel away mystery from events.

Just because human beings have a subjective sense that they are units capable of deciding to do other than what antecedent forces dictate they should, this does not mean that they actually have such an ability. We also believe that we are acting in dreams; but on awakening we know we are not. Why could not consciousness of human decision be similar to that of dreams? If we have been taught to value free will, we may deliberately reject the easy decision to which a situation would normally incline us in order to prove to ourselves or others we are free. But what does this prove? This rebellion is just as likely to have been determined by the interaction of chance thoughts, antecedent training, and our particular situation at the moment as any of our other actions. (Again we encounter, however, the paradox of the determinist social scientist: Since one's decision concerning determinism is, in this view, also determined, the determinist argument is itself determined.)

If the actions of all persons are actually determined, and their power to escape this net is illusory, then there is no moral responsibility. Some determinists, such as Hume or Skinner, have tried to assure us that this is not so, because insofar as a person can be taught to do something and then does it, he is responsible. In this use of language, responsible action merely means action that can be trained into, or out of, a person through reward and punishment. A responsible person is a trainable person, and an irresponsible person is intractable. But then the judicial system becomes primarily an educational system, and to punish a man because his training was wrong and reward another because it was right replaces the ethics of justice with that of efficiency. Since this eliminates the notion of freedom and the responsible human agent, as I use the language this is the strictest form of determinism.

Opposed to determinism are the concepts of freedom and free will. The central belief, which must be accepted, is that of emergent levels or emergent evolution. It is supposed that as we cross significant evolutionary boundaries, as from inanimate matter to animate matter or from unconscious life to conscious, a level of organization is reached at which units act in ways that could not be predicted from knowledge of their constituents. The existence of the previous antecedents of the new organization is a necessary but not sufficient condition for its functioning, for it now operates by its own laws. Psychologically, this position is based on the common facts that as individuals we seem to be making decisions and that we cannot imagine how we would act if we thought we could not intervene in our own decision process. How could a theory of determinism be right when we obviously could not act in its terms? There is also a good deal of discussion in the literature of the well-known indeterminacies in all scientific prediction, although the degree to which these are due to incomplete heuristic models is not clear. Of course, the fact of irreducible chance does not say much for free will, for random man is not more of a moral agent than mechanistic man.[8]

How then does the argument come out? Like most persons, I want to believe in free will, yet I am uncomfortable. A weakness of the doctrine of free will is its inability to present a coherent story of why evolutionary processes would have made selections for an organism that can decide independently of environmental feedback. Flexibility is of survival value, and therefore the evolution of an increasingly complex sensory and computing system is of survival value. But why free will? For free will must lead to missing the optimum survival response of the organism as computer. The optimum response would by definition be a predictable response once the values, information, and variation of the organism were deciphered.

This reflection leads us to note that the same evolutionary mystery surrounds the evolution of consciousness. Why does awareness help? The resolution of complex problems through intuitional flashes shows us that reflexive thinking does not require consciousness. Consciousness only seems to get in our way. For example, while fears common to all animals have survival value, what survival value has human knowledge of individual mortality?

Monod (1971, pp. 154–158) has suggested that there is survival value in being able to simulate situations that have not yet occurred. For example, before beginning a hunt, a hunter might think out where the game would be and in which direction it would go if he chose a particular approach. If selection gave the hunter the ability to visualize this kind of future event, it may be unavoidable that evolutionary processes also give him abilities to visualize the past or the more distant future, and even to play with this visionary ability. Thus, there arise the paranoic (or perhaps better, schizoid) features of man that Koestler (1967) refers to as the "ghost in the machine." In addition, the development of language had a survival value for men in groups, because it strengthened their ability to gather inputs for planning and to organize subsequent group actions on the basis of planning. As Monod points out, once developments of this kind begin, they may through positive feedback push on to develop new survival values based on the new abilities.

But what does this explanation do for free will? It seems to me that we must go back to Monod's explanation of the emergence of life and note that life is characterized by purposive behavior, directed toward survival and reproduction (Monod, 1971, pp. 8–22). This behavior is, in a sense, in the whole organism, not just in the nervous system, yet it is in the directive and coordinating role of the latter that we place purpose, and this location seems more and more appropriate as evolution proceeds. This biological goal-directedness can be thought to provide a first buffer, or question mark, between determinism in the physical-chemical sense and life, for each unit of life has its own autonomous determinism.

A second buffer would seem to arise with consciousness, for now the organism senses itself in a way the amoeba does not. It knows fear. A dolphin or a chimpanzee may come to develop apparently autonomous interests in other beings and characteristic or individual forms of play. In human beings, we may say that primary abilities for pleasure or pain may become transferred to activities no longer related to their original purpose, or they become functionally autonomous in relation to their original etiology (Allport, 1937).

But this separation of the organism from its biological ground only adds decisively to freedom when it leads to the third buffer of reflexive consciousness, or the ability of an organism to consider itself as though it were separate from itself—to become, in effect, two or more interacting, conscious selves. This partial or apparent transcendence of the primitive self would seem to be a necessary concomitant of the ability to simulate, for if we can simulate a scenario for the hunt, we can simulate alternative futures for ourselves.

Notice that on this level we are playing with and manipulating images of reality, and since thinking is behavior, we are for the moment engaged in activity (such as daydreaming) that may have little reality feedback, and consequently little survival value. But reflexivity is not all play. We may decide, for example, to commit suicide because our consideration of alternative possibilities has turned up little that is attractive and much that is not. It has been suggested that for some creatures, such as lemmings, the existence in the gene pool of a tendency to suicidal behavior under conditions of overcrowding is helpful to the species as a whole (Wynne-Edwards, 1972). However, there is no evidence that in human history overcrowding has been such a problem that individual suicide would have been adaptive for the group; this is certainly not true of suicide in the late teens. Yet suicide at this age has a long history. This does not tell us that particular suicides are not determined, but it does reinforce the point that evolution may produce new abilities, perhaps such as free will, that up to a point have no selective value.

The fourth buffer to simple determinism that man possesses is culture, or the learning traditions that have proliferated in every human group, until they form an important part of the context in which each person develops and begins to think. For an individual, his culture is part of the deterministic nexus that surrounds his actions, but for the group (seen analogously to an organism), a culture buffers the freedom of those within the group from outside forces. One of the most outstanding characteristics of cultures is the degree to which they are *not* adaptive in a simple, naturalistic sense. Food taboos and preferences are a good instance.

The development of functionally autonomous interests, reflexive consciousness, and cultures and civilization makes possible the dedication of a human life to the composition of music even when this composition brings no external reward. Is not the composer deciding to dedicate his life in this way? Still, where is the composer or the human agent? Among the synapses and the neurons of the brain he seems to vanish. Of course, we can speak of higher levels of organization not reducible to their constituents. Yet in fact, Monod (1971, p. 87) points out that in nature higher levels are reducible in the sense that the necessary and sufficient condition for the next higher system exists already in the structure and valences of its constituent systems. New creation is revealed in the higher structure, for it was chance variation in one or more of its components that predetermined it. If, to stretch the point, the potentiality of the decision to devote himself to composition exists in an individual's memory traces of prior experience with music (that is, of reward and punishment), his perception of present opportunities, the characteristics of his personality, and his natural talent and coordination, then what part has he played? Does his consciousness of himself make him more than a deluded observer forced to participate in a life in which he really has no part?

The buffers are, then, only partially convincing. In principle, all may reduce to what went before. We have, it seems to me, an insoluble mystery, and one that by its nature cannot in the foreseeable future be empirically decided one way or another. The chasm between what science knows and what it needs to know to add substantially to the argument is too great, and the subjective claim of our apparent decision-making ability too insistent. So we have what may be called a *rationally bounded mystery* at the heart of our concern. Most of human behavior may well be explicable in terms of a rational social science such as that in the model explicated in the first part of this chapter. But it is at least plausible to argue that some human behavior, and I would argue its most important part—the part that really makes us human, the part that repays us for the pain of consciousness and seeming choice—lies in the ability of individuals to establish functionally autonomous principles and realities and to respond to these as in a separate, transcendental world. On the basis of this plausibility, we must act. If there is no agent, then there is no point to the game. And so in his ignorance the social humanist opts for belief in a partially free human agent, just as an earlier generation opted for belief in the traditional concept of God. If we are right there is much to be gained, and if we are wrong there is nothing to lose.

Notes

1. Most might agree today with Moynihan's (1969) conclusion that in the present state of ignorance, "the role of social science lies not in the formulation of social policy, but in the measurement of its results" (p. 193). However, this is a minimal form of science. At the opposite extreme, Wilson (1975, pp. 43-63) sees social scientists as primarily interested in discovering the causes of action. He believes that because most social scientists are looking for the causes of behavior and most policy makers are looking for what to do about it, social scientists are often not useful in devising policy alternatives.

2. I am arguing that social science theory goes little beyond common sense (although social scientists can organize this common sense in a model that, when fleshed out with "uncommon knowledge," can be socially useful). It is true that the man in the street could not have written Kuhn's *Logic of Social Systems* (1974), but I suspect he would find little in it that was very surprising. Most surprising, counterintuitive results of social experiments are surprises primarily to social scientists with little experience in dealing with people.

3. More generally, the following discussion is based in large part on Kuhn. In Kuhn these system capabilities are called the detector, selector, and effector subsystems. Kuhn's approach is, in turn, very close to that of Homans (1961) and Blau (1964), both of whom have also profited me.

4. The basic bargaining model must, of course, be supplemented by knowledge of the biosocial tendencies of persons in bargaining situations (see Rubin and Brown, 1975). It is significant that Rubin and Brown seem implicitly to accept the model sketched here as the point of departure for experimental refinement.

5. The contrast of *exit* and *voice* as controlling alternatives in organizations (Hirschman, 1970) is equivalent to that of transaction and communication here. Exit is the primary mechanism emphasized by the economist, as in the case of the choice to buy or not, while voice is the primary mecha-

nism emphasized by political scientists, as in the ability of different segments of the population to make their desires known or to compromise differences. However, it is important to note that even in politics it is exit, that is, the leverage obtained by the threat of withdrawal, that makes much communication effective. Hirschman and Kuhn (1974) are right to emphasize the importance of communication, but it is, after all, a secondary process in society.

6.   It is important to note that human biology has also made remarkably little progress beyond common sense in understanding the working of the mind and brain (see Norman, 1970, especially pp. 375–387).

7.   Of course, personality differs from culture in having an individual, biological basis as well as a personal learning tradition. The reader should realize the following discussion is part of my continued exposition of a modified Kuhn systems model. Many of the individual deductions are not empirically verified; by their nature some cannot be.

8.   Some analysts distinguish between free will, an essentially uncaused or chance response, and free action, an action based on the personal reasons of the actor (see Bermant, 1970). However, in this discussion, I am using free will in the sense of personally determined action, and determinism to refer to the doctrine that actions are fully explainable in terms of a chain of events outside of personal control.

THREE

The Society: A Model of Organization, Variation, and External Relations

The Rational Source of Affiliation

Biosocial man lives in groups that establish rules and expectations by which he must live. In the model, he stays in a society and pays the price of the loss of freedom this entails, because this allows him to achieve his interests more efficiently than by any alternatives he perceives.

Figure 1 summarizes the systematic concept of mechanistic man presented in the last chapter and begins to relate this concept to interpersonal and organizational behavior. (The figure is modified from Kuhn, 1974, p. 11, as is much of the following discussion.) Indirectly, the figure suggests that human organizations may be seen as merely higher levels of organization than individual human beings. In these terms, the relationships of organizations internally and externally are built up analogically from an understanding of the individual. Each unit or system, whether the human brain within the individual, the individual within the corporation, or, more tenuously, the corporation within the society, may alternatively be explicable in

terms of its supersystem requirements—the functional explanation—
or of the rational goal-seeking behavior of its parts—the reductionist
explanation.

In order to understand social affiliations, it is first necessary to
understand the rationale for a person belonging to an organization.
In a simple organization, the persons who make a major bargain of
affiliation with one another do it because it is in the interest of each.
Returning to the business analogy, let us imagine I have a store and
no employees. If the business grows, I may soon find that customers
are going elsewhere because I cannot wait on them. In this case, I may
calculate that I can afford to hire an assistant at $20 a day, expecting

Figure 1. Basic Processes Within and Among Social
Units.

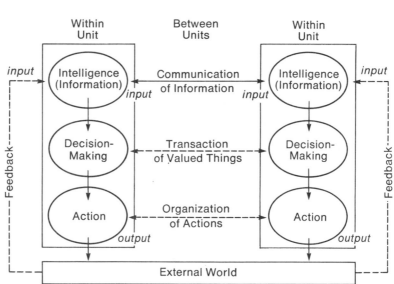

Within Unit
Input (Stimulus): Information about environment
Decision (Organism): On basis of interests of the unit
Output (Response): Actions impinging on the environment

Between Units
Communication: An interaction analyzed with respect to its in-
    formation content
Transaction: An interaction analyzed with respect to its value
    content
Organization: Joint actions by two or more persons and a super-
    system relative to those persons

(Input ⟶ Decision ⟶ Output = Stimulus ⟶ Organism ⟶ Response)

that this will lead to a net daily increase of $20 in the store's gross income. But why should I increase the size of the store and my headaches for no additional return to me? Therefore, I may attempt to hire an assistant at $15 a day, with a hidden willingness to go to $18, but no higher. If there is an acceptable person who wants to trade his time for as little as $18, he will then become my assistant, and both of us will profit from membership in the resulting organization.

In a complex organization, the major bargain is struck between an individual and an organization, so that direct personal transactions are no longer the primary cement. In such an organization there are sponsors, staff, suppliers, and recipients. The organization serves the values of the sponsors with the aid of the staff, while suppliers provide inputs and recipients receive the products, or outputs. A profit corporation, for example, is an organization in which sponsors (investors) invest money in resources (labor and capital) to produce products or services for customers. Such a corporation is a fictive person, in which basic decision-making is controlled by the sponsors and the feedback of customer actions leads to corporate learning. In the major bargain, the staff employee agrees to perform a specified role. He is responsible for performance to the person who can apply sanctions (for example, fire him), and that person, in turn, is responsible for his own performance to his superior. The employees work at the best wages and in the best positions they can get, and the sponsors offer the least they can to get the people they want. In any case, sponsors in a profit corporation employ persons only in numbers and at salaries that leave something over for themselves, and workers only accept positions that offer them more than their alternatives. If wages get too high, the investors may switch from labor-intensive to capital-intensive operations, or dissolve the organization. If wages get too low, workers will change jobs or, in a welfare state, drop out of the labor market.

The Reason Groups Must Organize

When we go beyond the level of the biological individual, we can, for the purpose of analysis, regard organizations within larger organizations or groups within groups as individual social units.

However, in *The Logic of Collective Action*, Olson (1965)

reminds us that group behavior is quite different from organizational. Too often vague theories of collective action and group interest have led us to misperceive reality and thus falsely predict and prescribe. For individuals in a group will not follow common interests, even if there is perfect consensus. (Olson rejects the idea that this means the person will act selfishly, but nearly all his cases suggest he will.) In a group, the individual has no rational reason to act in the group's interest unless his personal contribution will make a significant difference and the collective benefits from the difference achieved will reward him sufficiently to cover his personal costs. In very small groups, this may result in the more powerful or wealthy individuals working for the group's interest in spite of the lack of a guarantee that others in the group will do their share. Olson illustrates this exploitation of the strong by the weak by reference to organizations such as NATO, where the stronger regularly bear proportionally heavier burdens (Olson, pp. 34–36). It is partly for this reason that small groups are more efficient than large, as studies of decision-making groups show (Olson, p. 54).

In large groups such as labor unions, the best strategy for the individual will be to reduce his costs to zero and enjoy the rewards that accrue to all members of the group. The chance of the individual's actions making a difference is too small. As a result, in these groups, collective goals simply will not be attained unless individuals are given specific rewards for their help or are forced to help. The need for compulsion is the reason for both the closed shop and compulsory professional guilds (for example, the state bar associations). These rewards and compulsions, or, in Kuhn's (1974) terms, *goods* and *bads*, may include the emotional rewards of praise and blame, but in many groups these are weak motivators.[1] As an example of the general weakness of collective interests unsupported by these pressures, Olson describes a case in which attendance at union meetings declined drastically when fines for nonattendance were removed. Nevertheless, a subsequent poll of the members showed that nonattendance at meetings was considered one of the primary problems facing the union (Olson, p. 86). In Olson's terms, the members were both acting and communicating rationally. Failure to realize that individuals would rationally not pursue group goals was, in Olson's view, one of the fundamental mistakes of Marx's analysis of the inevitability of class struggle, and the reason Lenin later replaced this theory by the concept of a small, vanguard "sponsor" party that would make the sacrifices and reap the direct rewards of revolution (Olson, pp. 98–110).

Organizations, then, result from the biosocial need to overcome the natural inability of groups to sufficiently motivate their members by appeal to collective interests. By developing leadership positions and offering services, organizations offer special goods to particular members to raise their stakes. To become effective, organizations need to develop coercive mechanisms to prevent free riders. As Olson says, no state has ever managed to exist by voluntary taxation.

Individual Compliance and Role Definition

Societies, then, consist of individuals and groups of people, generally in organizations, with a variety of functions coexisting in one area at a time. People become members of families, businesses, governments, churches, and fraternal organizations. For any particular society, traditions have developed on how each of these types of organizations should be arranged and of the proper relations among them. A distinction must be made between active, formal *organizations* and the passive sets of cultural patterns that sociologists refer to as *institutions*.[2] Institutions are groups of assumptions about how specified persons ought to behave in a certain context. As a citizen on voting day, I have learned I should vote, and I would condemn myself and my fellows would condemn me if I did not. While in Olson's terms my vote is irrational, since it probably makes no difference, I vote to achieve the largely internal rewards and avoid the internal punishments of not voting. Institutions can, for a time and for some people, overcome the implications of Olson's analysis of collective behavior. Thus, when two people marry, they establish a new family organization and implicitly agree to follow the expectations of the institution of marriage. Persons in a society must participate in several organizations. In order to do so, they must learn to behave in terms of a variety of institutional roles and to accept outwardly the regnant assumptions as to what should be the relation among these roles. Metaphorically, the sponsors of institutions are usually the whole society, but they are particularly its religious or ideological leaders.

The relations that an individual has to his cultural tradition and the institutional roles that others expect him to play within that tradition are much disputed. Surely they vary widely from individual to individual in all societies (Hart, 1954) and greatly between societies and over time. Wallace (1961) suggests that each person adjusts through learning a cultural maze, while Riesman's (1950) other-directed, inner-directed, and tradition-directed trichotomy offers three forms of adjustment. Etzioni's (1968) concept of utilitarian compliance bridges the gap between cultural and self-interest models, for it is certainly true that most of us learn that we will satisfy our interests most easily and thoroughly if we do what is expected of us most of the time. In traffic, I drive in one lane not because it is morally right but because others expect it; casually changing lanes may cause arrest or an accident. Do I refrain from murdering my enemies for much the same reason? We need imagine little more, because the calculation of gain and loss for most potential murders weighs very much against them. We are so conditioned not to murder and to follow the rules of our society, that most of us would botch the whole thing, and we know it.

Yet organizations and societies also manage to develop communicated traditions of right and wrong that attach to all affiliated persons and to specific roles. Surely these exist on a verbal level, and in a public situation, they can be invoked to change the actions of others. The extent to which they are automatically accepted is open to a great deal of doubt. This is one reason why asking a person's attitudes or beliefs on a polling form may be of little predictive value, unless the questions are as specific as those relating to expected voting preferences. However, as is pointed out in the discussion of humanistic man in Chapter Four, inculcation of verbal cultural ideals provides the basic training that a person later uses to reevaluate his life goals in terms of an "alter ideal."

In the appendix, I suggest that a central problem of our time is the breaking down of the cultural consensus of our society, or, perhaps more precisely, the breaking down of the consensuses within the subgroups of our society. In a pluralistic society, it is not necessary that all live by the same institutions, but it is necessary that most people usually live within a nexus of relationships with people using similar sets of assumptions about the nature of reality and the human values with which decisions are made. This is, at any rate, widely believed by social scientists. Although as with most global beliefs strict proof will be hard to find, the disorganization of personal behavior in cases of acculturation or deculturation, indicated by phenomena such as alcoholism, have been well documented.

On the national scale, the collapse of the nineteenth-century social consensus in Europe between the world wars has often been noted. But the inability of the Weimar Republic or of France to stand up to the more unified, less relativistic value systems of the Nazis was only the latest in a long history of failure of the overcivilized to resist more unified barbarian groups (Ibn Khaldun, 1950, pp. 117-126). Of course, the Nazi-Weimar comparison documents the case that it is preferable for a society to fail rather than adopt just any belief system. It is partially in recognition of the alternate dangers of disorganization and evil organization that the concept of social humanities has been developed as a basis for a justifiable consensus.

Class and Status

Societies are uniformly characterized by status systems, or divisions into classes differentiated by differences in generalized power (Berelson and Steiner, 1964, pp. 453-491; Gastil, 1973a). Mechanistically, classes emerge and are maintained as a by-product of the pursuit of individual interests. Of course, abilities that increase individual productivity will vary from context to context. At the most primitive level, the physically stronger person often had more general power than any other, and so strength came to be the main basis of status differentiation. Very soon, however, other skills, such as eloquence, manual dexterity, and organizational ability, came to have at least equal importance. Soon people with power invested it in the future by distributing their wealth or influence among their children, other relatives, or friends. In this way, the power of one generation became the basis of the power of the next.

The maintenance of power relations may be explained in interest terms. If an individual has high status, this means that he has more power to obtain what he wants than those of lower status, and, conversely, that one can get more from him than can be obtained from a lower-status person. The benefits others can confer on one because of their general power are quite various, but include gifts, property exchanged through marriage, the quality of social entertainment, and contacts through which employment at various levels may be attained. Over time, the separate classes tend to develop particular standards of speech and behavior; these secondary features of class then reflect the power of the higher classes or the weakness of the lower. For this reason, all persons will tend to want to deal with persons of as high a status as possible. For those at the top, this will mean that they will wish to have relations primarily with those of their own status, while those below will wish only for contacts with people of their own status or higher. Since a lower-class person wants contact with a higher-class person more than the latter does with him, he must "pay" for the contact through deference, which is often paid with ambivalence. For this reason and because lower-status persons are not wanted in many interactive situations, groups of people with relatively open familiarity among themselves include only those of roughly equal status.

Societal Change and Differentiation

Just as groups of people tend to differentiate themselves on a class basis in a complex society, they have also tended to differentiate themselves from one another on a territorial basis for reasons of economy of communication and the distribution of power. Let us imagine that you are a man of power in a community, and you refer to a certain dangerous animal as a "combi," while everyone else in the community has their own word for the creature. Soon those wishing for a closer relation to you will note that if they call the animal a combi, you will be pleased; gradually a speech community emerges with this usage. As it emerges, usage of the word becomes standardized, and to use another term may, in a crisis, lead to harm for both the speaker and those in the group with whom he desires to communicate. For analogous reasons, all of those who regularly need to communicate will tend to develop the same language, because it is in the interest of all to do so and the costs are very low. But insofar as there is a choice, change will be in the direction of the usage of the powerful.

In a similar way, cultural groups develop distinctive traditions in most areas of potential learning. Children learn that adults think them wiser if they believe what adults believe; colonels, if they believe what generals believe. If an advisor to a leader agrees with the leader's judgment the leader concludes: His judgment has been confirmed; the judgment of the advisor is of high quality (because it is confirmed by another, that is, himself), and his judgment in choosing the advisor is confirmed. The leader feels good about the whole thing, and the advisor notes this feeling. After a few iterations of this pattern, it will take quite a shock of negative feedback from the real world to break up this autistic world of communication between the advisor and advisee. It is simple enough to imagine how even the strangest belief systems may become widely diffused and persistent once a persuasive leader has enunciated them, and a coterie of followers has developed.

There are, of course, countervailing forces to both the spread and the persistence of new belief systems. The first countervailing forces are those of communication barriers, competition, and random change. Because of actual or sociocultural distance (Sorokin, 1943) and the imperfect nature of communication, there will be a decay of similarity as one moves from the center to the periphery of societies. This basic assumption of cultural diffusionists is perhaps best illustrated by the relation of dialect variation to distance (Bloomfield, 1933). Some people also have a natural tendency to try to improve their status position by breaking out of their position in the traditional hierarchy and successfully communicating aberrant symbols, beliefs, or practices. If they can get others to follow their lead, then their personal power will be enhanced in ways they believe it could not be within the hierarchy. To take a recent example, if homosexuality is discountenanced in our society, then the response of most homosexuals will be to discountenance it as well. They may hide their feelings or live in fear with consequent loss to themselves. In a context of liberalization, however, some homosexuals may note that they might gain more by offering a public doctrine that homosexuality should be regarded as of equal merit to heterosexuality. If generally successful, they will increase their power in the whole society, in part by increasing the power of their friends; even if generally unsuccessful, they may develop a group of true believers that increases the power of its members to satisfy their interests over what it was before the group "came out."

Related to this countervailing force is the heterogeneity of messages that people receive in all cultures, but especially in complex civilizations. Spin-offs into opposing cultural groups may represent the results of spiraling disputes based on the slightly different reception of a tradition in a community, as well as the often conscious exploitation of those differences by leaders or followers to serve personal interests. Finally, the most important countervailing force stems from the fact that human beings are naturally propelled to try to make sense of their world and to go beyond what they have received. Every time they try, they potentially establish a new tradition.

Ultimately, the most important control over change or the direction of change in a belief is the feedback from actions that are based on the belief. If there are no actions that follow from a belief, then it can be as bizarre as human imagination allows. Yet if we include thoughts as actions, as they surely are for philosophers and scientists, then there is almost no belief conceivable that is not directly or indirectly related to the real world through intervening actions. In other words, all beliefs are embedded in patterns of belief, so that if any part of a pattern is tested by its effect on action, all parts of the pattern are tested. If a belief in a magical theory of illness leads to less improvement in health than the germ theory of disease, then the magical theory will be replaced; for every new disease, we will look for causative germs or analogous agents. Of course, in the most arbitrary symbolic systems, such as language, feedback from the physical and biological world is of only limited value in explaining change and persistence. Here, fashion can have its freest play, yet it remains constrained by the desire of individuals in any community for effective communication.

The Selective Pressure of Social Inequality

While status systems are inevitably developed out of the struggle of individual interests, they survive historically because in the struggle of groups, they evidently helped, or at least did not hinder, group survival. Thus, the rationale for one person driving a new car while his neighbor drives a clunker goes back to the fact that men have different abilities. The lazy and fearful or stupid and weak always tend to receive less in life. On the most primitive level, the man who hunted regularly and risked his life intelligently for the group was rewarded with status if not wealth. The best girls were offered or offered themselves to him as brides; for instance, among the Siriono of Bolivia the one who brings home the meat of the day gets the girls that night (Holmberg, 1969). Rewards for effort are granted by all groups, because groups would starve or be destroyed if everyone were allowed to live equally on the efforts of everyone else. Children in all societies are rewarded for helping, because if the connection between work and reward is not established when the person is not yet grown, it will be difficult to establish later.

Most economic theory, especially that associated with the market behavior of capital and labor, is based upon the assumptions of this model. In particular, those who oppose the welfare state assume that as unearned welfare benefits rise, increasing numbers of people will simply drop out of the labor market and live on the benefits, while the motivation (or discipline) of those who continue to work will be lowered. This is particularly true when welfare systems reduce benefits as recipients increase their earned incomes. Critics of this analysis claim that the poor prefer work to welfare and accept welfare only if there is no other course. We can agree with the critics that there is little experimental or other proof of the economist's assumptions, although there is a great deal of case study and common sense evidence (Gastil, 1973a). The reasons for the difficulty of obtaining hard evidence are evidenced by the almost complete methodological breakdown of even large, heavily funded experiments, such as the New Jersey Negative Income Tax Experiment (Peckman and Timpane, 1975). This experiment showed that there was a slight reduction in the amount of work done by those receiving increased welfare benefits. However, there were too many people who left the system, the sample was too skewed by design, and the change in the rest of the welfare system in New Jersey during the course of the experiment overwhelmed many of the results. More generally, all large-scale, non-case studies of people on welfare are bedeviled by two insurmountable problems: A great deal of money earned in the world of people on welfare goes unreported, and those living off the welfare checks are often persons not officially on the welfare rolls (especially boy friends and grown sons).

However, the reader should note carefully the complexities of our theory in this regard. It assumes that successful cultures will teach the principle that all healthy adults must earn their living and will reinforce this principle with appropriate reward and punishment. Therefore, in most societies, a person living off the work of others will generally look down on himself and be looked down on by his neighbors (unless he has very high status). In a normal community, this would surely mean that most people will prefer work to welfare benefits, for if we count the nonmaterial rewards of the approbation of a person's fellows, his overall return will be much higher if he works. But if there develop subcommunities in which many people become accustomed to receiving welfare benefits and not working becomes accepted and even praised as clever by some, then over a period of time learning (feedback) will produce a population in which many members will simply not work unless there is a large differential monetary reward to be obtained through it (Caudill, 1962; Gazaway, 1969; Leighton, 1959).

A great deal of nonsense has been written about work. It is not automatic or fun—much of it is not rewarding in itself. It is true that for some people work does become a hobby. But if your work was a hobby, you probably would pursue it with a great deal less intensity and regularity, and according to a quite personal scheme of value that others might not find useful.

An implicit reason for inequality, then, is the desire of a society's sponsors to motivate each individual in the group to contribute as much as possible toward the well-being of the whole. Those who contribute more, get more. In a fairly loose society, every individual has his own scale of values, and he can choose fame and fortune or personal ease. But of course, the limits of reward are different for each individual. Since the average person is neither physically nor mentally strong enough to excel, if he strives he will do only somewhat better than others. With enough effort, a man with a relatively poor mind can find two jobs and attain salaries the equivalent of school teachers' or even assistant professors'. But some in society will see no justice when a bright person receives five times this level of income because an inherited ability or social position made it possible to enter one of the higher paying professions or businesses.

However, it may always be necessary to give a differential reward in terms of contribution to society, for the alternative may be to literally apply the whip to everyone's back and mobilize society as a slave state. Even communist states are coming to realize this dilemma, this tension of ideals and reality. One suspects that no matter how productive our society becomes, there will be little change in the necessity to motivate economic activity by reward and punishment. Maintaining the computers of the twenty-fifth century will require a level of dedication and attention that will be higher than the average monitor of that age will be willing to give simply out of a sense of personal responsibility. There will always be dull jobs and more exciting things to do, although what today seems exciting and easy will be considered drudgery by our descendants.

Reward and punishment is in many respects a universal requirement for the organization of personalities and society, as animal psychologists such as Skinner have tried to demonstrate. Policies for the prevention of poverty, crime, or war must all be developed in terms of this fact. The less punishment is feasible or the less society chooses to use punishment, the more society must reward, and vice versa. The situation is not perfectly symmetrical. Toward the reward-only end of the spectrum, the demands of recipients are apt to run up against the limits of available supplies, while recipients become increasingly ungrateful and demanding (compare Paddock and Paddock, 1964; Caudill, 1962). On the other hand, with extremely effective, Nazi-type repression, the victims often become quite docile and the repression can even be relaxed somewhat. In a middle range of approaches, there is a choice between forcibly preventing an action or threatening punishment and offering bribes or buying out the opposite party. Of course, it is hard to orchestrate the solution, for the very offering of potential rewards suggests a weakness, in either force or determination, which may then be exploited.

This brings us to the principle of *scientific limits* that Sorokin (1947, pp. 699-700) expounded so effectively to generations of sociology students. Every social law, every relationship we believe we see between two social factors, will turn out to be valid only within specified limits or boundaries of application. For example, a market economy achieves efficiency by establishing a natural price through the equilibrium established by fluctuations in supply and demand. Yet Hardin points out that left to itself, such an economy will also drive out the less efficient companies with each dip in price. While at first this guarantees efficiency, where economies of scale are decisive it will eventually result in monopoly (Hardin, 1968a; compare Samuelson, 1969). This result is initially the victory of the most efficient, but it may be maintained in the face of inefficiencies if the concentration of economic power in one firm makes the entry of others too difficult. One may think of the American auto industry (excluding imports from quite different economies) or of newspapers in single-paper cities. In these cases, monopoly evidently destroys the market system, which can only be reestablished by regulations that work against concentration. But over time the regulators will also amass power, and they too can wreck the system. So the free market system only exists in a limited social space characterized by negative feedback and not in those areas on either side where positive feedback generated by aspects of its operation would destroy the system. The reader may think of other perfectly reasonable social propositions, such as, "the society succeeds best that is best able to defend itself," or "the most effective teacher will be the teacher that is most open with his students," that on reflection will be found to be true only within certain limits, boundaries, or conditions.

Legitimacy and Social Determinism

Societies and organizations originally developed to serve the goals of their sponsors (which may include most of their members), and they change to meet the changing interests of these persons. In sociology, structural functionalists have analyzed how organizations and social institutions serve the members of a society, but Marxists have analyzed how institutions and organizations serve their sponsors. While tradition will not in itself maintain an institution for long, a small group may support the maintenance of obsolete institutions or roles that serve them personally rather than the interests of the whole society. One may think of a shaman who, by maintaining the fears of his people, ensures their support, or of an army that, through supplying misleading intelligence on neighboring armies, ensures large appropriations for its support. However, in general, role definitions are traditionally legitimized compromises between the interests of those likely to be concerned in their performance and their performers, and express in a salient form the power of each side as meliorated by the ideals of the general culture.

Every cultural group has built up a social system with governmental and economic subsystems that is backed by both religious and secular traditions and handed down from generation to generation. If a person attains power and wealth by means that are acceptable in a particular system, then it is conventionally said that most people in the society believe that he has legitimately attained his position and respect him for it. However, the more we look at history and life around us, the more we find legitimacy questioned and questionable. Often a sudden revolution shows that what appeared to be an accepted social order was only the product of general acquiescence while waiting for an apparently superior alternative.

Every social group, even the family, needs leaders and followers, and the group will do better if the more competent members are selected to lead. We have already established the necessities of status differentiation and reward and punishment, but this does not explain why the most competent and altruistic people often do not become leaders. Because functions are served by political organizations does not mean that men have generally enjoyed or accepted the way concrete hierarchies have been established. An examination of history suggests that most men have seldom felt their rulers really had their interests at heart. Rulers have generally been seen as a necessary evil, facts of life which most people at most times lived with as well as they could.

An examination of this thesis might start with a rough categorization of men in any society into the *rulers* and the *ruled*. The ruled should be subdivided into a generally supportive mass and a small number of persons who consciously think of themselves as oppressed. Within the ruling class, there are perhaps only two completely satisfied men, the most powerful and the most wealthy, and often each is trying to earn both appellations for himself. Generally, any ruling class will have one or more *factions* that bitterly resent the fact that other individuals or factions are currently ruling or are more wealthy, but at the same time believe in the existing social system, in the structure of society that provides them with privileged status. Such dissident factions within the ruling class may stage coups or temporarily ally themselves with oppressed classes to achieve changes in personnel, but they do not intend to cause a general class inversion. The *supportive mass* is made up of those who act as though they have decided that struggle for change in the system or its personalities is not worth the danger and exertion. Generally, they have adopted various defense mechanisms to avoid noticing their surrender or acquiescence. If they do not identify with their rulers, they may encapsulate their activities in little worlds, such as clubs, so that success in these worlds becomes for the average man a reasonable substitute for more general success.

On the basis of his study of the English, American, French, and Russian revolutions, Brinton (1965) found that a revolutionary situation is characterized by a rising standard of living, particularly among those directly involved in the revolution's planning, and bitter class hatred between the rising classes and those established before them. Also critical to the prerevolutionary syndrome is a transfer of allegiance by intellectuals from the established system to the proto-revolutionaries. (Although this is the most reliable indicator Brinton found, he also remarks that the alienation of intellectuals is endemic in modern western society.) In addition to this transfer, the old ruling class loses faith in itself and its right to rule, while its members tend either to lapse into dissolution or to become revolutionaries themselves. Equally important is a failure of the governmental machinery to cope with the prerevolutionary situation. This failure becomes most dramatic when revolutionary violence develops, because in this process the observer is impressed not so much by the ability of the revolutionists as by the inability of the government to effectively oppose the often weak revolutionary forces that challenge it. Apparently, for a revolution to succeed, a government must lose the capacity to use force either to maintain order or to suppress opposing force.

From a general perspective, we can say that there are two conditions under which the support by the mass for the established order becomes so weak that revolution may succeed. First, if there is a noticeable rise in insecurity and danger in the lives of average men, then their support of established order comes into question. Only if this order shows signs of reestablishing security or of still offering better security than available alternatives will most people be willing to continue to actively support the order. If it does not, large numbers will stand aside under conditions of stress, even though most men will still not become active revolutionaries. Their calculation pertains to personal, or at best family, gain and loss, not group gain and loss. The second reason for a deterioration of the support of the majority is that economic, material, or cultural expectations are not met. In most times and places, expectations have been limited to a rough justice and the availability of necessities, but since the seventeenth century, revolutions have often been caused by failures to meet the expectations aroused by rapidly rising benefits (see Davies, 1969; Olson, 1963).

Revolutions are almost always pursued by *dissident minorities*. In normal times, these minorities within the mass are made up primarily of those persons who, while regarding themselves highly, have no way to rise with satisfactory speed within the current structure or have personally failed to do so through bad luck or incompetency. The numbers of those actively disaffected will swell if the ruling class seems weak or vulnerable or if the rewards of acquiescence in the system seem to be diminishing.

Dissidence will also be common among those who have been expelled from one social system and are not yet a part of another. On the personal level, this implies that dissidence will be most common among those who have left the family they grew up in and have not yet formed families of their own. On the societal level, the proposition leads us to look for dissidence among those who have been cut off from an earlier way of life and have not yet constructed a new pattern. In both cases, these are circumstances in which the advantages of conformity have lessened, while expectations and possibilities of both success and failure seem limitless.

All will agree that we have discussed an aspect of reality, but there will be a good deal of disagreement about the extent to which we have described the most important aspects of social structure. The foregoing is essentially a realist, or conflict, analysis often associated today with Marxist theory,[3] while the most common social scientific theories in academia in the 1950s were structural-functional or culturological. According to the latter, men in societies were brought up to believe in those values, beliefs, and norms that characterized their culture, and these had such a strong hold on persons in the society that they could hardly avoid playing the roles ascribed to them or competing for those roles they could achieve. Both rulers and ruled acted in terms of their culture, ultimately for the benefit of one another, out of a desire to play their expected parts in the social drama.

One of the most striking examples of the clash of realist and culturological interpretations is in the interpretation of the Australian male initiation ceremonies. These ceremonies involved circumcision and often considerably crueler mutilations of the male genitals in the context of a great deal of ceremonial verification of the mystical powers of the older men. According to the culturologists, these ceremonies were conducted generation after generation because they were the "culturally defined norm," and the forms surrounding the initiation gave meaning to the life of the whole group. According to the realist view, the ceremonies and the operations were designed to overwhelm the impressionable young males (and all women) with the powers of the old men, so that the old men could continue in undisputed mastery of the group long past their physical prime (Radin, 1955, 1957; Spencer and Gillen, 1966; Berndt and Berndt, 1951; Hart and Pilling, 1960). It seems significant that for their extremely low level of technological development, the Australian aborigines perhaps had, of any culture that has been studied: the most elaborate ceremonies and mutilations; the most power in the hands of the old, some leaders being over 60; the most inequitable division of the women, the old men getting the young women, and often several, while young men were often given women of 30 or 40 (who were considered more able to introduce them to sex).

The structural-functional approach is essentially a variety of the culturological approach. It grants that the normative structuring of society is crucial, but it specifically tries to show how the structuring of certain groups is determined by the interaction of economic, social, and technological situations with the biological nature of man. In other words, while cultural norms determine behavior in the short run, the norms are themselves usually the product of predictable interactions of biosocial factors with changing situations.

Cultural explanations may or may not admit that structural-functional, or biosocial, factors are crucial in the formation of cultures, although they surely play a part. Some culturologists see the development and diffusion of ideas and things as historically (situationally) determined, with biosocial factors placing only the broadest of limits on the results. A people may have a trait because it is functionally adaptive or because they happened to borrow or invent it. Of course, the truth is usually in between, but this is a very important continuum on which to place the thought of social analysts. For if we believe that current societies are structured almost entirely by necessary, internal processes of readjustment and adjustment to changing circumstances, and that what is not functional is necessarily discarded, then it is foolish, for example, to try to teach democracy to the Gabonese. If democracy is right for them, they should evolve it themselves, or at least readily choose it; if it is wrong, they will adopt some other system, such as one-party socialism. Similarly, military actions within and among countries would have no long-range significance, since the society of the future is foreordained by natural biosocial processes. One can be a pessimist or optimist about these processes, one can hope to ease transitions, but in the end structural-functional thinking should lead to passivity. Indeed, much of the criticism of and withdrawal from this approach in the 1960s resulted from the fact that structural functionalism did not lend support to violent action or rapid change.

My belief is that although there are no doubt biosocial pressures for the adoption of certain forms under certain conditions, the range of alternative group responses to any situation is not adequately suggested by structural functionalism. At the most primitive level of technology and ecological relationships, the Australian aborigine was not typical. Australian tradition developed in a fair degree of isolation. It was a good culture for the old but unusually oppressive for the majority. Maybe, on balance, it was a good system. But the young Eskimo or Paiute or Bushman male certainly was glad it was not universal. Today, in the developing world, we are told that central planning and some totalitarian controls are necessary for the inevitable process of development to occur. The extent to which this position is pushed can be seen in the following quotation from a leading American structural functionalist:

> *In this sense the cultural background of the West permitted* laissez-faire *government. . . . The second pattern applies to many of the countries that have more recently*

*entered the path toward industrialization. Here I lump
together Russia and China, as well as some of the developing
nations in Southern and Southeast Asia and Africa. (Note: For
a variety of reasons I exclude Japan, the Middle East, and
Latin America.) Many of the new nations have inherited very
conservative religious traditions . . . consequently they have
had to manufacture . . . a cultural background favorable to
industry, in the form of vigorous nationalist movements. . . .
These countries have required strong governmental action.
. . . This feature is especially marked in the communist countries, but is evident also in Southeast Asia and Africa.
[Smelser, 1966, pp. 257–258]*[4]

This is a purely functional explanation—communist government was caused by the situation rather than vice versa. Ideology
plays no role in this world of ideas; it is rather an epiphenomenon.
There is no serious attempt to see if the religious situation was different in communist and noncommunist countries; in fact, one could
make the opposite argument and suggest that religion was generally
weaker and more discredited in those underdeveloped countries in
which communism has spread rapidly. The author also seems
unaware of how hard it is to find correlations among rates of development, systems of government, and types of economic planning. At the
time he wrote, outside of Europe and America, the countries of
Lebanon, Greece, Colombia, Malaysia, Thailand, Taiwan, and
Japan had been doing much better than many states that had emphasized planning or given less attention to democratic forms.

Forms of Political Organization

While in the corporation either sponsors or employees may
pull out at any time, this is not true of more permanent organizations,
such as political states. Here the population as a whole serves as both
a major supplier, in its role as a tax base, and the major consumer of
system output. In the state, there is always overlap between sponsors,
staff, resources (including tax base), and customers, and the general
population may or may not be willing and able to play its roles. In a
democracy it is assumed that the sponsors are the whole people. They
hire employees (representatives and bureaucrats), who then utilize the
tax base to provide services for the sponsors. Since the sponsors, the

tax base, and the customers are largely identical, there is rapid feed-back from undesired governmental actions either in the collection of taxes or the provision of services. In a democracy, there are also civil liberties, which may be thought of as constitutional (major bargain) limitations on staff control over individual actions. In a dictatorship, whether personal or party, the sponsors are only a minority of the people, while the tax base and the customers are the whole people. Since satisfying the interests, monetary or ideological, of the sponsors is the goal of the dictatorial governmental organization, decisions are easier to arrive at and enforce than in a democracy. However, feed-back from governmental action is generally of lower quality and of a different nature. In an ideological dictatorship, the goal is to improve the power of the state and change the beliefs or actions of its people with their personal wishes secondary.

In each type of governmental model, there is a basic under-standing between the people and those who govern them. Fundamental to government is the assumption that a government controls the expression of violent force in the country. In a democracy, this force is never to be used by a government in power simply to keep itself in power, because this would replace the people as sponsors with government staff as sponsors. In a dictatorship, on the other hand, the use of force both to maintain the governmental system and to maintain a particular group in power is understood, because the sponsors and the government staff stand together, while the people are only to act as suppliers and recipients.

Of course, in the real world there are no pure dictatorships or democracies, but many states lie close to one or the other end of the continuum between the ideal types (Gastil, 1974b). Democracies are never pure because staffs are composed of people whose self-interest lies both in playing their assigned roles and in exploiting these roles for personal benefit. Yet the positive feedback of power accumulation will be persistently checked by institutionalized competitors or publics who have an interest in seeing staff roles defined narrowly. It has been argued that since public opinion is easily manipulated, the sponsor role of the public through elections is merely a facade. However, detailed studies of the relations between voter judgment of both personal and societal interests and voting behavior often show that the outcome of elections reflects to a remarkable degree the interests of the voter as he sees them, particularly as these reflect his judgment of the recent record of the party in power (Key, 1966). On the other hand, within the democratic framework, private organizations adopting democratic forms, such as labor unions, do commonly become facades in which the staff usurps the sponsor function. This is so for a variety of reasons, including member disinterest and the large gap between office holders and members, and makes the leaders willing to do almost anything to stay in office (Lipset, Trow, and Coleman, 1956).[5]

Dictatorships are never pure because the staff-sponsors will find it in their interest to respond to feedback from the tax base and customers, and they treat the people at times as quasi-sponsors. An ideological dictatorship is also impure because the personal interests of the staff-sponsors often overwhelm ideological interests, as in the "new class" phenomenon in communist states (Nove, 1975).

A dictatorship is stable to the extent that the people are convinced they have no alternative, and this is most easily achieved by the consistent application of force whenever the least threat appears, especially whenever a competitive coalition begins to form. In a system in which force is the basis of a particular group's rule, using transactions in Kuhn's goods beyond a certain point is dangerous, because it would communicate the fact the people have power and excite their use of it. If a sufficiently cross-checking hierarchical structure can be established and communication within the structure sufficiently inhibited, one or a few people at the top of a dictatorship can hold the system together with minimal effort at positive communication or transaction in goods and a consistent control over the use of bads. This was, for example, the achievement of Duvalier's administration in Haiti. Another way to put this is that sponsors of dictatorships (or profit-making governments) can lose repeatedly in their efforts to control through the preferred methods, but they are aware that they dare not lose in their calculation of force balances. To offer better arguments or more goods to the population may be a useful way to supplement their control of force, but these actions can never substitute for it; nor can the leadership sleep if they allow this softening to go too far in the area of civil rights.

Natural Democracy

History suggests that there is a biosocial pressure in groups toward democracy, if not constitutional democracy, and in dominant individuals or ruling elites toward dictatorship. For the average person, democracy has a universal, primitive appeal. The feeling for primitive democracy expresses itself most often in the idea that all— or at least all adult men—should agree to a course of action before the group pursues it and that leaders should be chosen by the group. (Because of superior physical strength, aggressiveness, and common interests resulting from the division of labor based on these facts, men have historically formed the dominant coalition in most societies; see note 7 of this chapter.) Of course, such unanimity often leads to the coercion or expulsion of the individual who stands against the group.

Any individual or group that rules against the real or apparent will of the people requires a special doctrine to disprove the appearance of injustice in its rule. Much of the elaborate ritual, theory, theology surrounding nondemocratic systems appears to have been created in a desire to answer the nagging questions "Why do I?" or "Why do we?" rule.

There is a sense in which most governments in recorded history have been illegitimate and so regarded by their people and even at times by the rulers themselves. There has been a guilt in ruling which, combined with the fear of dissent, often makes a system fearsome in its oppressions. This point may be illustrated by mentioning certain aspects of Middle Eastern history. About 500 A.D. a religious reformer called Mazdak arose in Persia. According to tradition, he gathered about him a considerable following and finally attained the confidence of the Sassanian emperor. Mazdak taught that it was not right that there be rich and poor, rulers and ruled. Since this doctrine threatened their position, the nobles and priests developed a scheme by which they were able to eliminate Mazdak and his followers. But for hundreds of years, long after Islam had come to Iran, the ruling classes still lived in fear of Mazdak's ideas and the remnants of his following (Brown, 1951, pp. 166-172, 310-313; Firdowsi, 1931, pp. 361-367; Christensen, 1944). Rulers under Islam were even more explicitly illegitimate; after the first four caliphs, power in Islam was maintained by legal fictions that were only provisionally acceptable to the religious leaders. Rulers should have been elected by the body of the faithful; they were not. They should have been good Muslims and have abstained from alcohol; generally, they drank, often to abandon. Most often, their only right to rule was conquest, and the doctrine finally came to be that whoever was mentioned in the Friday prayer as ruler should be so regarded. About one ruler of eastern Islam, the chronicler writes that he was a coppersmith in the bazaar but well liked by men. He set up a gang of highway robbers. Succeeding in this, he was appointed a chief of his district. Then he displaced the governor and finally reached for empire. He was a good leader of men in the business of violence (Gardizi, 1948).

Mazdak was hardly a unique figure in early history. Cohn (1970) has documented in great detail the antipriest, antinoble movements of the Middle Ages in northern Europe and England. Conspicuous behind all of these movements was the assumption of the illegitimacy of those having wealth and power. The ease with which peasants could be convinced of this and the fact that the top strata had to rely on mercenaries to help them against the mobs attest to the weakness of the average man's belief in the legitimacy of the system he was forced to live under throughout this period.

Historically, most princely houses have been based on tyrants who had little more than their control of violence to recommend them. Yet historically the princes were important men, and their foibles left an impact. Many illegitimate rulers changed the cultural norms, the rules of behavior, for those who came after. The relation of the religious innovations of Henry VIII to his marital difficulties was not unusual—just more spectacular than most.

So it was that when the English masses began to rebel under the guise of religion in the seventeenth century, many disparate groups quickly came to the same conclusions as Mazdak. All men are equal; there is no kingly right to rule. If the king is not an efficient servant, he is nothing. Sooner or later the English revolution ran its course; the desire for liberty and equality was less strong than the desire for stability, and for a time the people again bought protection with their liberties (Gooch, 1959). The sense of injustice had run up against the biosocial fact that a ruling group, even a poor and unjust one, is preferable to chaos. In Wallace's (1961) terms, no one can live in a maze without walls.

Violence and Internal Order

The discussion of democracy suggests the importance of violence in determining what group will rule and often which individuals within the ruling group will be on top. Since even the directions in which cultures develop have been determined by violence, we should expect it still to be playing an important part today. Communism, fascism, and constitutional democracy became models in the world because they succeeded through violence, and to a considerable degree, their violent successes determined their further appeal. Fascism lost its appeal when it lost in arms. Rebels in Hungary in 1956 lost an appeal to arms, and when they failed potential rebels even in the People's Republic of China abandoned hope for revolution against communism (Loh, 1962, pp. 228–233). Americans have the society they do today because they killed the Indians, defeated the British, and crushed the Southern threat to national unity. That "noble experiment" Israel exists only because of excellence at arms and the thorough mobilization of its people for war. The best, the most progressive, the sentimentally most appealing often lose, because they fail militarily. As Taylor has pointed out, Germany might rule Europe today if Hitler had not been carried away by the dream of conquering Russia (Taylor, 1961). It was hubris that destroyed the fascists. Athens was crushed by more and more simplistic peoples until its genius finally disappeared. But much of the greatness of Athens was made possible by the repression of slaves and the barbaric destruction of neighbors so that a few Athenians might enjoy a rather ideal democracy for a while. This should all be obvious, as is most good social analysis. Yet people need to be reminded, because analyses of national and international problems often seem oblivious to this common fund of human experience.

A second lesson which we might learn is the inevitable tension between ideals, such as equality and democracy, and their practical application. Ideally, force and violence are not used by one man against another to secure rule over a state or to secure a larger share of the goods of life. Men do not by right take the lives of one another.

Then these—democracy, equality, and pacifism—are the recurrent doctrines of those free intellectuals who are not dedicated to preserving the institutions of a particular society. However, men in more direct contact with affairs know that people are not as they should be. They are often selfish, cruel, and greedy, as well as occasionally altruistic, dedicated, and high-minded. They know that to prevent a person from being dominated by his less attractive traits, he must be rewarded for good behavior and punished for poor behavior. The punishment can be of different kinds, but it must be there. It is strange that people who would agree with this statement for developing a growing person often disagree when visualizing the structuring of adult life. Education is a lifelong process; even in senility we keep learning what we can and cannot get away with.

Experience suggests that many individuals must be forcibly and violently suppressed in every society. There are numerous types of insanities and mental deficiencies that require control for the protection of others. If these individuals do not respond to many of the normal social pressures, this suggests another biological requirement for counterviolence.

As discussed above, democracy is based on the idea that the community should not let a few people attain power against the wishes of the majority and then stay in power by violence or the threat of violence. Once this idea becomes well established, only foreign occupation or extreme degeneracy is apt to allow the system to be broken. Historically, however, most communities have had a small, elite group that tenaciously defended its power by violent means. In both democracy and dictatorship, the punishment of those striving for power through channels not acceptable to the ruling group has generally been violent. The record suggests that in most states, stability has required the use of violence; when the military and police capacities of a state weakened, and the certainty of defeat and punishment for disaffected members of the elite or masses waned, chaos followed (Brinton, 1965). The reluctance of a government to suppress violence too often merely permits those who are willing to fight to decide the issue violently. Similarly, in the relations between states, unwillingness to fight by one party too often merely transfers the load to another.

As we will see in the section on ideas below, because of the power of ideas and the ability of men to make meaningful choices among ideas, change can occur without violence. The fact that there is biosocial pressure for violence and change to occur together does not make their association inevitable. In particular, it is not true, as some social scientists believe, that underdeveloped countries cannot progress rapidly without bloody revolutions (Heilbronner, 1963). While this may be true of some rigid societies with a small ruling group, social structures that rapidly adjust to changing majorities are able to accommodate changes of direction without violence. In any situation, personal abilities and cultural norms will determine the amount of violence that will accompany change. However, if a group of people believes, is taught to believe, or finds through experience that violence is rewarding for it, then it will practice violence. With practice, violence will become the habitual means of achieving social objectives. This is as true of police as of criminals, rioters, or aggressive ruling groups.

The costs to a society of internal violence, even if it achieves change, are often greater than the advantages gained. The scars of violence inhibit orderly process. The comparative ease with which Americans gained independence in the eighteenth century made more likely the creation of a flexible, democratic process. The French revolution of 1789 or the Vietnamese struggle against the French in this century established traditions that left legacies of hate and repression, which have been difficult to overcome. In the American Revolution, the remarkable lack of serious in-fighting among the secessionists created a firm ground for continuing compromise for eighty years. Yet within any society, when a threat of violence does develop, it is often contained only by the use and threat of counterviolence—the South revolted only once.

International Relations and War

Although the interactions of organizations are analogous to those of individuals, organizations are less likely than individuals to depart from the neutral transactional mode. Organizations do not have human emotions, and so cannot receive pleasure from the pleasure or pain of others nor benefit from communication by itself. Moreover, an organization usually has a mixed and changing group of sponsors, whose most salient common goal is apt to be narrow organizational self-interest. Although there are widely varying definitions of organizational self-interest, staffs in most organizations can rely upon that community of interest between themselves and their sponsors that is based on organizational survival or expansion.

The most important organizations are national governments, and the most important external interactions of organizations are those that take place between national governments. Again, as in the relations between individuals, the preferred means of reaching agreement among governments is communication, that is, the attempt of one state to point out the advantages to other states of a desired policy or action. Communications might then be used to initiate transactions in goods in which both states would be equally pleased. If these approaches are insufficient, an additional means of achieving international objectives is to initiate transactions in bads, either through threats, the application of stress (increasing loss), or simple dispossession. Since personal heroism in war is no longer a highly valued good in itself, in the modern world states will generally prefer transactions in goods to transactions in bads, but bads will be preferred when the probable benefits relative to costs are greater.

Peace is a particular major bargain among contracting states by which subsidiary communications and transactions take place. It is strongest when all the parties to the bargain have approximately an equal interest in maintaining it. Should one nation have a greater interest than another in peace, its bargaining position in subsidiary transactions is eroded, just as the person most interested in maintaining a marriage has the poorer bargaining position within the marriage on other issues. This leads to the dilemma that faces all peace movements that are not equally strong within all states that are parties to a major bargain of peace: The more successful they are in convincing a people to prefer peace to war, the more likely they are to upset the balance of interests in peace, in which terms the peace bargain is maintained. This works to the disadvantage of the more peaceful state or causes a severe rejection of the peace position when its population sees the results of continued appeasement (and has not yet seen the results of war).

Any successful strategy to prevent war must include both force and accommodation. To prevent wars, each country must give opponents some hope for continued prosperity and give little reason for continued apprehension. At the same time, the actions of a state must not suggest the possibility that an opponent can move forward militarily or politically without incurring the danger that the state will block such moves, or at least make them too costly. The critical task of those involved in the foreign services of the world is keeping the national actors informed of one another's willingness to accommodate or to use force.

If one state violates or threatens to violate the territory of another, then the ruling group in the threatened state must respond to preserve its position, in much the same way as it would against internal threats. An elite is able to use its subjects to defend its system by inspiring acquiescence through a mixture of terror and persuasion. Propaganda stresses all of those myths with which an elite normally tries to legitimize its position in peacetime. In addition, most people are motivated to support their government in war because they know that national defeat will harm their interests, even if they have not personally supported the war. Thus, rationally, the average man may feel that considering everything, his chances and those of his family for success and reward are better if he goes along with his government's plans for war rather than opposes them. In a democracy, the same process is involved, except that there is the additional motivation that the democratic system may be changed by defeat, and as we argue above, most people prefer to be sponsors of their own government. (In fact, however, as the appendix suggests, the individualization and demystification promoted by civil liberties may enervate individuals in a democracy facing war more than their sponsorship inspires them.)

The problem for the independent intellectual has always been that in war individuals are fighting, dying, and killing, even though their interests as individuals seem to be in no way involved. Leadership groups have repeatedly mobilized their peoples for aggression, even when the people had very little stake in the outcome. Yet without destroying those pawns who are the tools of aggression, defending states have not been able to stop the aggressors. If all states were of the same quality or evolved according to uniform laws of social evolution, then there would be less rationale to opposing the forces of an aggressing nation. There would be that special oppression that defeat is apt to carry with it, but that would be all. This oppression might be more than compensated by the lack of killing on both sides, and the help that a nation's surrender might give to the goal of eventual world unity. However, our analysis has suggested that no system is inevitable and that democracy will exist only when there is continued willingness to struggle against its internal and external enemies.

In this regard, it must be admitted that the reasons which can be legitimately used for participating in war may not be the reasons that many people do participate. There are instinctual feelings of biological aggressiveness, and the restricted information available to both sides tends to free these instincts. Although rational explanations of behavior are more significant than many Freudian social scientists believe, introspection should easily convince us of their inadequacy to fully explain an emotional and rational process such as war.

The Immanent and Indeterminate Force of Ideas

In the final analysis society is formed by man, and in Chapter Two we provisionally granted men free will. The forms of society and social change result from an interplay of mechanistic man with humanistic man. The fact of change is not what needs to be explained by this broader view, for the constant interplay of the personal interests and abilities of changing human actors and the need to bring changes in one area into harmony with those in another imply continual change. The problem becomes, then, the directions and forms of change.

New ideas come into being through innovation or recombination, through playful mulling or direct analysis (Barnett, 1953). New ideas may or may not represent solutions to problems previously posed. But if adopted, they will produce changes that will in turn raise new problems that will find answers, because it is in someone's interest that there be answers. We can think of the progress that has been made in medicine and agriculture leading in time to better health and rapid population growth, leading in turn to the development of easier birth-control methods. This has allowed an acceptance of certain liberal attitudes toward sex that were always present at the fringes of society but could not be generally accepted because of their disastrous personal and social consequences. Yet these new attitudes also affect the concept of the family, with obvious ramifications.

Let us think of another change in which indeterminate man plays a more obvious role. In the course of the modern history of western Europe, there developed out of renewed interest in classical traditions and ancient Germanic institutions the concepts of political and civil rights. Men came to be seen as individuals that in a political sense should be regarded as equal. Once that idea became implanted in the imagination of the intellectual elite, there was no stopping it. Gradually the electorate was expanded, gradually the contributions of the classes to the state were equalized. Finally all men had the vote, then all men and women. Inexorably this meant that the majority would exploit the minority, that is, the wealthy and the very poor, for they now had the power, and this was in their interest. It was an educated, minority doctrine that all men should be equal, but the uneducated majority reaped its benefits. As the majority were educated to understand the full implications of democratic doctrine, they became willing to extend this doctrine even to minorities below them. For this reason, it was possible in the 1960s to pass poverty programs that helped the poor with the majority's money.

Why was this inexorable? First, it was because the communicators and thinkers of the eighteenth and nineteenth centuries had a theory that the process should go on, while those who wanted to stop it had no generally acceptable or coherent doctrine. Of course, ideas were not enough. At each decision, some individual or group had to press for an enlargement of the electorate or for a higher tax on the wealthy, because they saw it in their interest to do so; sometimes, they found they succeeded. Those who tried to move society in the other direction because it was in their interest usually failed, because their forebearers had accepted a principle and each new stage of democratization was only the unfolding of the principle. In addition, when a new stage was reached, power was distributed in a way that made reversal very difficult, at least until the majority came into power (Schumpeter, 1950). (The reader should note, however, that the particular relation of ideas and their consequences that drove this process may be relatively unusual.)

The process was also inexorable just because it was not inexorable in terms of material interests alone. The determinate progress toward democratization was due to the fact that some ideas dramatically expand the future. Once we see ourselves as liberal and open-minded, we must consider all propositions that are rationally put forward. Once we accept the principle of the political equality of all persons, we must accept all reasonable proposals to extend the franchise. I am not judging that the progress from an abstract principle to its general acceptance was necessarily right, but only that most well-meaning and thoughtful people since the eighteenth century in Europe and America have held beliefs that made this progress inevitable, given the tendency of men in marginal situations (where their other interests are uninvolved or balanced) to attempt to satisfy the interests of their alter ideals (see Chapter Four).

This understanding of society will also lead us to emphasize two other approaches to social change that the more mechanistic approach underestimates. According to mechanistic sociology, change occurs primarily to fit the requirements of the situation. In a peasant society, ideologies and social structures develop that are appropriate to the peasant way of life, while in an industrial society, ideologies and social structures develop that are appropriate to industrial life. Today, popular prognosticators claim that future ideology and social structure will surely be the natural result of "postindustrial civilization." It naturally follows that in essentials all peasant societies are like all other peasant societies, and all industrial societies are like all other industrial societies. But of course what one regards as essential is determined by what one's theoretical inclination asks him to look for.

An alternative view is to recognize the functional determinants of society and culture as only one group of determinants among many. Equally important is the effort of individuals to maintain coherence between their cultural traditions and changing circumstances or to try to develop a new synthesis out of whatever comes to hand. In mechanistic terms, this is the theory of change implied by Festinger's (1957) emphasis on the importance of the natural drive to eliminate "cognitive dissonance" from our thinking. In this vein, functionally autonomous intellectual innovation and determinism have played a key role in social change.

The difficulty in proving that individuals decide on the basis of alter interests is that social events are usually so muddy that it is very hard to find a clear case of the influence of rational indeterminism. It seems to me that a reading of John F. Kennedy's *Profiles in Courage* (1955) affords some of the best documented examples of allowing alter ideals to determine one's actions. For example, when Edmund G. Ross voted against the conviction of President Johnson in 1868, in spite of his personal political interests and enormous pressure, it was because his internal alter interests were dominant at that moment. Another good example is the recent history of the interference of the Turkish military in Turkish politics (Haddad, 1965). When military leaders overthrew Menderes and Bayar in 1960, the military objective appears to have been the defense of the constitution against very real threats. Since that time, the generals have stepped in several times to avert political collapse. But given experience elsewhere, it is remarkable that they have repeatedly striven to maintain or reestablish authentic democratic processes, even to the extent of allowing their opponents to rule. The Turkish military was not forced by the power of the people to return to the barracks. In terms of popular attitudes toward the military, Turkish generals could take over and rule Turkey more easily than Greek generals could rule Greece. Yet they have chosen not to, for until now military rule is not the pattern of government they and their coterie feel is acceptable.

The interpretation of individuals and society as indeterminate will also lead to an emphasis on action rather than contemplation. Taken seriously, functionalist and mechanistic social science understands events as determined by external patterns, with men playing parts that are essentially foreordained by previous events. In particular, in this view, a free and an unfree modern society are not fundamentally different. On the one hand, no one is really free in any society, and on the other, all modern societies react essentially to the same basic structural requirements. Wars, similarly, are maladjustments, unfortunate breakdowns in the progress of affected societies toward unavoidable conclusions. It is true that by a wonderful ability to segment thinking, determinists are also often activists in their personal lives. May not this irrationality account for the fanaticism of movements such as the early Calvinist and modern communist, which are shot through with this contradiction?

To the indeterminist, on the other hand, there is an obvious point to action, to decision, for we are here and now the ones making the decisions. If we let others decide, they will decide differently and perhaps not so well. We know what we intend, and believe it is best; yet we can always be wrong, we could always do better were we to think more or have more information. We do not necessarily have the keys to the future, but we are going to act and study and consider and go forward. We are only a few, but what little we can do is ours to do.

Levels of Organization

But let us return to the beginning of the chapter where we borrowed from Kuhn the idea that the basic model of man was also the model for any controlled system or social unit. Perhaps the most important point to learn about organizations is the extent to which they are analogous to individual persons. In *Essence of Decision,* Allison (1971) has addressed the problem by considering three levels upon which analyses have been made of an international event, such as the Cuban missile crisis. On the most general level, analysis has often been carried out in terms of the clash of national interests. On the next level, the analysis may be seen as one in which national interests result from the clash of bureaucratic or subgroup interests within each nation. Finally, the result of the clash of the interests of individuals within the subgroups may be seen as defining bureaucratic interests. Allison concludes, as is generally the case of students who get down to the details, that the last level, that of personal interests, is the most critical.

However, Allison went too far. The fact is that each level controls and defines the others. We may think of the relationship between levels as mediated by culturally accepted role definitions. It is true that the parts define the whole, but the parts are also necessarily defined by the whole. If I am a schoolteacher, I will express through my teaching my idiosyncratic intellectual, decision-making, and action capabilities, but I will also guide this idiosyncrasy by what I understand to be the role characteristics of a teacher in the school in which I find myself. My intelligence may sense that a certain pupil makes me uncomfortable. It would be in my interest to eject the pupil and calm my nerves, but unless the pupil commits flagrant acts that allow me to eject him or her, then I will not actively pursue this goal. It would not fit my understanding of my job or the reciprocal understandings of those around me. I may decide, however, to make the pupil want to leave of his own accord, but even in a campaign of this sort, I will be careful to restrict my actions to those acceptable within the teacher role. On a broader scale, the school as a whole has a role to fill in the larger society, and while this changes over time, at any one time the actions of the school, that is, the output of the cumulative decisions of all those in it, will lie within rather narrow limits. Moreover, a study of schools over time and space will suggest certain uniformities or biosocial regularities in these limits that will affect schools everywhere.

Similarly, in the Cuban missile crisis, individual persons worked to promote their interests within the confines of knowledge of what was expected of them, and on the next level of organization bureaucratic interests were likewise restricted. No matter how interested the CIA may be in promoting a particular line of action in a situation, those who guide its affairs must act or propose action in ways that a variety of publics can be convinced are both in the national interest and appropriate to the CIA. When a bureaucratic analyst describes the national interest of the United States or of the Soviet Union, he is describing what are likely to be the acceptable arguments that will be made by responsible individuals expressing the concerns appropriate to their roles within a national pyramid of decision. Generally, the larger the number of individuals involved, the more conservative the decision, for faceless bureaucrats are much less likely to be criticized for doing the expected than for doing the unexpected. Conservative action is generally the best road to bureaucratic survival.

Incidentally, this failure to understand the essentially conservative nature of complex hierarchies in modern states is what led liberal writers, such as C. P. Snow, to imagine in the late 1950s that the world would surely blow up before 1970 without far-reaching arms control (Osgood and Tucker, 1967). I do not mean to be complacent, but it was their mistake to overemphasize the importance of the individual interests and irrationalities of leaders within systems as organized as the U.S. and U.S.S.R. While Stalin lived, the Soviet bureaucracy was often short-circuited. But even Stalin in most cases had to decide, reward, and punish in terms of established role specifications.

Is Our Approach Subject to Scientific Proof?

In Chapters Two and Three I have attempted to establish a basic framework within which we can consider the behavior of men and societies. The framework is built on a systems model essentially

adapted from Kuhn, but Kuhn in turn is summarizing a long history
of social thought and, in particular, generalizing from the rational
man approach that has long been the basis of microeconomics. Some
social scientists will agree with the usefulness of the model while
others will disagree, but most telling will be the criticism that it is
not a useful scientific model because it is not subject to proof or disproof. Let us then consider in some detail how we would answer the
criticism.

The model we have presented can be seen as of both termino-
logical and generative significance (Gastil, 1975c). It offers an alternative set of terms for understanding; in this sense, the model is not open
to proof or disproof unless it can be shown that a designated category
has no reflection in reality. For example, if someone could prove that
there is no example of negative feedback in human behavior, then the
model would be disproved. However, the only term in the model that
is likely to be open to such rejection is *free will*, and our discussion
has already suggested that this does not appear to be a hypothesis subject to definitive proof. From another perspective, as terminology the
model obviously does not claim to supply all terms that might be useful in describing human behavior, but it does claim to cover with
some general terms within its framework all of the types of considerations that must be covered in a theory of human behavior. If there
were a section of explanation not covered, then this would be a fault.
But the suggested framework is so elastic that this seems unlikely. We
can conclude that terminologically the model is unlikely to be subject
to disproof and, in this sense, has relatively little explanatory power.

However, as a generative theory, the model makes much
stronger claims, for by emphasizing some factors more than others the
model asserts that they will be more important. On the one hand, it is
saying that each of the factors defined in the model is of more than
trivial importance (for example, variations in information, values,
and biological inheritance), but on the other hand, that certain factors will generally be found to be more important in explanation than
others. The model asserts, for example, that individuals will try to
exploit situations for their own personal benefit; once advantages are
achieved, they will try to structure institutions or organizations to
maintain these advantages. I have noted that not realizing the invaria-
bility of this proposition was the fundamental mistake of Marx, who

mislabeled the sins of man as the sins of capitalism. This is also the mistake of functionalists, who imagine that a society is primarily the result of an efficient adaptation by a group to its situation.

The model does not imply that altruistic motives do not at times move leaders or that roles cannot be specified so as to dampen the tendency of revolution to merely restructure tyranny. However, the model would lead us to question the arguments that so many new third world states have military tyrannies because "no other system can work" or because the military is the best-educated elite. The model would predispose us to accept the argument that the military so often rules in the third world because there are not sufficiently institutionalized norms held by sufficiently powerful groups to block the assumption of force by those leaders that directly control violence. In the universal struggle for power, the absence of strongly institutionalized norms must give the power to those with the most guns. The model would lead us to suspect that the reason these military leaders so often adopt Marxism is not because of its intellectual superiority (in fact, they often do not understand it). It is rather because Marxist rhetoric and communist example offer the best legitimization available among the younger generation in the third world for maintaining a ruling group's position by force.

In another generative area, the model incorporates the obvious fact that there are strong biological drives and that frustrating these can be dangerous. However, the model makes the claim that most human behavior can be explained in terms of learned patterns that have resulted from myriads of rewards and punishments interacting in individuals with conscious calculation of self-interest. Marriage, for example, has a biological base, but marriage is not produced by the base but rather by certain biosocial processes (discussed in Chapter Six) as shaped in a variety of cultural traditions. Individuals marry because this is a means of satisfying a variety of social and personal interests that is also regularly rewarded by society's sponsors, while failure to marry will result in loss of esteem as well as loss of security later on if the individuals have no legitimate children. One might decide to marry a particular person because of love—that is, altruistically[6]—but this is not the motive for a generalized decision to marry.

Men are generally built more powerfully and more heavily than women, and they also have more hormones that aid in the expression of force. In fact, difference in aggression is the major bio-logically defined psychological difference between the sexes, which was confirmed in a recent summary of the evidence (Maccoby and Jacklin, 1974). Our model would suggest that women will, therefore, be subordinated to men, and especially that men will control the political system (which, among other things, is the means by which violent power is institutionalized). Again, the records of history and anthropology bear out this assumption.[7] If the evidence were reversed, we should consider the model in doubt. I am not saying, by the way, that a society could not have existed where women domi-nated public business, only that it would have been very difficult to maintain such a pattern. Biosocial factors are only one group of fac-tors that determine human behavior, but they are generally the strongest group. In modern life, the decline of the importance of indi-vidual physical strength in most relationships suggests that there may no longer be a biosocial basis for male domination. However, recent experience in Israel certainly leaves this in doubt (Tiger and Sephar, 1975).

Cultures or learning traditions play an important role in social life. However, the model generatively would lead us to expect that individuals and groups in the aggregate will have rather similar interests and responses everywhere. The model would lead us to hypothesize, for example, that all cultural areas would develop pat-terns of behavior analogous to those that we call war, insofar as the social groups in the culture area become large enough to get beyond individual or family fights. This is because in all societies some indi-viduals will inevitably learn how they can use the threat of force to achieve their interests cheaply, and this experience will then prompt them to notice the same possibility between groups. Unfortunately, it takes very few people or groups making this calculation to make other groups ready and willing to use force in self-defense. As long as it profits them, powerful groups will expand until they meet equally powerful groups.

Perhaps we can demonstrate the generative nature of the theory most explicitly if we contrast our treatment of war as a neces-sary universal alternative in relations between independent political groups with the more optimistic treatments often found in social sci-ence. In a recent review of the anthropological literature on war,

Otterbein (1973) considers eight causes of war. These include innate aggression, frustration-aggression, diffusion of the idea of war, the exigencies of the physical environment, war-promoting aspects of the internal social structure, the evolutionary level of the culture, military preparedness, and the "goals of war." In contrast, the theoretical approach of this chapter would look on these eight theories as raw material for reorganization using a more systematic approach. (However, the reader will note that the discussion below does not criticize Otterbein's work, but rather the material he is reviewing.)

Let us begin by considering the goals of war. In Otterbein's review, these goals are generally seen as culturally and situationally specified particulars, such as a need for young men to collect scalps, revenge for a previous attack, or the need for more horses. In our approach, we should turn this around and define as the *primary goal* of war the achievement or maintenance of the interests and values of the society. The *secondary goals,* then, are the specifics that attend a particular society or war-generating situation. Once a war pattern is begun, it may lead to a predictable frequency of war through a combination of positive and negative feedbacks. In some cultures and for some individuals, aspects of the war pattern may become functionally autonomous and therefore goals in themselves. But for all groups, as long as war is easy and relatively cost-free, it will increase in frequency as long as there are appropriate enemies. As costs escalate, war may become less prevalent. Sustained patterns of war will also produce higher levels of military sophistication and larger political units (through conquest or the necessities of offense and defense). Ways to fight war technologically and organizationally will, of course, diffuse and change cultural patterns where they are received, either through passive or enforced imitation. Capabilities for war include the mental and emotional potential that make group organization possible and the physical and physiological accompaniments of war, including capacity for anger and a degree for pugnacity, and in particular some of the reactions that follow frustration. These characteristics make war possible, but they do not cause it; they are necessary but hardly sufficient.

One further generative result of this theory would be that preparation for imminent war should reduce the chance of a society losing its values through war or defeat. Otterbein decided to examine statistically the hypothesis that military preparedness prevents war (the deterrence theory) and the alternative that military preparedness causes it. He found proof for neither theory, but he did find that cultures with high military sophistication were more inclined to engage in offensive, external war. Of course, it defies common sense to try to test theories of this type statistically without detailed analyses of particular prewar contexts. Lack of military preparation is generally going to characterize a situation in which either there is little threat of war or the society involved prefers surrender to fighting. Deterrence theory rests on consideration of the probable outcome of being prepared or not being prepared in a situation of threat where surrender is not considered an acceptable alternative. Broad statistical surveys cannot test this theory.

How would our model be tested in regard to war? One way to disprove the model would be to find a cultural area with large, totally independent organized societies that do not fight wars with one another. However, we do not find such cultural areas anthropologically or historically. Otterbein (1970, pp. 21–22) concludes:

> It appears from this study that for cultural units and their constituent political communities to remain social entities, they must have the means, through capable military organizations, to defend themselves from attack. A cultural unit composed of political communities whose military organizations are unable to defend them will either be annihilated and absorbed into the political communities of other cultural units or will flee and seek safety, not by arms, but by hiding in an isolated area.

It is important to note that all four of the societies in his sample that chose to hide had chosen this alternative, in part, because of previous destructive experiences with other primitive peoples (see also Service, 1968; Turney-High, 1971).

A related disproof of this theory would be to show that failing to respond to the threat of war or being willing to risk less in its prosecution was an adequate group response to preserve its values. However, Otterbein demonstrates that the higher its degree of military sophistication, the greater a group's success, as measured by expanding territorial boundaries; he also shows that political centralization alone does not promote such success, while willingness to accept casualties does.[8] If war was simply an irrational, learned pattern, as some anthropologists have claimed, it might be fought as a game or arranged between leaders for their entertainment. However, most societies in Otterbein's sample preferred to initiate war by surprise attack; they used diplomacy for war termination rather than initiation. Fatalities from war (and the fighting between individuals of different groups that preceded war) in the primitive world were in fact much higher than in civilized societies: 15 to 50 percent of adult males in primitive societies compared with 0.5 to 10 percent of adult males in modern societies since 1750 (Livingstone, 1967; for examples of the situation in the few areas that remain primitive, see Chagnon, 1967; Service, 1967; Matthiessen, 1962). The pandemic slaughter in many societies untouched by larger civilizations was no doubt one of the major reasons for low population densities and lack of cumulative change in the primitive world.

Another critical disproof would be to show that wars are not generally related to the achievement of societal purposes beyond those of catharsis, that is, to show that wars are irrational. However, the evidence goes the other way. For example, Tibetan nomads have historically been more warlike than their neighbors. Gorer (1967) felt his evidence showed that people dependent on crops fought less than Tibetan herders, because if the farmers had enough land, more land was only a burden. Herding people, however, were more likely to fight because animals that they had stolen could be moved easily and converted into money (Otterbein, 1973). On the other hand, Ekvall (1961) thought that nomads in Tibet were warlike because their peacetime life prepared them for it and that fighting was therefore easier for Tibetan pastoralists (more gain for less effort) and less risky, since they could often escape if they were defeated.

Obviously, I would not expect the model advanced to be easily disproven. It was selected as my favorite model for social humanities because I see its broad thrust confirmed by the general experience of man as well as the best social science research. However, I would expect the continuing body of research to improve our knowledge of how the model is expressed in particulars. Behavior therapy, for example, would be predicted by the model to be useful, but just what forms of behavior therapy should be used in particular cases must be decided on the basis of an interplay of developing theory and experience (experiment). The free market should be an efficient way to allocate resources in terms of the model, but what interferences will become endemic in certain situations and how to deal with these must be decided by experience guided by theory. On the other hand, since efficiency is not the only criterion of society, all markets must operate in terms of nonmarket norms, and the effects of alternative norms must be closely studied both scientifically and humanistically.

The reader accustomed to the natural sciences may still be unconvinced, since the predictions generated by the model and the confirmations attested may seem discouragingly nonquantitative or slippery. They are, and yet too often the attempt to become quantitative has led to unjustified concentration on numbers. An important reason we cannot quantify our theoretical tests is a lack of appropriate units. Physical distance can be measured in a way sociocultural distance cannot; the most important aspects of love cannot be quantified; even units of dominance elude us. Perhaps more important, understanding or intelligent participation of human beings in human action quickly makes real-world situations too complex to handle by methods appropriate to the physical sciences. In physics, when a heavy body hits a light body it will displace the light body, and the character of this action is quite predictable. When a large lion attacks a small one, it too will generally win, although the prediction will be slightly less reliable. When a large human being struggles with a smaller, he too will generally win, but now the prediction is least reliable and the number of possible outcomes becomes infinite, and each form of winning or compromise will lead to different feedback (learning) for each of the people concerned. Since most important events are the result of complex chains of previous actions, quantitative prediction and precision become impossible. The student of human affairs must inevitably accept this imprecision.

Notes

1.   There is, of course, a large literature on group or crowd behavior. Much of this is summarized by Smelser (1962). For special studies of crowd behavior that indicate how individual values and preferences may change in group situations, see the literature on the "risky shift" in social psychology (for example, Lewin and Kane, 1975). However, evidence of this kind does not

contradict Olson, because it relates to fleeting situational changes in behavior rather than more fundamental, group-determined changes.

2. In this distinction, I completely depart from Kuhn's definition (Kuhn, 1974, p. 403). While I sympathize with his attempt to reject the use of *institution* for *social pattern*, I feel the definitions given here preserve in less cumbersome language the essential distinctions.

3. Of course, Madison, Hobbes, Machiavelli, and many others espoused this position long before Marx. In fact, most nonacademic intellectuals have probably thought this way. In recent years, the position has been associated especially with the works of Mills (1956) and Dahrendorf (1959).

4. This is a very common interpretation; for example, "In the North, as expected, the struggle for economic survival and industrial progress [after Geneva] barred any retreat from the hard communist dictatorship" (Buttinger, 1967, pp. 843–844). This is the same mode of interpretation that allows Wolf (1969) to subsume the Vietnam War and similar situations under the heading *peasant wars*. However, communism cannot be categorized under other labels as an inevitable part of the development process. Although there are dissatisfactions among people who revolt and communists are often best able to exploit the situation because they are better organized and more selfless than other groups, this does not mean that the equivalent of a "hard communist dictatorship" is inevitable or that the label *communists* does not tell us more about the militants in a developing society than labels such as *peasant revolutionaries, modernizers,* or *mobilizers of popular dissension.*

5. It is interesting that union oligarchy is justified by union leaders in almost the same terms as oligarchy is justified by the leaders of the socialist pseudo-democracies. *Union Democracy* (Lipset, Trow, and Coleman, 1956) is, of course, primarily a study of an exception, the International Typographical Union.

6. Altruism and love are equated here in that both assume a generous transactional relation in which the individual wishes for the other person's gain as well as his own and will give up his direct interest to gain the secondary benefit of another's pleasure. Of course, in our model, one does not act without satisfying some form of self-interest.

7. As Mead (1967) points out, the significance of the physical difference has been reinforced by the fact that in the known human record, the use of weapons has been almost entirely restricted to males. For a discussion of the extremely rare instance of female soldiers in primitive war, see Turney-High (1971). A recent study (Tiger and Sephar, 1975) of the development of woman's role in the kibbutz, a setting designed to ensure equality and female emancipation, shows that there has been a steady movement toward reestablishing traditional sex roles, particularly in regard to leadership. This has apparently reflected the choice that the women have made.

8. Referring to a different kind of competition, Gorer (1967) reported that the Lepchas of Sikkim had to be protected from their neighbors and isolated because "their almost complete suppression of competition and aggression, causes an inevitable breakdown of their culture in any mixed community" (p. 37).

FOUR

Humanistic Values: A Framework for Social Analysis

What should be the interests of men? In asking this question, we step beyond the considerations addressed in Chapters Two and Three to consider what should be the basis of individual conduct, of judgment of the conduct of others, and of evaluation of the quality of civilization. In other words, in this chapter we will shift from concentrating on intellectual understanding to concentrating on how men and societies should use this understanding to decide upon action.

Until now, our discussion of man has emphasized a rational model according to which man acts to maximize gains and to minimize losses in terms of a simple set of values. By and large, people want pleasure rather than pain, life rather than death, high status rather than low, and wealth rather than poverty. The model puts the burden of proof on those who believe most people simply follow cultural dictates, the dictates of their fellows, or the dictates of irrational forces (whether altruistic or destructive) that emerge within their own personalities as the interactive effects of genetic and environmental factors. The foregoing analysis admits these influences but suggests that most behavior is primarily guided by cost benefit comparisons.

In this view, the main difference between animal and man is man's greater complexity of understanding, evaluating, and action mechanisms. In particular, man is more flexible, more able to adjust to change and reevaluate experience, and so to solve problems that inhibit the efficient operation of the mechanism. Social organizations are merely higher-order systems, incorporating individual human systems to expand the power and thus the rational attainment of goals by at least some of their participants.

Against this hypothesized scientific background, a central problem of social humanities becomes the specification of the sense in which there is more than a mechanistic element in human behavior. Since the eighteenth century, an influential doctrine has developed that questions of morality or normative decision are indistinguishable from those of scientific fact. If we can prove that certain institutions or practices make men happier under particular external conditions, then these should be the institutions of society. But what is happiness and pleasure? For the neutral social scientist, an obvious answer is to ask, or poll, the public. Over time, and perhaps with sufficient experimentation, these and other social indicators will assure ever-increasing quantities of human happiness for the short term. Longer-term happiness will of course remain doubtful, but according to this doctrine, as information and theory develop ever more adequate models of man and society, this problem will eventually find a technical solution.

While the doctrine developed in the preceding paragraph is popular among social scientists (and many natural scientists and engineers), most philosophers are convinced of its fallaciousness by arguments such as those of Moore (1903). In the early twentieth century, Moore attacked Mill and Bentham for the "naturalistic fallacy" of confusing the discussion of good and bad with the discussion of particular goods or bads, such as happiness or pleasure and pain. While the general and the particular were obviously related in some degree, these are quite different dimensions of reality. Personal happiness may be based on evil (Moore, pp. 216–224). The pleasures of many people are derived from cruel practices, such as the torturing of opponents or the brutal slaughter of animals. These are evidently pleasurable evils, yet only a moral system that distinguishes between the "is" of pleasure and the "ought" of good can condemn them.

Accepting, then, Moore's contention that there is a nonpositivist problem of good and evil, what are its dimensions? A good beginning is to consider Gehlen's (1969) anthropological discussion of four bases of morality. First is the ethic that is developed out of the reciprocal relationships necessary for society. For the benefit of all, societies come to surround both transactions and communications with culturally specific assumptions and conventions. Second, Gehlen points to the more or less instinctual, ethological ethics that emphasize the happiness and welfare of others. Although better studied in lower animals, an outstanding example in humans is the tendency of most persons to aid the helpless, particularly infants, as well as the tendency (under favorable conditions) of people to become extraordinarily helpful in a crisis situation that envelops the community (Janis, 1958; Fritz, 1961). A third basis for ethics grows out of the experience and assumptions of the family situation, in which ideally all members work for the interest of all and love other members simply because they are in the family. Finally, Gehlen distinguishes the morality that grows out of experience in social institutions, particularly in governmental affairs. If we combine the second and third bases, Gehlen leaves us with three quite different moralities: those based on *reciprocity, humanitarianism,* and *social responsibility.*

It is Gehlen's thesis that the crisis of our age stems in large part from the tendency to replace social responsibility with familial humanitarianism. In any event, we should examine social responsibility in more detail, for it is from this realm that a fully conscious human morality must develop. As pointed out in Chapter Three, it is instructive to analyze human lives and society in terms of the concept of the social role. (A particularly interesting treatment is that of Sorokin (1947), especially pp. 714–723 on personality seen as a collection of roles.) Some social roles, such as the role of mother, are very broad and involve many layers of personality, while others, such as an occupational role, may be very specific. A man on an assembly line must put in a particular component; the work is not very demanding physically or mentally, but he must do it. Similarly, the soldier has a job that the society assigns him, and if this means machine-gunning enemy troops as they cross the border, he must do that. If he will not, he should not have accepted the responsibility of the role (assuming he did so voluntarily). Without specifying roles and assuring that occupants live up to the specifications, complex society could not exist. Much of world literature is concerned with the conflict between the demands of differing roles, particularly public and private roles. Antigone had a responsibility both to the laws of the state and to the memory of her brother; for her, a successful resolution was impossible. In our time, the failure in family life of the successful businessman is the cliché of overemphasis on a public role.

By suggesting that the development of a variety of roles allows human beings to emancipate themselves from a narrow dependency on role definitions, Plessner (1964) carries the discussion a step further. While the roles a person plays in the course of his life help to define his personality, they never exhaust the potentialities of the person, and the inevitable conflict of roles opens up an arena of choice among alternatives that a comfortable accommodation of roles could never offer. Through the concept of role, we are brought back to the fact that no amount of predetermination by either biology or society can take away the responsibility to decide.

Accepting freedom of will as a rationally bounded mystery (Chapter Two) makes it possible for the social humanist to employ science in understanding man without eliminating humanity. In particular, he is able to imagine a man that can act responsibly and creatively, because his decisions and efforts are to some extent really his. To the social humanist, humanity is defined by the abilities to project, to empathize, and to see oneself as another person. A human being is granted the capability not only of imagining his own death and those of others, but also to create imaginatively thousands of lives and worlds that never existed.

Yet man is to a large extent determined by both his internal and external histories, and in his daily life he must respond to the roles imposed upon him. The result is that, in the words of Francis Schaeffer quoted in the appendix, grace is always in danger of being swallowed up by nature. On the plane of individual life, this means that moral decisions are always in danger of evaporating under the twin pressures of rationalization and inattention, while in social analysis, theoretically describable and predictable relationships continually threaten to exhaust the discussion.

In order to keep the ground we have gained by the discussion of free will in Chapter Two, it will be necessary to erect on personal, social, and analytical levels modes of expression and self-understanding that emphasize the distance between man as mechanism and man as free agent, even though we realize that, in real life, these are intertwined.

To Kuhn (1974), morality was developed by societies to enhance the efficiency of transactional relationships; moral rules are primarily codifications of transactional necessities. This implies that each individual must to some extent recreate the process that provided the moral code, thereby raising reciprocity to the level of conscious responsibility. In particular, each person symbolically establishes within himself proxies for both sides of the transactions in which he takes part. If a person internalizes transactional logic so that every benefit has a cost, he may feel off balance when he receives benefits without cost. Such an imbalance can only be set straight by guilt and resulting self-punishment. Alternatively, if one feels that he has paid costs without expected benefits, he may attempt to reestablish a balance through theft or other antisocial behavior.

Within his own head, everyone has his own moral universe of learned moralities and interests, with personal rationalizations for both. Within this universe, most deserving of our attention is the human capacity to create *alter egos*. The extreme form of this ability is found in psychological disassociation, when a person no longer recognizes himself. Schizophrenia originally meant split personality, and a person with a mild form of the condition is referred to as *schizoid*. Yet to a degree it is this ability to reject rational man's reality, to disassociate, to daydream, and to create fictional worlds, that is distinctively human. It is the other side of what Koestler (1967, p. 312) refers to as the tendency of man's overdeveloped brain toward repeated bouts of paranoia. It is not necessarily paranoia, but it is a stepping back from normality, from the rational calculation.

We may imagine that it is this ability that ultimately led early man to people the world with spiritual beings that finally coalesced into the figure of God. That these figures had, and even in the most developed religions continue to have, attributes of humanity, that is, of rational, preschizoid man, is understandable, for the models for the cosmic drama had to be taken from ordinary human experience. God was given the desires and willfulness of an earthly father, but like a father, he also came to represent the conscience of the community and thus to be seen as the giver and sometimes the enforcer of its laws.

Perhaps the most important implication of the ability to create an alter ego is that it makes more understandable and probably more feasible freewill moral and ethical action. If anything can, man as alter is able to operate independently from external inputs, to create ideals, and then to preserve the independence of those ideals in internal transactions. This schizoid, transacting partner is comparable at first glance to the Freudian superego. Yet this superego was just another product of conditioning—an unconscious, normally unexaminable control over action. For the schizoid personality, on the other hand, the alter ego as ego ideal is an independently created, examinable, and reformable quasi-being. This alter ego comes to have laws and principles of it own, and these have weight in the internal transaction.

As long as the ideal is seen as a separate reality in transaction with our everyday lives, it will not decay into a simple reflection of our rational calculations. Were it not to be projected out and kept out, it would decay, because in the rational transaction, the individual can only use what pays off. This analysis may stem from no more than slavish adherence to the variety of social science we have selected, but I think it is more than that.

For most persons, the alter ego is, of course, recreated in a form not too different from that learned by each individual in his cultural tradition and his particular experiences with ideals. But if he is no longer within a fixed religious tradition, he will have considerable freedom to let his imagination play with and expand upon what the ideal person should be. This freedom is not necessarily desirable, but it is a fact with which we must deal. However, as the rational theory of Kuhn (1974) suggests, persons within the same communication net will establish similar alter egos. We can hope that if we retain our humanity, the often-predicted death of God will not make the reestablishment of a moral community impossible.

The argument may become clearer if we consider an incident in Willa Cather's *A Lost Lady*. Forrester, a retired railroad contractor, is suddenly called away to close out the affairs of a failing Denver bank, of which he is a director. Since many of the depositors are working people whom he encouraged to deposit money in the bank, he insists that all depositors get back their deposits in full. Since the other directors do not agree, he is forced to exhaust his own fortune in order to repay the full amount. His lawyer does not like to see him ruin himself, but since he is doing what the lawyer also thinks is right, the lawyer cannot interfere. Upon his return, Forrester suffers a heart attack. For he had, after all, materially lost everything.

Why did Forrester do it? According to the simple form of the rationalist analysis, he must have felt that his apparent generosity at this moment would be paid back by improvement in his station and support from the community whose expectations he fulfilled. Yet Denver was a long way from his residence, and he seldom visited there. His fellow directors did not expect his sacrifice, and few of his wealthy friends would ever know of his heroism. His wife accepted it, but not happily, and he had no children. The lawyer would have been satisfied if he had made somewhat less of an effort to do right by the depositors.

In the novel, it is simply stated that Forrester acted this way because he felt this was the way a man should act. He had a picture in his mind of himself, and he resolved to live up to it. According to the Kuhn model, Forrester must have acted as he did because this brought a higher return to him than the alternatives. But the return was mostly from himself, provided through an internal transaction with his alter ego. Perhaps this is what Riesman meant by the distinction between other-directed, inner-directed, and tradition-directed behaviors (Riesman, 1950). In traditional behavior, the alter ego comes ready-made: While its nature may have been the result of the imaginings of the prophets of the past, the ego is now encapsulated, an external, spiritual guide beyond reformulation. For the other-directed person, there is essentially no alter ego controlled by the personality. One calculates the costs and benefits in external terms alone, including, of course, the moral and ethical expectations of others, and then acts accordingly. For the inner-directed, or schizoid, personality on the other hand, there is also an internal transaction so that the individual acts, or sometimes acts, as his alter ego directs.

It may be evident to most readers that a person who lives on two planes, who projects beyond his interests as a rational economizer, is a more valuable achievement for himself and others than a person who does not. But if a reader is not convinced that it is better to be inner-directed, what is the argument for inner direction? The best I

can do is to try to relate my understanding to the Maslovian ideal of
self-actualization that is commonly accepted by this generation
(Maslow, 1954). Self-actualization means the attempt of the individual to be all that he can be. If we see ourselves as a particular species, this should lead us to desire to maximize the unique attributes of
that species, that is, to be as specifically human as we can. If only
human beings have the capacity to escape from the rational model of
an integrated organism, then it can be argued that human self-
realization requires the strengthening of the alter ego or an emphasis
on reflexive transactions between ideal and rational egos that is parallel to the external transactions of the whole person. In saying this, we
are confining our attention to the technical dimension. Human self-
realization also implies the possibility that the mechanistic ego can
transcend its rational self in all areas of life, particularly those areas of
the imagination and creative arts. Of course, being human also
implies exercising human capacities for evil. It is partially because of
these too-human capacities that the framework developed below
includes a region of control.

Beyond a Theory of Justice[1]

If we assume that humanistic man is inner-directed, or directed
by his ego ideal, what guidance can we give him in the construction of
this ideal? Moderate philosophers today might point to Rawls' *A
Theory of Justice* (1971) as the best available guide. Although Rawls'
objectives appear limited in his title, in using the achievement of justice as the basis for an evaluation of society, *A Theory of Justice* is
meant to form the groundwork for a general theory of the good society.[2] Rawls' approach is to ask what a man behind a "veil of ignorance" (concerning his own or future position in society) would
choose as the rules of the society in which he would later live. From
this "original position," Rawls deduces that he would choose a broad
range of political and civil liberties, as well as full equality, including
equal access to positions of status and opportunity. The fundamental
principle of this society would be equality of all primary goods. Any
departure from this principle would be justified only when it would
benefit those in society who would otherwise be least benefited. In
this way, Rawls seems to differentiate himself from classical utilitari-

anism (where the measure is the good of the whole society), from extreme egalitarianism, and from those who would trade liberty for equality.

Rawls' theory is based, however, on five apparently mistaken assumptions: (1) The most acceptable ethics are derived from a single, compelling origin or insight; (2) ethical behavior must be universal; (3) ethics are necessarily consequential in a quasi-quantitative sense; (4) the "primary goods" of interest are closely bound to the desires of individuals; and (5) both the model of the ideal society and rules for individual behavior can be derived from the same compelling, rational ethics. Although these assumptions are closely interconnected, they should be examined separately.

Rawls' exposition of the original position and its derivative principles is only the latest in a long series of attempts to find the key to ethics. Marcus Singer's (1961) generalization principle, the several utilitarian principles, and Kant's categorical imperative are all based on the idea that there must be one critical discovery or rational position from which everything else is deducible. This is paralleled in religious ethics by the reduction of all rules to guidance by single principles, such as love or faith (for example, Fletcher, 1966, where "agapeic love" becomes the principle behind a utilitarian calculus). Once the principle and its derived rules are specified, there can be little theoretical conflict, although there can be conflict of application. Such conflicts are in fact invited by the very nature of the abstractness of the basic principle or position. However, as Moore (1903) pointed out long ago, "We have no title whatever to assume that the truth on any subject matter will display such symmetry as we desire to see. . . . To search for 'unity' or 'system' at the expense of truth . . . is not the proper business of philosophy, however universally it may have been the practice of philosophers" (p. 222; see also Nozick, 1974). Categories such as ethics and morals are likely to be cultural constructs, with the limits of meaning of comparable terms varying from culture to culture and philosopher to philosopher. Conventional mathematics has developed tidy systems for analysis, but why should this experience be more appropriate to ethics than that of aesthetics or musicology on the one hand or sociology on the other?

The desire for neatness, for a quasi-mathematics, is probably one of the reasons for the ethicist's insistent universalism. In ethical analysis, everyone is regarded as an abstract person (an *A* or *B*) brought into relation to another abstract person or an abstract society. An explicit example of the universalist tendency is Peter Singer's (1973) recent discussion of our responsibility to famine victims. He argues that:

> *If we accept any principle of impartiality, univer-salizability, equality, or whatever, . . . it makes no moral difference whether the person I can help is a neighbor's child ten yards from me or a Bengali whose name I shall never know ten thousand miles away. . . . [If necessary] I ought to give as much as possible . . . perhaps . . . to the point of marginal utility, at which by giving more one would cause oneself and one's dependents as much suffering as one would prevent in Bengal. [pp. 231–234]*

Singer considers, only to reject, the case that we should not go so far as the point of marginal utility. He also considers and rejects the arguments of those who make a distinction between duty as a minimum, negative morality and charity as what would be good to do but not necessary. Yet nowhere does he seriously consider a doctrine of non-universal obligation. The flatness of his map of obligation and responsibility is suggested by the remark, "unfortunately most of the major evils—poverty, overpopulation, pollution—are problems in which everyone is almost equally involved" (p. 233). To diffuse responsibility this broadly not only offends common sense, but is apt to render most people passive in the face of a burden they can neither understand nor bear.

Real human relations, of course, involve concrete patterns of interdependency, and duties are fulfilled by accepting personal responsibility in appropriate spheres. The relations of greatest practical interest are relations of *particular* husbands and wives, fathers and sons, employers and employees, sergeants and privates. Ethicists such as Fingarette (1966) do not seem to realize that for most of us the problem is not that Samaritans often do not help Jews, but that often Jews do not help Jews, colleagues deceive one another, and husbands run out on wives. Jesus was referring to an ethical standard far beyond the reach of most, and the philosophers have followed him. Partly because of this lack of the specification of the concentric spheres of

moral responsibility that differentiate those most dependent on ego
from those in enveloping regions of diminished responsibility, the
gap between the paper ethics of most philosophers and those of average men remains unbridgeable.[3]

The unidimensionality and universalism of this ethical tradition are also closely related to a consequentialism that results ultimately in a quasi-quantitative calculus of moral good. The most
recent form of the utilitarian methodology is cost-benefit analysis.
Tribe (1972) has argued cogently that, in spite of important exceptions, Rawls "reduces complex, structural entities to essentially
homogeneous, or at least smoothly exchangeable, characteristics" (p.
94), while at the same time he measures all in terms of an "end-result"
calculation.

Rawls' (1971) work is also essentially materialistic and individualistic. In theory, the spiritual good of liberty is placed by Rawls
ahead of all other goods. Yet, as Barry (1973) points out, this is only
Rawls' "official doctrine." His operating doctrine is suggested by the
statement that:

> As the conditions of civilization improve, the mar-
> ginal significance of our good of further economic and social
> advantages diminishes relative to the interests of liberty. . . .
> Beyond some point it becomes irrational . . . to acknowledge a
> lesser liberty for the sake of greater material means. [Rawls,
> 1971, p. 542]

But, of course, people in every age will change the "point"; even
Rawls places it beyond where the Athenians would have (Marnell,
1971). By comparing Rawls' thinking on primary goods with that of
the young Marx, Schwartz (1973) points to Rawls' individualism and
materialism, while Tribe (1972) points to his restricting goods to
individual rather than group ends.

Finally, Rawls adheres to the tradition that moral and nonmoral value judgments are distinct; then he develops a moral theory
and proceeds to establish a theory of the good society on this only
half-adequate value basis. "Justice," Rawls tells us in the beginning,
"is the first virtue of social institutions, as truth is of systems of
thought" (p. 5). As he develops this idea, we never learn of any nonmoral values (that is, values outside of his ethical system) that might

condition the ethical concerns. Rawls is forced to this stance by the aspects of his approach that we have already mentioned. The demand for a compelling, rational derivation from a basic premise and its related, universalist consideration of abstract individuals with primarily individualistic needs leave little room for the incorporation of artistic or other nonmoral values. In spite of this omission in *A Theory of Justice,* Rawls is more interested in the good society than in interpersonal relations.

On reflection, the problem of restricting attention to what ethicists may call moral judgments not only is unsatisfactory for evaluating the good society but is also unsatisfactory for evaluating interpersonal ethical behavior. The larger arena of general humanistic judgment must be decisive when there is a conflict between the two more limited kinds of judgment. For example, if one placed a high value on art, he might judge the good society to be one that produced great works of art, regardless of its oppression of people. For these persons, Renaissance Italy contained societies preferable to many modern welfare societies. In terms of personal behavior, a person making this judgment might deny that a great Renaissance master should have risked his life to minister to the sick in a plague or have aided a swimmer in distress.

Ethical overemphasis in this regard is tied to the bias of Rawls' approach. It would be possible for the individual behind the veil of ignorance to ask some less individualistic questions about what societies and personalities would be like under different ethical and social systems. Irrespective of the humanistic everyman's chance to be a Mozart of Shakespeare, he might wish to support a system that produced great artists. The spiritual ecologist as everyman might wish to ask what relationship the society might take to nature. The humanistic planner might wish to know if there is to be one society, one mass, or a variety of societies pursuing and developing different values. In other words, a moral man is not only interested in hypothetical shares of goods for himself and others; he is also interested in what civilization might become with alternative rules.

Rawls (1971) admits there are other bases of evaluating a society besides justice, yet in practice he gives little importance to these. The limitations of concentrating on interpersonal ethics to derive a good society have led some ethicists to adopt perfectionist principles that bring in the values of science, art, and culture for the judgment of behavior and institutions. But Rawls (pp. 9, 325–332) is quite explicit in his rejection of perfectionism, either as a priority principle or as one among a set of intuitionist principles. He admits that there are standards of excellence in the arts and science: "Indeed, the freedom and well-being of individuals, when measured by the excellence of their activities and works, is vastly different in value" (p. 328). However, Rawls does not allow his theory to be tempered by this fact (or the more important but unmentioned differences in values existing apart from individuals), because behind the veil there is substantive ignorance of value, and the political principles derived from the theory of justice do not reflect value differences. The only exception to Rawls' suppression of perfectionist values is that once all of the libertarian, primary good, and distributional aspects of life are taken care of, citizens may decide to tax themselves for public goods in the arts as long as the agreement is unanimous. Rawls writes that:

> The principles of justice do not permit subsidizing universities and institutes, or opera and the theater, on the grounds that these institutions are intrinsically valuable. . . . Taxation for these purposes can be justified only as promoting directly and indirectly the social conditions that secure the equal liberties and as advancing in an appropriate way the long-term interests of the least advantaged. [p. 332]

And elsewhere Rawls suggests that:

> There is no more justification for using the state apparatus to compel some citizens to pay for unwanted benefits that others desire than there is to force them to reimburse others for their private expenses. [p. 283]

Rawls' exception is, therefore, not much of an exception. It would appear that most state support would be for popular culture, for the elite cannot even argue that they know what is in the long-term interest of the disadvantaged. And we must remember that in an ideal state dedicated, at least theoretically, to egalitarianism, there is not going to be a great deal of private surplus to support elite cultural interests.

This discussion suggests that critics who have argued that Rawls is essentially another professor protesting against the quality of life in bourgeois society (Kristol, 1972b) have failed to notice that Rawls' liberal guilt at his own good fortune and his theoretical proclivities have caused him to propose principles that would result in a populist and materialist society. Indeed, one questions whether the cultural traditions of disinterested speculation that produced *A Theory of Justice* could ever have been developed in Rawls' just society. For he would require that universities not be subsidized for their intrinsic value, and surely Harvard's nonprofit status is such a subsidy—at least as far as the philosophy department is concerned.

A Pluralistic Framework for Humanistic Evaluation

To achieve general acceptability, the philosopher must proceed more modestly. As Rawls (1971) says in his preface, most working philosophers end up with some variant of the utility principle circumscribed by "ad hoc intuitionist constraints." He wants to do better, but his "better" is essentially to construct an elaborate system to reinforce the particular intuitions he has about the primacy of justice and, within this, of liberty. A preferable alternative is to posit a series of basic values and intuitions and then to build up understanding of the pattern of their relationships, conflicts, alternatives, and justifications. In this approach, the first step is to establish a pluralistic framework for humanistic evaluation, in which ethics is not considered a separate category. Eventually, these developed intuitions may fall into reasonably coherent and defensible patterns of humanistic or evaluative doctrine. We can doubt whether there will be only one pattern that will convince all rational persons; but within a framework of common assumptions, conflict will be more creative and less destructive than that which we often encounter.

Once we have identified our intuitions of right and good (which include, of course, utility) and have accepted the likelihood of conflict among them, we must then develop a few principles to guide the analysis. I would suggest first that we accept the moral and intellectual limits of man as a part of his moral condition. Universal principles suffer by asking for too great a departure from ordinary existence. As Gehlen (1969) suggests, there must be a moral basis in the normative pattern for differentiating between obligations to persons in traditional and emotional relations of dependence, obligations to persons who only have a universal claim on us as men, and obligations to the society in which we live. St. Augustine warns us that although all men are in theory to be loved equally, one should "pay special regard to those who, by the accidents of time, or place, or circumstance, are brought into closer connection with you" (in Ramsey, 1950, pp. 157–158).[4] Samaritans are not being egoistic in preferring to help Samaritans, or Jews in preferring to help Jews. Still Samaritans have some obligation to help Jews, and the balance and gradations of these conflicting levels of obligation must be developed.

The same reasoning applies to the concept of irreducible moral limits. Man's rationalism is too weak and his desires too strong for him to live in a world of free-ranging consequentialism. There must be moral limits to life that are not open to question. For example, no matter how much societal utilitarianism might help men in general, it must be limited by refusal to do certain things to other human beings. We must have reverence for individuals, reverence that the man behind the veil of ignorance would not necessarily justify rationally, for his own cost benefit calculation might well show a positive balance for a more experimental attitude toward the physical or mental manipulation of individuals than is intuitively acceptable. The concept of moral limits parallels on the humanistic plane the concept of scientific limits proposed in Chapter Three.

The analysis should next develop a framework for achieving agreement on valuational issues relating to moral and nonmoral judgment, rather than a method of achieving any early agreement on solutions to these issues. In terms of this framework, we can then illuminate the alternatives and conflicts of our humanistic life. Finally, the approach should develop the degree of interdependence between alternative patterns of humanistic judgment and alternative scientific or descriptive analyses of the issues in question.

In the pluralistic framework presented in Figure 2, alternative values are arranged in terms of two intersecting oppositions. The first opposition is that of the action principles of utility and transcen-

Figure 2. A Pluralistic Framework for Humanistic
Evaluation.

dence versus the control principles of distribution and moral limits.
The second opposition is that of the material concerns of utility and
justice versus the spiritual concerns of transcendence and moral limits (or reverence). *Utility* values are related to social maximization, to
growth in wealth and technology. A *distribution* ethic of justice considers principles of fairness, such as concern Rawls (1971), and of control over the fruits of one's effort, such as concern Nozick (1974).
Transcendence values measure success in terms of accomplishment
that goes beyond narrow biological satisfaction; whether the accomplishments are in religion, art, or science, they are not measured in
terms of utility. Similarly, *moral limits* are values in themselves and
are not defined in terms of utility or justice; for this reason, adhering
to them is also a value in itself—whether a dietary restriction or an
unwillingness to kill another no matter what the provocation. Of
course, an individual may spiritualize economic growth and egalitarianism, yet the fact that change in these areas can be quantitatively
measured and rationally criticized in terms of universalist, rationalist
principles makes the material region fundamentally different from
the spiritual. It will be noted that utility and transcendence are both

areas of action in the Faustian sense of changing, making, or doing. It is the action principle of Blake or Nietzsche, or of T. S. Eliot when he wrote, "It is better to do evil than to do nothing: at least we exist" (in Williams, 1971). Justice and reverence are values of control, of moderation of action. Societies emphasizing these values will be creative only within a narrow range and will not be characterized by material growth.

Each area and region potentially modifies the others. In a slowly changing material world, religion and philosophy ignored the demands of progress, for progress was hardly noticeable. In a more rapidly changing world, it is only too possible to overemphasize the significance of material progress. For the materialist, social justice is the first and most obvious control. But improving material distribution may lead to gray monotony and fail to emphasize those individual rights that stand above material rights. This consideration leads us across into the region of spiritual concerns, which are beyond an easy calculation of trade-offs.

Within the framework of humanistic judgment, *utility* is defined in hedonistic terms, as is implicit in most uses of the term. For many analysts, the most obvious basis of the good society is that its ethics and institutions should be utilitarian by serving the most general interest of mankind. Those who emphasize utility are able to bring humanistic and scientific analysis closer together, because utility is the implicit basis for judging social action prudently as well as ethically. This approach is the underpinning of the claim of positivists that there need be no difference between positive and normative (humanistic) judgment (Skinner, 1971). What one man thinks is useful, another man will deny, so that to say that one is interested primarily in utilitarian ethics is not to resolve the humanistic problems, although it does narrow the discussion and make it more amenable to potential agreement. It should be reiterated that since the framework offers several alternatives to the utilitarian approach, utility can be defined narrowly. In these terms, unless people are scientifically wrong about what is useful, they cannot be wrong in their definitions of utility. (For example, fast-food service chains are useful if people utilize them in the presence of alternatives.) In this area, it is only insofar as the individual is asked to think in terms of group or universal utilities rather than personal utilities (see the discussion of exten-

sion below) that we go beyond the prudential to the ethical and normative. Within utility, the primary distinction is between *productive*
and *affective* utilities; these might be thought of simplistically as the
utilities achieved through work and the utilities achieved outside of
work activities. There is also a secondary distinction between the pursuit of *long-term* and *short-term* utilities.

While utilitarian argument is based on enhancing the good of
the whole society, a *distributive* ethic concentrates on the way in
which social goods are allocated. There are many possible distributive ethics, if perfectionism or other goods outside of distribution
itself are to be enhanced. But if just distribution is central to one's definition of the good society, then an ethics will be devised that will tend
toward a more egalitarian society, whether in terms of goods or
power. The area of distribution lies within the area of control; it is
significant that so much of the current philosophical concern as
expressed by Rawls (1971) or in the pages of the new journal *Philosophy and Public Affairs* should represent the area of control, of revolt
against Faust. In the area of justice or distribution, the primary distinction is between concern for *equality of opportunity* and concern
for *equality of result,* with most academic analysts favoring the latter.
The distinction in distributive ethics that parallels that of the productive and affective utilities is that between *material distribution* and
affective distribution, which is an important question, particularly
within the family.

Nozick (1974), however, has developed powerful arguments
against the advocacy of any pattern of distribution. Since preferred
"patterned distributions," whether of opportunity or result, deny
individuals the right to distribute what they receive, their attainments
will ultimately require aggression against individual rights. Nozick
perceptively reminds us that Rawls sees distribution as reflecting only
accidental distributions of talents and abilities. Thereby, Rawls evi-
dences a deterministic view of man that denies him the right or ability
to choose his life pattern. By ignoring completely how people have
chosen to develop their natural assets, Rawls threatens man's ability
to give a coherent meaning to his life or to the lives of those who pre-
cede or succeed him. Nozick, therefore, rejects arguments over the justice of alternative patterns and seeks justice instead in *entitlement.* He
asks us to turn our attention from the merit or virtue of a societal dis-

tribution at a particular time and instead ask about the history of the particulars of any societal distribution. To Nozick, if the modes of acquisition and transfer of a particular good were legitimate, there should be no question of injustice. If not, then the question is how to rectify the historical error. An acquisition would be unjust only to the extent that its occurrence resulted in net harm to the interests of others. Thus, the wealth of a thief and his victims should be rectified, but not generally that of a millionaire inventor and his customers or of a popular entertainer and his audience. Because it adds dignity to life and accords more fully with the common sense and complex nature of man as described in Chapters Two and Three, entitlement arguments are prima facie preferable to arguments for justice based on pattern. Nevertheless, because of the murky record leading to the present state of affairs, and because our humanitarian concerns in practice are not exhausted by Nozick's approach, we cannot ignore the distributional patterns that concern Rawls. To some degree, both distributive and entitlement arguments need to be balanced by Ramsey's (1950) concept of "redemptive justice," that is, justice that would fulfill needs simply because they are there.

Parallel to the material and rational areas of concern are the nonmaterial and spiritual. The first of these is that of transcendence, or the positive value that human beings place on "going beyond," on defying *normal* (see Chapter Two) accomplishments or definitions of personal self-interest. We might measure transcendence by the degree to which human beings go beyond purely animal, prehuman existence. Ethics and social philosophy deal primarily with interpersonal concerns beyond this level, while the humanities as a whole are concerned with creation and judgment in all areas of transcendence.[5] It is only by including this broader range of concerns that we can speak of a framework for social humanities as a whole. The area of transcendence can be analyzed according to two analytic schemes. First, it can be subdivided in terms of the *barriers* being overcome (defined in Chapter Two as biological, biosocial, cultural, and situational). Second, transcendence may be subdivided in terms of the *means* of transcendence, a list that would include concerns such as life pattern, aesthetic creativity, intellectual activity, spiritual activity, and monumentality.

In the development of man, consciousness and symbolic

memories made possible the transcendence of place and time, and eventually led to symbolic systems defining and exemplifying truth, beauty, and good. Most transcendence is not ethical, but it is all of humanistic concern. To worry about ethics at all is an important form of transcendence, but the resulting ethics may or may not offer a moral basis to go further. For example, the elite may not believe that turning the Metropolitan Museum into a high school is in the interests of the "people" in the long run, but if the people really want this (as indicated by polls or voting), Rawls' (1971) system offers no moral basis to try to circumvent it. From the viewpoint of those who would emphasize nonmoral transcendence, the challenge to the humanities is to develop and sell, at least to an effective minority, values that are not reducible to utility and fair distribution. At all times many men have devoted their lives and the efforts of their fellow men to nonutilitarian goals. In ancient times, the Australian aborigines devoted an astonishing part of their meager resources to ritual behavior, the Greeks to learning, sculpture, and architecture, and medieval Europe to monasteries and cathedrals (and modern America to moon flights and mountain climbing). It can be argued that these activities had utilitarian functions, and their promoters often so argued, but there were, in fact, more obviously useful ways to spend resources. Implicit in these expenditures was a value placed on creativity and achievement, to which questions of use and distribution were subordinated.

Most important may be the transcendence of the fact of human mortality. The desire to have children and grandchildren identified with one's name is nearly universal. On a broader plane, from at least the time of the ancient Egyptians, the attempts of men to preserve their name have been both magnificent and pathetic, but always persistent. We may also burrow back to establish new links through archeology, history, or more immediately, the family genealogies traced by so many older citizens. It is in this sense that the study of history is a moral undertaking, and not, as Smith (1964, p. 229) asserts, that the historian must render moral judgments on the events that he studies. Indeed, the historian plays the transcendent role the more he frees himself from contemporary cares and concerns to re-create lost meanings and values; he is engaged in the work of immortality—or as close to immortality as any of us will come.

Transcendence is the extension of interest beyond one's immediate interests. As we have pointed out, social extensions may involve a wide variety of differing roles, from the immediate responsibility for one's child to one's general responsibility as a human being. While the role conflict involved is central to great literature, in recent years academics have rarely dealt with the universal human fact that the definition of the good society, whether in terms of utility, distribution, or prohibition, varies greatly in its generality. When idealistic concern goes beyond the self, it should not necessarily become universal. There may legitimately be a careful grading of concerns from immediate relations of reciprocal obligation to obligations to society at a variety of levels up to nations and beyond. (To extend symbolically beyond the self is a special form of transcendence, for it requires that the individual accept moral responsibilities to other persons and things that often conflict with personal interest or instinct. This is the basis for all ethical concern. However, it should be noted that extension is not itself a critical concept for understanding other forms of transcendence, since transcendence is by definition a phenomenon of humanistic significance beyond ethics.)

One of the best discussions of social extension in terms of what might be called *role-dependent moralities* is that of Emmet (1966). To Emmet, the notion of role provides a link between factual descriptions of situations and moral statements about them. For the average person, morality only has meaning in relation to those concrete relationships by which he defines himself. Figuratively, he tells himself that if he is X, then he is also $X + Y$, where Y describes the norms that attach to X (Emmet, 1966, p. 41). This is, of course, Gehlen's (1969) institutional responsibility. Professional codes are formalized institutional role attachments of this kind (for example, see the laws of war discussed in Chapter Eight). There is in such morality a different mode of universalism, because the person merges his interests with those of society as he performs expected roles. In doing so, he joins those who have gone before and will come after him. Just as one accepts the costs and benefits of life, he also accepts those of the roles he agrees to play as a kind of moral contract with his fellows (the moral requirements of truly involuntary role playing are, of course, quite different). *Role* is a surprisingly appropriate term for this moral side of normative behavior; if I accept the part of Hamlet in a play, I implicitly accept a greatly narrowed and largely predetermined choice of activities and responses during the run of the play.

Emmet's concept does not cover all of the role dependencies of social extension, for she wishes to see roles as existing only in named relationships (pp. 167–170). However, as St. Augustine suggests, all relations, even the most transitory, establish moral responsibilities that are greater than those of universal man to universal man outside of the range of personal contact. If I pick up a hitchhiker, I have a responsibility for that person's welfare that goes far beyond my responsibility to him before I picked him up, and this has no relation to whether I particularly like him. Conversely, roles offer particular moral rights to those who play them. As Melden (1959) points out, anyone who accepts the social role of parent earns a lifetime right to special consideration from his children. It is a right attached to the role and within broad limits is not dependent upon any particular actions the person takes or does not take. Together, the duties and rights ascribed to roles provide the predictable framework for most social life.

Beyond those extensions that are role dependent, social extensions can be thought of as radiating from the person to his age group, class, or sex, or on a different level, to his family, community, or ethnic group. Ultimately, both of these directions of extension would converge at humanity and interests beyond. Another extension is to future generations, a concept that especially applies to the ecologist's worry that we are not justly distributing utilities to our descendants. Ethical utilitarianism only differs from prudential utilitarianism in that in the former, the individual extends his interests beyond his purely self-related interests. The moral evolution of mankind and of each individual is characterized by a gradual development of an ability to overcome egoism. In personal and historical time, man's interests grow from the person to the family, the local group, and finally, the larger society. Recent research has suggested that to the level of the primitive band, man did not greatly transcend the inheritance and experience of many other species. Yet man's symbolic ability made the structure of this moral relationship qualitatively different. Man could, for example, remain consciously concerned with his group's fortunes when separated from the group, either spatially by thousands of miles or temporally by periods even longer than his own lifespan. This moral sense allowed man to build up a universe of responsibility that extended to tribe, nation, all mankind, and beyond.

Social extension is, then, a special form of transcendence that we need to consider for all areas of evaluation. Interest in social extension leads us to ask: "For what group are we interested in applying rules of distribution, utility, or substantive limitation?" This is, of course, not a simple question; on some issues we may have a very broad scope, and on others a narrower scope. There will be differences of intensity. In particular, there will be differences in the degree to which a closeness to ego or a special relationship to ego engenders moral responsibilities that take precedence over more general responsibilities. In many cases, an overriding sense of responsibility to someone very close—child or superior or friend—leads to immoralities from a more universal position. This may be the judgment even of those with otherwise identical structures of moral concerns.

Finally, as Vickers (1968b) points out, all systems must eventually call a halt to the infinite regression of "why" questions. At this point, the system's sponsors must simply say, we do this, or we use these criteria, because this is the way we are. Most human groups have established a distinction between the sacred and the profane that requires not only a sense of transcendence of the human situation by action but also the curtailment of action through a sense of *reverence* or *moral limits.*[6] The sacred, ancient prohibitions were many and specific to each culture. Modern man thinks of moral limits on certain kinds of affronts to the sacredness of human beings, for example, in medical experiments. To the new breed of ecologist, reverence may mean denying man the right to eliminate a species. A wide variety of social ideals based on the preservation of what is regarded as necessary to human life at its most ideal derive from emphasis on this area. The Christian may believe that man is not fully human outside of a family-centered society; a socialist, outside a community-centered society. Rawls (1971) sees liberty as basic to human life. He thus places moral limits on depriving man of rights, whereas others would speak of preserving the sacredness of human individuality, family, or community. Unfortunately, as Bell (1975) points out, the problem of such liberal answers is that they are developed within the framework of traditional ethics that "dissolve the parochial into the universal" (p. 412). Bell believes, and I suspect he is right, that a sense of the sacred, of what is out of bounds, is based on a less-than-universal social extension without which moral structure collapses.

Moral limitations may be *legalistic* (obeying laws because they are laws); *moralistic* (obeying cultural proscriptions and prescriptions because it is a cultural assumption that one should); or *rationalistic* (obeying rules because they prevent a pattern of behavior that can be considered undesirable in terms of other areas of concern). Moral limits may have idiosyncratic and transcendent origins and only fit one of the foregoing categories at a later time. Rationalistically, moral limits are open to discussion, so in this sense they are not primitive rules. Yet the point is that the limits are not open to day-to-day calculation of their influence on the other areas of concern. An analogy between axiomatic limits and other ethical rules is that between the Constitution of the United States and the ordinary body of federal law.

In his discussion of situation ethics, Fletcher (1966, p. 37) quotes Kenneth Kirk, who despairingly reaches the conclusion that, in ethical matters, "Every man must decide for himself according to his own estimate of conditions and consequences; and no one can decide for him or impugn the decision to which he comes." Fletcher adds that this is "precisely" the moral freedom that situation ethics affirms. If so, then situation ethics is wrong both scientifically and humanistically. As individuals we have neither the time, information, nor moral strength to decide everything for ourselves. No matter how inner-directed we may become, we need the reinforcement of the approbation of our fellows when we do right and their condemnation when we do wrong. My attempt here is to develop the basis for a doctrine that assumes that if we are serious and right-minded, we do have the right to impugn the decisions of others and to try to convince them of their errors. In this way, we may gradually work toward areas of consensus that keep the community from dissolving entirely. This is not to say that in a free society there should not be restrictions on the right of a majority to compel conformity (Gastil, 1976a, 1976b).

Reverence for man limits the doctrines of utility for most of us. In Nozick's (1974) language, these limits are the "side constraints" within which we pursue personal or social ends. We might imagine that with the development of human cultural traditions, it became possible to develop a principle of benevolence that could then be applied to both social utility and distributional justice. Men were no longer interested merely in what works best but in what works best without violence to the interests of particular people. For example, it might be best for the survival and development of the species to kill all but the best babies at birth, to eliminate all persons over forty, or to allow only selected men and women to breed. But by the principle of benevolence, these actions have not been allowed in moral societies. Within this framework, then, one important principle is that human beings are to be treated in all but specified contexts (see Chapter Eight on war) as possessing absolute individual rights to respect regardless of the larger social good of the moment.

Historically, reverence has led to moral limits that go beyond living humanity, either to the ancestors or gods of the past or to all nature. Tribe (1972) points out that Rawls' (1971) approach is man-centered and suggests that an additional ethic that takes into account man's relation to animals and to nature as a whole is needed. Today, with the ecological movement, many feel a need to respect nature as a supplement to the respect for man. This movement echoes Albert Schweitzer's (1923) "reverence for life."

The result is that we cannot derive acceptable valuational or even limited moral principles by appealing to the morality of egoistic, presymbolic man, no matter how we ask him to rationalize his actions in social terms. We must ask him rather to create limits that constrain the play of free rationality. Every great religious system has had prohibitions and constraints. These are severely tested when they contradict rules of utility and distribution, but they must sometimes be upheld if man is to remain fully human.

Through attempting to define the quality and balance of the four areas of humanistic evaluation sketched above, a more adequate moral basis may be developed for society than is possible through limitation to one or two areas. One concern may contradict all of the others and yet at the same time supplement them. It may be possible to reduce all bases of value judgment to an expanded concept of social utility. Yet there is a difference between the theoretical possibilities of expansion of a principle and the central direction to which it generally leads analysts.[7] The full scope of human concerns is probably best served by establishing opposing principles and then working out compromises between the demands imposed by each.

Balancing Concerns Within the Framework

The purpose of the exposition to this point has been to establish a format for understanding humanistic issues. Ultimately, individuals will want to develop evaluative guidelines that will aid them in using the framework to help resolve questions of personal or social concern. It has been established above that there is a prima facie case that for every issue each of the areas in the pluralistic framework is of some importance. Therefore, for any decision concerning the relative desirability of a particular situation or action, the humanistic analyst must give some weight to each of these areas of concern. Wherever there is a choice, he should consider the following:

1. Among available alternatives, does this choice provide for the people concerned a satisfactory probability of general happiness (as they now understand happiness) in the short and long term?
2. To what extent am I satisfied with the inequalities in happiness that will be found among individuals and groups in a community with this choice?
3. To what extent do I think this choice sufficiently affirms the transcendent nature of man or affirms his existence?
4. To what extent am I satisfied with the moral limits that are recognized, proposed, or ignored by this choice?

It will be seen that the guiding principle is implicitly the achievement of a humanistic balance, although analysts will disagree on when a system is in balance. If the situation seems to an analyst to be out of balance, he will prefer choices that restore the balance. Obviously, John Rawls' *A Theory of Justice* (1971) is predicated on the need to restore balance within the material side of the equation. Some may accept his judgment that utility has been overemphasized at the expense of justice but still see that both are overbalancing the spiritual dimensions. In the 1970s, my judgment is that both transcendence and moral limits tend to be ignored in our society in favor of an emphasis on egalitarian and utilitarian goals. Ours is a world of economics and sociology rather than of humanities. My choice would be to redress this balance whenever resulting dislocations would be acceptable. At times in the past, I might have judged the society was out of balance through spiritual overemphasis and therefore have chosen a material emphasis wherever spiritually acceptable.

The importance of balance is suggested by Moore's (1903) attack on his profession when he says:

> The chief defect of such attempts as have been made by philosophers to construct an Ideal . . . seems to consist in the fact that they omit many things of very great positive value. . . . Great positive goods, it will appear, are so numerous, that any whole, which shall contain them all, must be of vast complexity. [p. 185]

But when Moore specifies the greatest good, he commits the same error of oversimplification of which he has accused his fellows:

> By far the most valuable things . . . are certain states of consciousness, which may be roughly described as the pleasures of human intercourse and the enjoyment of beautiful objects. . . . It is only for the sake of these things—in order that as much of them as possible may at some time exist—that any one can be justified in performing any public or private duty. [pp. 188–189]

The apparent inconsistency is resolved by Moore in terms of the contrast of means and ends. Yet if certain means are necessary for certain ends, then these means become normatively as important as the ends themselves.

The best argument for stressing need for a balance of material and spiritual concerns is, then, their dependency upon one another. John Adams expressed this dependency when he suggested that he "must study politics and war, that my sons may have liberty to study mathematics . . . natural history, commerce and agriculture, in order to give their children a right to study [painting, music, and poetry]" (Adams, 1976). Adams suggests a hierarchy of values that crosscuts what we have suggested. Instead of the squares of the pluralistic framework, Adams described three concentric circles. In the outer circle he would place politics and national security—indeed, all activities that protect and give a framework to the social space within which we plan our futures. At the farthest edge of this circle is national defense. As pointed out in Chapter Three, societies historically disappear that fail to defend themselves. Some hope this is no longer true, but recent events in the world and our biosocial analysis do not support this wish. If problems of defense can be solved, then attention may turn to improving the standard of living, or the activities that directly support such improvement. Science and mathematics are placed here, because in Adams' mind they seemed closely related to engineering and the full range of practical arts.

In an inner circle, Adams placed what we have defined as the humanities. In spite of ingenious and misplaced arguments, these make little direct contribution to the other circles. Great achievement in one circle may or may not mean achievement in the other. Some scholars would judge both the United States and Russia as rather weak in humanistic transcendence, irrespective of their material power (for example, Leonard, 1976; Kramer, 1976; McDonald, 1962). In Islamic history, the Turkish tribes excelled as rulers, while the Persians excelled in the aesthetic arts. In a profound sense, without this inner circle human life is hollow. If there is not great music, architecture, painting, poetry, and literature, if the society does not have or does not produce transcending concepts of man and his place in the order of things, if it does not help the individual to understand his condition and purpose, then the civilization is to that extent a failure.

Moore (1903) added human intercourse to beauty in the inner circle. To Moore this was a refined intercourse closely connected to his ideal of beauty. It is surely true that for most people, the outer world exists so that there may be an inner world, Gehlen's (1969) familistic world, in which both convivial and aesthetic values predominate. Therefore, another way to think of the circles is to see material, impersonal public activity as the outer circle, and personal, interactive or aesthetic activity as the inner. Note the word activity. To Moore, aesthetic contemplation was the highest good, yet for many the realization of beauty is through the achievement of form in its manifold possibilities, from skiing facilely down a slope to baking a great cake. It is for the perfection of this world of action that we work at dreary jobs or diaper babies.

In this sense, the two circles are supportive. If the outer circle fails, there will be no inner circle; indeed, society would lack all definition. If the inner circle is weak the society rots, and there is nothing left worth fighting or striving for. The tragedy of our time is that too many who devote themselves to one circle are unwilling to admit the dependence of their lives upon the other.

The conclusion seems inescapable that great music, great art, and religious inspiration are the goals of civilized society, and private intercourse the additional goal of the individual, while armies, factories, and traffic laws are the means to achieve both goals. Many will object that the goal of civilized society must rather be the happiness of man, and that this first means good food, schools, hospitals, or housing. Yet is this not only another way of saying that the goal should be pleasurable stimulation of the senses? And if so, cannot this be achieved by the artificial devices of *Brave New World* more efficiently than by actually improving these services or facilities? It seems to me that ultimately we will find that all the economic and sociological improvement imaginable will not by itself produce a civilization in which man can take pride, nor may it improve the quality of private intercourse.

Utility and transcendence are, however, both virtues of action, and they must be balanced as a group against justice and reverence, the virtues of control. Perhaps the best example of the failure to achieve this balance was in the life of Jean Jacques Rousseau (Huizinga, 1976). Spending a life in pursuit of the pleasures of sex and success, and producing a lively if not always coherent flow of creative work, Rousseau was unable to understand his responsibilities to also satisfy the interests of those around him. We find it incomprehensible that he lived with a woman for thirty-five years and insisted that she send all five children to an orphanage. Although claiming that he did not have the money to bring them up, he made no serious effort to change his situation. This behavior becomes even more indefensible when we remember that this was a man continually examining his personal moral record, continually feeling the necessity to justify to himself and the world his every act. Rousseau becomes less confusing when we see him as merely the extreme case of the tendency of overrationalism in moral discussion to lead to no effective morals at all (Bradley, 1927). More cogently, it would seem to be a case where reverence for an absolute sense of limits, for a firm code of what one simply does and does not do, was necessary before an acceptable human life could be constructed. (Generally, the peasant has had such a code, but too often the intellectual has not.) Without limits, Rousseau flailed through life—and it may have been this moral incoherence that ultimately made it impossible for him to develop a coherent body of work.

Decision Rules

Within each area of humanistic judgment, we must develop decision rules to guide our lives and our attempts to influence society. In the area of utility, we must establish the weight to be placed on short- versus long-term happiness, defining each term appropriately. Seeing utility in terms of happiness, we should also develop appropriate criteria for estimating the comparative happiness of peoples or subdivisions of peoples, both in the present and after a variety of proposed changes. We would have to resort to information and models from the natural and social sciences, where useful, to estimate conditions or effects. Since other categories of the analysis probe beyond utility, here it should be sufficient to employ material indicators aided by polling techniques and perhaps social indicators, such as suicide rates.

We must also develop criteria for judging preferable or acceptable distributions of happiness or utility. Rawls' (1971) decision rule that any gain in utility must benefit those most poorly off in either goods or position or Nozick's (1974) that one is entitled to all that he has justly attained are two of the more attractive possibilities. However, we cannot quite accept Nozick's lack of concern with the general distributional outcomes of systems rather than the distributions affected by individual social or political choices; nor can we accept Rawls' lack of concern for persons who, because of environment or inheritance, are potential welfare dependents or criminals and yet successfully struggle to stay above these conditions.

Decision rules in the area of transcendence are particularly difficult, because they involve a detailed examination of most of the humanities and of the humanistic evaluation of the efforts of man beyond these confines. On the one hand, we might take positions in the aesthetics of painting, music, literature, and architecture. On the other, we must judge accomplishments in these areas in relation to those in science, engineering, medicine, social organization, and so on. The difficulty is that every effort of man potentially has a transcendent component. Organizing the Roman Empire or a multinational corporation can be judged as important an affirmation of man as building the Acropolis. Einstein may have transcended man's existential condition as much as Shakespeare. The pluralistic framework forces us to look at these questions, but of course does not resolve them. The analyst might strive only for balance within the category; yet civilizations have generally concentrated on only a few of the possible areas of transcendence at a time. My judgment would be to value most highly the efforts of man that seem most clearly to go beyond the utilitarian, to not meet material desires. It is the only way I can be sure that transcendence will not get lost in the unfolding of material possibilities. The man on a desert island who knows a hurricane will soon erase all trace of his work and yet builds the most beautiful and functional dwelling he can is expressing his humanity most fully, and his transcendence is in his persistence in the face of the realization that his efforts are ultimately impermanent. We are all, of course, on that island.

It is clear that in discussing social extension, I imply that I would favor some decision rules that are less than universal. There is a human responsibility to be concerned with the welfare of all men and a much more limited ethical responsibility to nature. (Of course, we may strive to preserve nature for strictly utilitarian reasons. For example, I like the natural world and would preserve wilderness for my utilitarian reasons, but this is not an extension of responsibility. Likewise, excluding actions simply because they go beyond intuitively acceptable limits of change may preserve nature, but this is a matter of moral limits rather than responsibility for nature.) However, as pointed out above, the highest moral priority is that people develop a heightened sense of role-dependent responsibility to those who depend on them for whatever reason within the framework of daily existence. For example, a rule that you should attempt to rescue a person in danger should be graded as follows: This is most incumbent if the person involved is in your family, next most if the person has some reason to expect help from you rather than others (for example, if you are a friend, if you have accepted a helping stance, or if you are a policeman), and least incumbent if you have had no previous relation to the endangered person and are not present in his danger. This doctrine is particularly important when there are several people endangered and one must make a choice. Although variable responsibility should govern most moral decision-making, it is less important for rules (established either for utility or as moral limits) such as "do not lie" or "do not kill" that can be applied universally, except where a person has conflicting responsibilities to people with different relations to him.

Finally, we must decide on the moral limits that we wish to bring into the analysis. The category covers both the absolute limits we place beyond individual argument and the extent to which limits are set. The latter raises the question of freedom. A common position is that moral limits should be primarily on society's right to interfere with the freedom of individuals. This may be either a libertarian position with overtones of the conservative economists or a position that would limit freedom only where it interfered with a just distribution of what is desirable in life. I would choose instead the position that society or an individual representing society should refrain absolutely only from controlling the expression of opinions on the nature of society, including opinions on what should be controlled. Thus, I would oppose political censorship and support social censorship, and, incidentally, deny that pornography is likely to be a political statement. In accepting the right to social limits, we would accept the right of society to impose negative limits but not to prescribe positive modes of action (Gastil, 1976a).

In these terms, I would accept the relativity of moral standards alongside the moral desirability of maintaining limits of some kind over social and artistic behavior. We forget that artistic creativity and style in human life is most likely to emerge from the interplay of human potential and traditional form. The great art of the past was produced under social and artistic pressures for conformity that would never be accepted by artists today. Too often a society or a person with all possibilities seems to have no possibilities. Social limits that should not be transgressed should emphasize the sacredness of human life, personality, and human responsibility. With growing human capabilities to affect life on both the microscopic and planetary level, we may need to establish new, fundamentally irrational limits on action in areas such as the use of nuclear weapons or the transformation of genetic material.

In attempting to live by a set of decision rules, we must not limit our focus to concrete instances. Because of the serial decision problem, many generally correct decisions can, in particular instances, lead to unwanted overall effects. For example, environmental statements for individual power plants that weigh the gains and losses of each may conclude in each case that the advantages outweigh the disadvantages; yet at some point, there will be so many power plants that they will exceed the thermal absorption capacity of available cooling resources. Because of the indefinite period between the proposal and the operation of new facilities, it will be impossible to pinpoint where and when the problem will become critical. In fact, the last plant may well be the best designed and most efficient. Similarly, we may, in individual instances, decide that chances for aiding a criminal offender will be best served by not sending him to jail. Yet after repeated decisions of this type, the deterrent effect of the criminal justice system may disappear with unfortunate consequences for society. Most generally, we may be able to justify on social grounds a wide variety of decisions that slightly erode personal freedom, with the result that personal freedoms have in large part been exchanged for scientifically informed administrative convenience.

The problem that we are considering is closely related to the "tragedy of the commons" (Hardin, 1968b), which is that individuals pursuing their own purposes eventually harm the overall purposes of the community. This is the reason for the development of the population problem, just as it was the reason for the hypothetical overgrazing of public commons. As pointed out in our discussion of group behavior in Chapter Three, in such a situation no individual can, by his isolated action, directly influence the outcome. Indeed, the conscientious citizen who keeps his cow off the commons may likely only hurt his own interest while failing to affect the larger interests. However, this problem should be distinguished from the serial decision problem suggested above; the serial problem is not a lack of community regulation, but the inability of the community to decide in terms of the whole, when the whole is not reflected in isolated serial decisions.

These considerations lead to the suggestion of two overarching *decision principles* that may modify the deleterious effect of isolated serial decisions by sacrificing isolated interests to more holistic ones. The first is the *principle of balance* among goods. When the matters with which we are concerned are "out of balance," then the analyst should arbitrarily favor decisions that will reestablish the desired balance. Alternatively, we might say that when a particular field of interest is saturated in certain respects, further action in the field should be in other directions. The second principle is that of *moral limitation*. We will set up certain rules as final, as not capable of being overridden, regardless of the individual interest.

It is, of course, paradoxical to speak of balancing against absolute moral limits. However, in a recent article, Walzer (1974a) has suggested one way in which this might be done. He suggests that although we sometimes must responsibly break a moral rule, we are not thereby absolved from the guilt or punishment accompanying our trespass. If, for example, we order the torture of a terrorist in order to exact from him information on where he has placed an atomic device that will blow up a city, we are making a right decision but one which is also immoral, and we should never forget it. This Catholic view of sin is far more attractive than the self-satisfied rationalism of situational ethics that accepts no absolutes (see Fletcher, 1966). Yet it is also dangerous, particularly for persons repeatedly faced with apparently urgent needs to transgress fixed limits or rules. For the positive feedback of successfully breaking limits may easily develop a habit of transgression unless the guilt or punishment accompanying initial trespass is severe. Thus, while in theory Walzer's solution works, given our model of man it is problematic. It should also be remembered that if limits are carefully chosen and specified, extreme cases in which breaking a limit is unambiguously required will be very rare. The number of solutions to most problems is large enough that if those solutions requiring breaking limits are eliminated from consideration, the mind will, in most cases, quickly find acceptable solutions of nearly equal efficacy.

The overriding principles of weighting, then, are those that will balance the several humanistic concerns. Paradoxically, one of the ways to achieve this balance has been to posit an area of humanistic concern, that of moral limits, that is beyond a question of trade-offs. Since particular limits are not open to rational argument, we cannot say that in a particular case considerations of utility, transcendence, or justice are sufficient to allow us to ignore certain limits. This is because the enemy of any system is cynicism, and cynicism is bred by the flux of unanchored rationality and the ease with which we may rationalize almost anything when our self-interests are at stake. To be effective, an evaluative system must force people to make hard choices —there must be costs to maintain the system. If there is a rule against killing except in defense against imminent attack, then starving men on a lifeboat do not pull straws to see who eats whom, even if this means that all will starve. One can argue about what the limits should be and how much weight the category of limits should have, but for limits that are accepted in this framework, there is no way to balance them off in particular instances.

Notes

1. This section is a revision of Gastil (1975a).

2. Although most philosophers and intellectual laymen are ideologically receptive to Rawls' egalitarian tendency, many do not find either the "original position" or what follows from it compelling (Choptiany, 1973; Scanlon, 1973). Rawls' original position of selected ignorance appears to some to be too removed from the real human condition to have meaning (Oberdieck, 1972). To others, the wealth and liberty that Rawls specifies as primary preferences are seen as the arbitrary preferences of a twentieth-century liberal (Schwartz, 1973). Critics point to the obvious fact that from behind the veil, the individual might be less conservative than Rawls imagines. He might see all units of good as equally valuable and thus prefer to maximize his probable return by accepting a maximum-utility principle. Or he might notice that his chance of being in the middle and upper classes is better than that of being in the least advantaged (lowest 20 percent), and thereby suggest a system that would maximize the goods of these classes, even at the expense of the least advantaged. If, on the other hand, we imagine that since this hypothetical man does not know his personal interests, he might decide in the original position to be more idealistic than in Rawls' model; he might choose the good (content undefined) of humanity in the long run rather than the fair share of primary goods that would accrue to his still-unknown individual personality. Rawls' refutation of this possibility (p. 327) is quite unconvincing; why would a person in the original position be concerned that he be free to follow a particular, less-than-best religious doctrine, ideology, or aesthetic standard? He would want to reduce the chance to become ego involved with an inferior symbolic system. Only if he were a real person, already involved, would he have Rawls' concerns.

3. In using the familiar model of the social contract, Rawls is, of course, theoretically thinking of the ethical relations among members of a cooperating unit (Scanlon, 1973, p. 1066). In fact, though, Rawls does not develop the idea of the distinction among obligations even across one boundary. (Actually, his approach is most appropriate for an instant one-world community.) The lack of discussion in the ethical literature of what I call social extension (see the following section) seems to have an analogy in political philosophy. Dahl (1970) points to the surprising lack of discussion of the definition of "the people" that is to be treated as a political unit. By what principle is the United States or the U.S.S.R. one country or two or ten? Yet surely the right to independence is one of the most critical rights of peoples. Intellectuals respond to the traditional problems of their disciplines more than to those suggested by their general experience.

4. Ramsey adds that in addition to universal responsibilities, "The permanent relationships [the Christian] has established with other persons within the limits of his particular calling have also to be taken into account" (pp. 157–158).

5. The reader might wish to compare the concept of transcendence developed here with the concept of self-transcendence in an integrative work similar to this one (Ulich, 1955).

6. In philosophy, this position is called *rule deontology*, or adherence to rules not connected to outcomes. In fact, the rules ascribed range from this extreme to the rule utilitarian position that a rule is adhered to because in the long run adhering to it can be shown to be advantageous. However, the area of moral limits should not be thought to include simple adherence to rules of thumb that must guide us provisionally in all areas.

7. This is the real basis of Tribe's (1972) criticism of policy science. Policy science theoretically includes all of Tribe's concerns, yet in fact it tends to quasi-quantitative, economic modeling directed toward comparing the material costs and benefits of achieving desired objectives.

FIVE

Putting Social Humanities to Work: Examples and Methodology

Chapters Two, Three, and Four have provided the basic models and framework with which one school of social humanities could develop its analyses, evaluations, and proposals. In this chapter we will recapitulate this material in two ways. We will provide outlines for analysis and evaluation derived from the previous chapters, and we will illustrate the ways in which the approach developed might be used to consider a wide variety of cases. Because the book has to this point been exceedingly abstract, instead of turning immediately to the development of outlines, it seems desirable to begin this presentation by considering a case history that may be familiar to most readers.

Magruder's Watergate

Magruder's analysis of how he came to act as he did in the Watergate affair is, on the surface, one of the most plausible and appealing of the Watergate stories (Magruder, 1974). It is especially significant because Magruder saw the moral aspects of his plight.

With the aid of his wife and the experience of humiliation in jail, he came to believe that his basic mistake in the Nixon years was emphasizing public over private life. He was unprepared for public life, for while his private moral sense was well developed, his public moral sense was not. Magruder came to what may be personally correct conclusions, yet clearly it would be a loss to society if all people as serious and capable as Magruder were to retire to private life. The problem remains: How do we create a means of morally strengthening men and women in public life?

Under the influence of his old friend, the Reverend William Sloane Coffin, Magruder contended that his mistakes stemmed from a characteristically American overevaluation of personal ambition, material success, and status. This is a very old charge, but a comparative study of a variety of cultural traditions and periods suggests that America is not particularly materialistic; in fact, Americans are more open to moral appeals than most peoples (for example, Almond and Verba, 1963; Banfield, 1958). (This is one reason Europeans failed to understand why Americans were so upset by Watergate.) In particular, Magruder's story does not seem to be one of material striving, but rather a story of personal moral inadequacy in an isolated institutional setting. To avoid this type of action, it is necessary to make a deeper analysis of why Magruder made his mistakes, an analysis that goes beyond generalizations about the moral tone of our society. We need to look specifically at the development of his situation as he describes it, to understand his story in terms of our psychosocial model, and to make a humanistic evaluation of his behavior.

Magruder's Story. Although from a Southern background, which his family never forgot, Magruder was brought up on Staten Island. While the family had been wealthy, in the early 1920s his grandfather went to jail for a business irregularity. Apparently, Magruder's dashing, recently married father suddenly lost his hopes and ambition as a result. Although the family continued to nourish upper-class tastes, the father's subsequent income as a printer was modest. Magruder's mother taught her boys that they should have lived at a higher level, and she emphasized the importance of the success that her husband never attained. In spite of their small means, Magruder went to Williams College, where at first he was made painfully aware of his social inferiority. His academic work fell off, picking up only after he had spent time in Korea. Since he always needed money, Magruder was self-supporting and experienced in business by the time he graduated. Although a business career did not appeal to him, he went into business, married well in California, and after a couple of years of struggling, was well on the way up the corporate ladder.

Yet he was perennially dissatisfied and changed jobs frequently. In part, this was because his real interest was political activity, particularly Republican campaigns. He enjoyed the excitement of politics, and the more he became involved, the harder it was for him to give it up, even though his wife objected both to his time away from home and to the changes of residence his activities entailed. In 1960, Magruder's involvement was quite ideological, guided by a strong belief in the importance of Republican victories; by the late 1960s this had moderated, and he no longer saw the world in black and white. Magruder was now as interested in winning elections in party terms as in ideological terms.

At this time, Magruder was recruited from his own small Los Angeles firm to become a member of the White House staff, working under H. R. Haldeman and Herbert Klein to improve public relations. In 1971, he was transferred to work with John Mitchell on the 1972 campaign. As an important lieutenant in the Committee to Reelect the President, he eventually was one of the people that approved the electronic surveillance of the Watergate office of Lawrence O'Brien, the chairman of the Democratic Party. Later, he carried the main burden of the Watergate cover-up: Magruder testimony provided the basis for the official story that Liddy and his men had acted without authorization.

Although there were a number of other immoral and illegal actions that Magruder ended up doing, the focus should be on the Watergate break-in itself. Here Magruder authorized breaking in, entering, and the surreptitious recording of other people's conversations without any satisfactory moral rationale. Of course, at the time Magruder gave very little attention to his actions. If they had not been part of a national scandal, Magruder might have seen his actions as careless errors made under the pressure of more important decisions. Yet why did Magruder ignore their implications?

Psychosocial Analysis. In order to answer this question, let us focus first on an explanation according to the biosocial situation—on what we would normally expect someone to do under the circumstances. Magruder, according to this analysis, would have been expected to maximize his self-interest by trying to convince others to do as he wants (communication) or by exchanging those values of which he has a surplus for those he needs (transaction). In a complex society, he would find it advantageous to accept both formal and informal affiliations to groups and organizations that would allow him to achieve more than he could independently or in other organizations. Such transactional organizational affiliations would have costs, however, and Magruder would pay these costs as long as he feels he is receiving compensating benefits.

An individual's basic affiliations in a complex society are to the family in which he is raised and the country in which he lives. He does not choose these affiliations, and only to a limited degree can he ever escape them. As he grows, a man will usually enter into a transaction with a woman to establish a new family and join other organizations for financial and other rewards. In the case of Magruder, when he went to work for the government, he increased his commitment to the Republican Party but also added a relationship to the White House staff and then to the Committee to Re-elect the President. As important as these formal arrangements, he also joined a small group of what we might call the *President's staff men,* whose goal was the success of President Nixon. So far, there is nothing unusual in this—these groups have existed in every administration. But it is important to note Magruder's particular position. After moving from Los Angeles to Washington, Magruder's transactions and communications were restricted largely to the formal groups from which he received his income at the time, the President's staff men as an in-group, and his new family.

Now we must bring Magruder's personality into the analysis, for it is only because of his personal values that he accepted his Washington work and persisted in it. (Although she objected at first, even his wife and then his children came to value highly their Washington life.) But in terms of what values? As an explanation for his attachment to the President's staff men, the accusation of materialism rings false, because Magruder could have made more money in private business. Most important was the glamour of being at the top. Supporting this were the proximity to presidential power, opportunities for more substantial political positions in the future, the excitement of the crisis atmosphere, which Magruder had long preferred to the calmer business world, and idealistically, the contribution to the country that he could make from this position. Perhaps in the background was the sense of reestablishing the Magruder name. Unfortunately, continuing to receive these benefits depended on his maintaining his position among the President's staff men. Since Magruder had been directly recruited and had little outside political support, it was most unlikely he could keep the benefits of Washington life outside of this group.

The first cost of the White House affiliations was the requirement of hard work, which demanded a great deal of time away from his family. But except for a guilty conscience about his family, at the time Magruder rather liked these pressures, so this was hardly a cost. (Again note the lack of materialism.) The second and more important cost was the necessity to go along with policies, decisions, and individuals that he did not like. In transactions with those above him in the White House, Magruder had his continued ability and cooperation to offer. This gave him some room to resist requests. But those above him had the power to simply throw him out. The longer he stayed, the less likely the President's men would carelessly dismiss him. Yet he knew that he was replaceable at relatively low cost to them.

Under these circumstances, Magruder tried to promote his values and perceptions by presenting them in terms of the values held in common with those above him (primarily the success of Nixon's presidency). For example, Magruder thought that taking a hostile attitude to the press was counterproductive and wrong. Yet since this was not the accepted line of the Presidential staff, what could he do? First he used communication to convince others to think as he did by appealing to common goals. When this failed, his next approach was simply to neglect hostile actions that were desired by his superiors and others with more power. But he could only neglect distasteful activities and contacts up to a point; he could not ignore a direct order. He had a limited number of negatives to play, and these could

only be used in the right context. He was in no position to employ the
threat of resignation, but his superiors did use the threat of dismissal.

Culturally, Magruder was trained in the American tradition,
particularly in its Southern and Protestant modes. These have a
highly moralistic component, especially in regard to patriotism and
traditional religious morality. However, experience in a wide variety
of jobs as a teen-ager and then in the army had taught Magruder that
success required an ability to deceive and to cut corners. Later, his
experience in the business world as an executive was at a higher moral
level; for a while, he had the gratifying experience of working for a
company, the Jewel Tea Company, that was dedicated to serving the
interests of both its customers and employees.

In Washington, Magruder's public morality was affected by
the subculture of politics and the sub-subculture of the men around
the President. Ultimately, it was because of the latter that he accepted
to a degree the set of perceptions that made Watergate possible. The
attitude accepted and developed by many of Magruder's superiors was
that in political struggles there were relatively few limits and that the
President was faced in the late 1960s and early 1970s with a particularly vicious set of opponents. Magruder and several of his closest
friends in the President's staff did not initially accept this view, but
inevitably the longer he remained a functioning part of the staff the
more he accepted it (see Kuhn, 1974; Gastil, 1971b). Regardless of
whether Magruder changed his mind, he came to see the views of the
"administration under siege" as those with which most of his professional transactions and communications must take place.

An aspect of Magruder's cultural position that he did not fully
realize was that there were legal dangers in his work for the Committee to Re-elect the President. He himself had no legal training, but
since he was surrounded by lawyers, he thought he could rely on them
for protection from legal missteps. Yet these lawyers saw themselves
at the top of a local system of law and order that had always treated
them carefully; after all, they represented the President. Since Magruder came from the middle class, the possibility of jail was extremely
remote. (It is significant that Magruder did not learn until 1973 that
his grandfather had been in jail in the 1920s.) Since in his world the prag-
matic dangers of illegality were almost never discussed, cultural control through the law (deterrence) had little chance to affect Magruder.

It was in this context that Magruder was told that the White House wanted more intelligence on the opposition. It was suggested that G. Gordon Liddy be appointed both to serve as a counsel for the Committee to Re-elect the President and to gather intelligence. Magruder wanted a full-time counsel but agreed to accept Liddy, a man of FBI background who was obviously more interested in intelligence. That Magruder would allow this to happen showed how little feeling he had for legal obstacles or for possible crimes that might be committed in the course of gathering intelligence. Liddy proceeded to develop grandiose, unacceptable plans, including the use of kidnapping, prostitutes, and wiretapping. Twice these plans were rejected. The third time they were presented, LaRue, Magruder, and Mitchell, all relatively "soft" members of the President's staff group in Magruder's view, accepted Liddy's proposal to set up electronic surveillance in O'Brien's office in the Watergate. They felt they had to be somewhat responsive to White House desires; they had no alternative available for easing White House pressure on them; and Mitchell did want something on O'Brien. In the following months, although Magruder was Liddy's superior, there was little contact between the two in the press of the election campaign until shortly before the Watergate break-in was exposed. In those last few days, Magruder and Mitchell received transcripts of tapes, found the material nearly worthless, and urged Liddy to come up with something useful.

At this point, it would help the analysis if we knew the extent of electronic surveillance up to this time among political parties. Liddy naturally thought it was ubiquitous, and his unchallenged conviction must have had an effect. Liddy's influence on Magruder can be inferred from the fact that he looked on Liddy as an expert in a nefarious world he wanted no association with, although he was half-persuaded that clandestine actions of doubtful legality were necessary. Magruder was aware that government agencies engaged in similar practices, apparently legally, and the President's staff in Washington, whatever their legal position, regarded themselves as part of the government. In any event, it seems true that the idea that there was something criminal or morally wrong about bugging O'Brien's office did not make much of an impression on Magruder. Did he believe that everyone else was doing it? Regardless of the facts, Magruder was caught in a situation in which he wanted to believe that they were. Clearly, the seriousness of illegal electronic eavesdropping was obscured by the weak moral glow that must have come from resisting the "really wrong" proposals that Liddy had initially put forward.

Magruder accepted the Liddy plan at the time because the expected personal costs of opposing it were much higher than the benefits of letting it go ahead, and he reckoned that the costs of approving it were very low. He barely noticed the possibility of cultural condemnation by others (including the superego), of damage to President Nixon, or of jail.

Humanistic Evaluation. To this point, I have been developing an analysis that would be sufficient only if Magruder were a self-interested mechanism responding to the costs and benefits of a situation according to his biological capabilities and cultural conditioning. But now let us see Magruder as a full human being, capable of reflection and responsible decision—capable of committing actions for which he may be justly punished. Let us assume that the values by which Magruder should have judged his actions were those of utility, justice, transcendence, and moral limitation. Because he is interested in moral questions, he recognizes the moral value of transcending his purely selfish interests. But if he transcends himself, he will be interested in securing utilities and justice for others. Because he cannot trust himself at all times to distinguish rationally between his interests and those of others, his transcendence of self must also include a willingness to place himself under those generally accepted rules of behavior whose purpose is to curb selfishness for the sake of the public interest. In other words, as a moral person, Magruder must transcend his mechanistic self and set up a series of extensions by which he may reflexively judge his conduct from a less self-interested viewpoint. Magruder, then, should not be concerned simply with interpersonal ethics but with what he is doing in terms of the full range of his nonselfish ideals.

Magruder saw himself as supporting an administration that was good for the country in both utilitarian and egalitarian terms. He felt that even in the social area it was doing more than previous administrations, and one of his chief frustrations was that this fact was not sufficiently known. He saw many of the personal shortcomings of the people involved, including the President, but he saw few faults in their nationally and internationally significant actions. He knew that for some of the President's men, policy accomplishments were so important that they could ignore the ordinary moral rules of society, but he never put himself in this camp. For example, Nixon and Haldeman might have done a great deal that was wrong from an ordinary ethical viewpoint, but they were pictured by Magruder as individuals who could justify these actions in terms of their values and the perceived alternatives. (This is a position that should not be lightly dismissed; it did, of course, play some part in Magruder's calculations. See Walzer, 1974a.) Magruder could not justify his own actions, and after he realized what he had done, he confessed his error. Therefore, adhering to moral limitations, the narrower ground of ethics, remained potentially important to Magruder, compared with calculations of national utilities.

He came later to realize that O'Brien and those around him had a right to privacy, and only exceptional conditions of immediate danger would give anyone the right to infringe on this right. From the point of view of justice, he could conceive that O'Brien's right was canceled by assuming that the Democrats were also planting bugs; but from the point of view of moral limits, cancellation of rights cannot be morally justified except under the most extreme conditions. In his book, Magruder accepts this latter basis for evaluation, and it is indeed the more useful protection of rights in a world where it is common to project our sins on others.

Parenthetically, I see a less serious moral problem in Magruder's subsequent perjury. That self-interest when facing jail overcomes the moral rule against lying should not be surprising. The relativism of the injunction against lying is recognized in the Fifth Amendment and in the concept of "white lies." While lies are surely wrong and there should be laws that deter people from lying before a court, there is a great deal of difference between limitations on what we will do directly to another (from killing them to deliberately invading their privacy) and limitations on how we will behave in situations that are less directly concerned with others (from committing suicide to lying).

In Magruder's case, his self-interest in lying was morally buttressed by a sense of loyalty, or an extension of interest beyond the self to friends, including friends he was responsible for involving in the affair. Thus, as a front man in the presentation of a lie, Magruder served the organizational purposes of the President's staff men, that is, fulfilled the last part of the "contract" he had had with them (and thus followed culturally determined, normative behavior), but he also morally subordinated his interests to those of the group. It is unrealistic for those of us unconnected with the affair to imagine that Magruder should have abandoned his role-dependent moralities in favor of larger abstractions, such as his affiliation to the government or the nation.

Magruder abandoned his false story only when subsequent events separated him morally from the President's staff and when the chance of further perjury succeeding became so low that its expected costs exceeded its expected benefits. Then, as his small network of governmental affiliations collapsed, he could clearly see his responsibility to the nation to tell the truth.

The next stage of the analysis is to consider how the mistakes of Magruder might have been avoided. However, in this case, their consideration will be postponed until Chapter Ten.

Generalizing the Process

The analysis of Magruder serves as a summary of Chapters Two through Four and as an introduction for the approach to understanding and advice that social humanities is meant to inspire. A full evaluation of a case would include: (1) a statement of the problem, (2) a narrative or descriptive account of the main facts, (3) a scientific analysis of the facts and their probable causes, (4) a humanistic evaluation within the pluralistic framework, and (5) consideration of possible ways to improve future outcomes.

In order to take these steps, we need to develop a standard checklist of concerns that can become as much a part of our day-to-day thinking as the less structured, common sense categories by which we usually try to understand the world. We need, in other words, a way to grasp reality from the social humanities point of view as surely as Marxists, Freudians, or Augustinians are able to understand reality from their viewpoints.

The basic concept for this analysis is the *social unit*. Denoting approximately what Kuhn (1974, pp. 25–26, 489) means by a "con-

trolled system," at least when applied to the human world, a social
unit can be found at any level from the individual human being up to
that of the nation. Of course, an individual may be a Jekyll and Hyde
united only by biology and so not a unit, and this may likewise be
true of a bureau or a nation. But if it makes sense to ask, "What will
Jim do?" or "What will China do?", then we are speaking of units
with describable means of understanding the world, making decisions in terms of their interests, and acting. Note that for this purpose
we are speaking of China as represented by the organization called the
Chinese government, not the Chinese people or even society. As Kuhn
says, a society is a semiformal organization and thus not amenable in
a strict sense to this kind of analysis. Nevertheless, societies do have
inputs and outputs, and we will wish to judge how these might be
improved; in Kuhn's terms, at least in a democracy, we are the sponsors of our own society; it was the society bequeathed to us and will be
our principal gift to our descendants.

The scientific analysis of a social unit begins with a *static
description* of the unit's biological or structural characteristics, its
intelligence and understanding, its interests as ego and alter ego, and
its capability to act effectively. While static in the sense that past and
present conditions are considered at rest, the description may be primarily derived from the history of the unit and the descriptions of
comparable units, for this information is often more predictive than
information we can gather through direct, contemporaneous
observation.

A *dynamic description* considers a social unit's interaction
with particular inputs or pressures that cause or prevent actions. We
will be especially interested in the communications or other inputs
that the unit is receiving, the interests called into play by these communications, the resulting transactions or other decisions the unit is
able to make, and the actions that then ensue. These actions may be
additional transactions or communications, as well as noninteractive
efforts. Finally, we would want to judge the feedback the social unit
receives from its actions and the extent to which this feedback results
in learning. Some dynamic descriptions will be holistic, for they will
consider the response of an individual or a society to its total environment over a span of time. In these cases, the static and dynamic
descriptions will merge.

The third stage of analysis is to evaluate a unit or the actions of a unit in terms of the unit's *output*. The analyst should first attempt to describe the external characteristics of the output. Straddling both sides of the scientific/humanistic boundary, he can ask these questions neutrally, although his humanistic concerns will play a critical part in determining what is examined. Second, in terms of the characteristics ascribed to the output, the analyst will consider the degree to which the unit has added to or subtracted from the utilities enjoyed by itself or others.[1] This is the classic form of cost/benefit analysis, although cost/benefit has usually been analyzed only in terms of the utilities of the acting unit. Such an analysis might also include the use of tools such as opinion polls to investigate how the output is perceived and evaluated by consuming publics. The analyst should also consider the extent to which the interests of the unit or of other units are changed or reinforced by the output; that is, we need to examine not only what happens to utilities directly, but what the existence or action of a unit communicates (teaches) to other units. A jail, for example, might fail to reform inmates but might teach many potential criminals that crime does not pay. Finally, in the area of humanistic evaluation, the unit's output will be evaluated by its utility (affective and productive, or direct and indirect), by the justice of its effects, and by its contribution to the transcendence of man or a structure of limits, as discussed in Chapter Four.

A summary checklist for social humanities includes, then, the following definitions, each of which should be used to develop the steps of our analysis.

1. A *social unit* is a person, organization, or society.
2. A *problem* is a hypothetically improvable condition that negatively affects the humanistic evaluation of a social unit, class of units, or their relationships. If the analysis is problem oriented, the focus of the subsequent analysis of the unit is on the unit description or output as it is affected by the problematic condition or context. Of course, different evaluations will identify different problems.
3. A social unit is statically described in terms of:
   a. structural characteristics,
   b. perceptual and intellectual abilities,

    c. interests of egos and alters, and

    d. capabilities to act effectively.

4. It is dynamically described in terms of:

    a. communications or other inputs to the unit, including those previously produced internally as outputs by the unit when described statically.

    b. unit interests affected by communications and other inputs,

    c. resulting internal communications and transactions,

    d. outputs, including communications, exchanged transactional goods, and noninteractive actions,

    e. feedback from outputs, and

    f. basic unit capability to learn from feedback.

5. Its output is also analyzed in terms of:

    a. external characteristics,

    b. utility cost/benefit to unit and other units, and

    c. effect on values of unit and other interacting units.

6. Unit output is given a secondary humanistic evaluation in terms of its effect on:

    a. utilities (affective and productive),

    b. justice,

    c. transcendence (including social extension),

    d. moral limits, and

    e. the achievement of an acceptable balance of these goods.

In going through this analysis, in each case we will be guided by our expectations in terms of our models of man and society, or in other words, in terms of the biological and biosocial "laws" we have discussed in Chapters Two and Three. These expectations are the result of pressures on the individual or groups that result from inherited structures, as well as the structure of the communication-transaction nexus. Exceptions will occur either because of the chance unfolding of events or because personal and cultural systems are created or maintained by individuals or groups that are willing to make sacrifices that are required of those who refuse to bow to the pressures assumed by the models. But exceptions should be explained after the general case and in relation to it. It need hardly be mentioned that the general case (or central tendency of explanations) must be continually revised by empirical and theoretical evidence.

It may be worthwhile to remember the additional determinants of human behavior as described in Chapters Two and Three. In order to understand the static and dynamic descriptions, we must try in each case to estimate the degree to which the observed characteristic or relationship is:

1. biological (in its regularity or individuality),
2. biosocial,
3. cultural, and
4. situational.

We will want to visualize the problem as an interactive framework in which there is:

5. positive or negative feedback, and
6. time lags of varying duration.

We will wish to understand units in terms of their transactional relations, particularly:

7. their general and bargaining power in relevant situations,
8. their generous or hostile mode of bargaining, and
9. their use of goods or bads to obtain objectives.

To understand individual and organizational behavior, we will need to know:

10. the roles played by the units,
11. the alter ideals of the individuals,
12. the major bargains of the participants,
13. the sponsors, staff, suppliers, and recipients of the complex organizations and their relative strengths and transactional modes, and
14. the relative influence of the perceptions and interests of lower or higher levels of an organization on its output.

There are, of course, a wide variety of different issues that might be approached in this way. These include *holistic evaluations,* which comprise the evaluation of the life patterns of individuals and the comparative evaluation of civilizations, *evaluations of institutional change,* and *evaluations of decisions or specific changes* at the personal and societal levels. Evaluations in any of these cases may be of known events, past or present, or of proposed or imagined events and conditions. In the following sketches, we simplify the process into a narrative, an analysis, and an evaluation (or solution) for one or more cases in each of the types of issues mentioned above.

Three Evaluations of Life Patterns

As a first case for evaluation, let us consider Mrs. Gerard, a black mother of the lower working class in central Illinois (Farber, 1971). She is surrounded by the influences of the black, lower-class American culture; objectively, her life and that of her family suffer from many of the conditions of poverty, such as large families and low-status employment, that have created that subculture. Yet she and her family cling successfully to a very different rural, black, working-class subculture that emphasizes the school, the church, and the family. Indicative of her success is the emphasis placed on affinal relatives (even after the separation and subsequent death of her husband) and several generations of forebears. It is obvious that this pattern is reinforcing and that her significant others, her cultural models, are lower-class persons of similar mind or members of higher classes. She succeeds in this pattern through her children, who are prompted to succeed in the attainment of middle-class goals by her support, by the home she creates, and by the validation of this pattern for them by the relatively high level of rewards they achieve in the external world both productively and affectively. There is continuous and positive feedback[2] confirming both her values and her actions. We should not be surprised by Mrs. Gerard, for her approach to handling poverty has been successfully followed by many (see U.S. Department of Labor, 1970).

In humanistic terms, this is a life that emphasizes long-range utilities, productivity as well as affectivity, and the family and its extensions; but more than anything else, it emphasizes the importance of rigidly holding to the moral limits of the Puritan ethic. Mrs. Gerard may not be able to explain this adherence rationally, but it is important to her that she does not, for she needs firmness to prevent herself and her family from sliding into the alternative lower-class pattern. Her transcendence comes through putting her family above her immediate personal interests and in successfully holding to a cultural pattern that inhibits the natural biosocial tendencies of her position (Gastil, 1973a). For her, this is quite enough transcendence.

As a second illustration, let us refer to one of the cases of Riesman's *Faces in the Crowd* (1952). Riesman's staff interviewed a variety of people, with particular interest in their political competency and affect in terms of Riesman's other-directed/inner-directed dichotomy. Among Riesman's cases was Harrington Wittke, a person in transition between other- and inner-directedness. He was vice president of sales for a large company, who, in his early forties, did not see his career going much further.

Culturally, Wittke came from a Protestant minister's family in the Midwest, went to a liberalizing college, and had only traces left of Christian fervor. He was intelligent, introspective, and in good health except for sleeplessness and worry at the time of the interview. Agreeable, talkative, but not too outgoing or friendly toward his business relations, Wittke felt he might not have been cooperative enough for "the team," but he lacked the courage to strike out on his own. In spite of doubts, he had evaluated staying with the sales job several times; his choices paid off in money, a good family, and a feeling of accomplishment. He had been following a culturally authorized life pattern, and his family, his bosses, and contemporaries rewarded him for it. At the time of the interview, however, his bosses were less supportive and negative feedback was increasing, which caused him to question both his actions and his values. He might have chosen to live with this level of satisfaction unless there were further negative assessments by significant others, but he might not have.

In the course of fulfilling his ambitions for himself and family, Wittke progressively narrowed his life until he lived for very little besides family and business. His dissatisfaction was exacerbated by his feeling that he had not really done very well in the job and that he was doing even more poorly as a husband and father. In both of these feelings, there was probably some feedback from the judgment of others, but he also judged himself in terms of what the culture and perhaps his own family experience (family cultural tradition) had led him to expect.

In humanistic terms, Wittke appears to be closely guided by moral limitations concerning his family and business life; even his political views reflect this. He sees his problem as being too utility oriented in the productive dimension, with a need to transfer emphasis to the affective dimension by spending more time with his family. A sense of injustice led to guilt over inattention to his family, and led him to recognize more fully than his superiors in the business world the rights of unionized employees.

The pluralistic framework (Chapter Four) suggests that Wittke suffers from a lack of spiritual transcendence. His interest in religion has gone; his politics have little affect. He has transferred social extension from his family of orientation to his family of procreation and identified to some extent with both his business and mankind (especially in a sense of liberal, understanding attitudes). But there is nothing he really wants to do, nor does he see any transcending value in his work and play other than perhaps loosely carrying on the cultural tradition that he received from his parents and his teachers. He thinks he would be satisfied if he could fulfill his family and business roles according to cultural expectations as he sees them. But would he? And if he would, should he? Or is not the culture wrong in expecting so little from a man of his talents? I would judge that his cultural training beyond his family of orientation has been defective in not cultivating more hope or concern for transcendence.

So far, the approach has been used to look at an individual working toward success for herself and her family and at an individual unable to bridge the gap between his self-image and his growing inability to live up to that image. In a third illustration, the methodology is extended to consider the interaction between particular individual and family histories and a social invention as an illustration of the varied meanings of human effort. The invention was the initiative and referendum as developed in the United States, and the lives were those of Seth Lewelling, William U'Ren, and their ancestors (Steffens, 1968; McClintock, 1967a, 1967b; Woodward, 1960).

The Lewellings were Welsh Quakers who had migrated to North Carolina in the eighteenth century. Meschach Lewelling, a physician and nurseryman, bequeathed several slaves by a relative,

moved to Indiana in 1825 so that he could free the slaves outside the
South. Here he reestablished his business and profession. In 1836, his
son Henderson moved to Iowa, where he set up a nursery on the frontier, prospered, and became a leader in the Friends' Meeting. But, in
1847, he took his wife, eight children, and a collection of seven hundred grafted trees to Oregon in a wagon so heavy and slow that they
had to travel alone most of the way. After seven months on the road,
they settled near Portland (Milwaukie) and by 1851 were again thriv-
ing in the nursery business, the first in the Far West. Henderson later
went on to more adventures in California and Central America, but
by this time his brother Seth had arrived from Indiana; it was he who
was primarily responsible for the nursery until his death in 1896. During this time, Seth developed a wide variety of fruit, the most famous
being the Bing cherry.

Seth had always supported the Republican Party, the Grange,
and other movements, but it was not until the early 1880s, following
the death of his only son and first wife, that, under the direction of his
second wife, his home became a meeting place for the leading intellectuals and reformers of Oregon, expecially of the populist Alliance.
During this period, a spiritualist friend of Mrs. Lewelling often
brought to the family destitute young men, who would live in the cab-
ins on the nursery grounds and take meals with the family. In 1891,
one of these young men was William U'Ren.

U'Ren was born in 1859 in Wisconsin, descended from Dutch
and Cornish blacksmiths and preachers. His parents had recently
come to this country to find liberty, and they hated slavery. Not liking
to be tied down to blacksmithing for a big outfit, his father tried
homesteading and ranching in a variety of places in the West and
upper Midwest without much success. Young U'Ren tried law and
newspaper work in Denver. Becoming very ill, he traveled for several
years in search of better health in California and Hawaii, and finally
came to Oregon, where his family was ranching near Prineville. He
was a rather weak young man, used to being alone a good deal, who
was a failure in his early thirties; but he was also interested in ideas
and hoped to help poor people, such as his family. His ideas were
those of the reformers of the day, especially the single tax and the
ideas of Henry George. When he arrived at the Lewellings, his confidence had just been boosted by participation in a successful

campaign for instituting the Australian ballot in Portland.

U'Ren quickly became a leader in the discussions at the Lewelling home, and because of this, he was soon made a business partner on very generous terms. Then one evening Alfred, Seth's nephew and also a partner, brought to an Alliance meeting a copy of a recent book on the Swiss system of the initiative and referendum, and its possible application in this country. Seeing this as the answer to the problem of the control of politics by professional politicians, the group immediately put together a joint state committee of the Grange and labor. U'Ren became secretary and the Lewelling family home became a center for the subsequent educational campaign (the many Swiss in the area were, of course, especially glad to help).

U'Ren plunged into a life of educational and political activity, and although he only served one term in the Oregon legislature, the initiative and referendum were firmly incorporated into law by 1902, and U'Ren used these tools to achieve a direct primary in 1904 and later the direct election of senators. But U'Ren failed to achieve a political position himself or institute single-tax legislation through initiative and referendum.

In achieving political success, the nursery had been bank-rupted, both by inattention and through Seth's donations. After Seth's death in 1896 and machinations by U'Ren and the 1897 legisla-ture that horrified many of his supporters but made success possible, Seth's widow and some of the other members of the Lewelling circle violently turned against U'Ren and fought him in his subsequent endeavors. But U'Ren never profited financially; he remained a poor, part-time country lawyer, and he never returned the hatred of the dis-appointed widow.

The convergence of two family traditions at a particular place and time made possible the campaign for the initiative and referen-dum. The leading figures were no doubt above average in intelligence and education, although they were mostly self-educated. Humanis-tically, both families emphasized egalitarianism and freedom, pro-ductive and long-term utilities, and transcendent achievement. In the last area, because of their greater ability to handle productive utilities or their greater decisiveness, the Lewellings were able to accomplish much more, first in plant breeding and later in supporting cultural, intellectual, and finally political reform. Both families also seem to have emphasized moral limitations, for their members exhibited a strong sense of right and wrong.

U'Ren himself seems to have been little interested in personal utilities. When he seized the chance to transcend his sense of powerlessness and lack of accomplishment by promoting egalitarian causes in Oregon, both his interest in personal utilities and adherence to moral limitations weakened. Hence, those in the Lewelling circle who were less dominated by the simple causes of U'Ren were no longer able to participate. U'Ren recklessly spent both his material and spiritual capital in the pursuit of a series of unique accomplishments. Yet if he had not had a family of orientation and later an adopted family that offered both utilities and a strong sense of moral limitation, he would never have been characterologically, socially, or economically able to achieve what he did.

If we place these illustrations in the societal context, reasonable employment opportunities, law and order, free schools, and environments that support a strict set of moral limitations would be sufficient to achieve the life plan of Mrs. Gerard. Here, the success story of American capitalism and the general direction of moderate reform would seem to be enough institutionally. But this was apparently not enough for Mr. Wittke. He wanted something beyond what his job offered, yet he did not have a clear enough understanding of what this was for his employer to help him, even if the employer would. His organization was either not transcending utility values or was not communicating this transcendence. But Wittke did not seem to notice the omission. He wanted to improve the balance of his life in the direction of affective utility, yet he had no way to change the expected productive utilities of himself and his company to make this possible. Finally, for Henderson and Seth Lewelling, business activities were an important means of attaining transcendence. The record suggests a loss of interest in the business after 1880; from this point, their business and material well-being were used to make possible a variety of other forms of transcendence for those most closely associated with the nursery.

The story of the Lewelling nursery is an ideal story of social responsibility at its best. One can say that there must have been people put out of jobs by the failure of the nursery, yet there were other nurseries that took up the slack; when the Lewellings were no longer creative, they should have been replaced in any event. Since managers of large corporations cannot responsibly allow their businesses to collapse for the benefit of noncorporate causes, the example is not helpful in many personal and institutional contexts. Yet perhaps the discussion has suggested the usefulness of judging achievement over time as it transmutes from one form into another.

Comparative Evaluation of Three Primitive Societies

Comparisons of civilizations could be drawn from contemporary society, but this would arouse much argument, as well as the irrelevant ideologies of both the author and his readers. To avoid this, let us place ourselves in the position of a cultural advisor trying to use the pluralistic framework as a basis for suggesting cultural change. (In making the following analysis, I am ignoring the dangers to the people involved of paternalism and acculturation, as well as the difficulty of adding isolated items to an integrated cultural pattern, where that exists.) For this purpose, I have chosen three societies at a very simple level of organization and technology.[3]

The Siriono of Bolivia live in very small, simply organized hunting groups in the jungle. The headman, who is but vaguely recognized as such, may have several wives; but within limits, women are expected to sleep with whomever brings them meat. The relations between siblings and between parents and their children are not close, and the weak and unfortunate in the group are largely ignored. There is little ritual, art, or religious behavior, minimal housing, and almost no clothes. Hunting is based on the bow and arrow, even though this is a very ineffective way to catch the numerous fish in the rivers. Work is minimal; people are generally hungry; life is short.[4]

The Australian aborigines (Arunta) live in larger, more organized groups, even though the environment is much less productive. There is both political and religious organization, but rule is essentially by a group of old men who have attained full, ritual adulthood. The old men have the most and often the youngest wives, and the old of both sexes are generally well taken care of. Both affinal and consanguinal relationships are taken very seriously, as are other ritual or economic relationships. The old are able to use religion and custom to rule, and young men must go through painful initiations. The aesthetic, religious, and intellectual culture is highly developed and intensively practiced, although representational art is not advanced in Western terms. There is little development of material technology, but both men and women have developed extensive means for obtaining food; the women, in particular, work hard. Hunger is frequent but tends to be seasonal.

The Polar Eskimo often live in very small groups, although this varies greatly with the season and location. Organization fluctuates and can involve little more than the individual family, but there are special leaders to take charge of religious ceremonies and boat crews. Although there are customary rules, force may be the only real arbiter of organization. A strong man might have several wives, steal another man's wife, or kill those who stand in his way. Recourse for those victimized by such a man is to get a band of men together and kill him. Feelings of emotional attachment or concern for one another are stronger than among the Siriono. The old and weak are helped, but if times are hard, they may be abandoned. Religion and music are individualized and not nearly as ordered and planned as with the Australian aborigines. Carving, of course, is highly developed, although there are only a few serious carvers in every generation to carry on the tradition. Technology for survival is very highly developed and complex for people at this level of organization. A variety of different houses are built, and clothes are very well made. Eskimos work hard and generally eat well, but occasionally they endure very hard times.

The cultural advisor would note that all three primitive societies have an unnecessarily unjust distribution of primary goods. Women have little status; every woman under thirty is given low status in Australia, and the old and weak are expendable among the Eskimos and Siriono (which has little justification if one compares the environment and technology of the latter group with those of Australia). For men, basic liberties among the Siriono are high; they are high among the Eskimo, too, if he can stay out of the way of stronger men. Liberties are available to women in both of these groups. However, liberties are quite constrained for everyone among the aborigines.

Basic rights are secured only in a society with moral limits that cannot be transgressed. However, among both the Siriono and

Eskimo, liberties and equalities result primarily from customary style and experience. The Siriono are easy-going, nonexclusive, and rather nonviolent; the Eskimo are anarchic, individualistic, and inclined to violence. Both of these stances support some rights and equalities and deny others. This results in apparent limits, but not firm moral or legal limits with a strong sense of right behind them. The Australian aborigine culture grants less equality and basic liberty, but what it does grant is backed by the community in a way analogous to law. There is an importance given to symbols in aborigine society that goes beyond biological and biosocial necessity. If a man is allowed to marry a woman, she is his wife and no one else's. If a man goes through the prescribed initiations, he is given the rights of the initiated and can rise through a series of known steps to be one of the wise old men that lead every group; most men who survive biologically succeed socially in this sense. Therefore, this rule-ridden society is at least potentially the freest and most egalitarian. It offers the most security and freedom to the weak and over a longer time span for both men and women, and it offers a basis of change. Therefore, if the chances of diffusion seem favorable, law or a more symbolic sense of the moral limits of right action would be important for the cultural advisor to promote in both the Siriono and Eskimo cultures.

However, how far should these people extend their sense of law, right, or responsibility? From the viewpoint of the pluralistic framework, the problem for the Eskimo and Siriono groups is that the individual's sense of moral responsibility is very constricted; indeed, for the Siriono, social extension goes little beyond that of mother to child. The educational task is to develop a firmer sense of reciprocal obligation among a wider circle of relatives and the band, and then to promote at least some responsibilities and limits beyond that. For the aborigines, the network of in-group and intergroup responsibilities is already developed and graded; the job here would be to add some sense of universal responsibility of man beyond the limits of the aboriginal sphere of relatives, friends, friendly bands, and ritual relations.

Finally, in terms of the pluralistic framework, it is significant that Siriono life achieves less in terms of human accomplishment, of transcendence, than either of the other groups. They are content to just "get by," and except for the common South

American hammock and an exceptionally large bow, their lives leave behind nothing distinctively human. (Rawls' [1971] only test here is that they should live by a "rational plan," and in terms of his criteria, who is to say they do not?) The Eskimos achieve transcendence through their artistry, but also through the style expressed in a wide ranging technology, whether harpoon points, hooks, kayaks, or igloos. The Australian aborigine achieves transcendence through a complex tradition expressed in art, myth, ritual, and social organization. Given his technology and the harsh conditions of his life, his achievement is remarkable. Aboriginal culture is so dissimilar to the Eskimo, and the achievements of both cultures so manifest, that ranking them is difficult; but in terms of the framework, the Siriono clearly rank below both. Therefore, in addition to the recommendations made above, they should be urged to improve their level of existence by actions such as deepening their sense of commitment to one another, to excellence for its own sake, and to a more extensive symbolic life.

Comparative Evaluation of Civilization in the Pacific Northwest

The author has recently completed a study of the cultural regions of the United States (Gastil, 1975b). One of the conclusions of the study was that it would help the quality of American life if more people took their relationship to the regions in which they live seriously. Therefore, after establishing the case that the Pacific Northwest could plausibly be considered a region (Gastil, 1973b), I turned to the problem of trying to understand in more depth the quality of this region of six million persons. While conventional quality-of-life studies would emphasize the short- and long-range utilitarian values of the Northwest, the concept of quality of civilization emerges from the foregoing analysis as a more encompassing and critical point of departure.

Let us compare the Northwest with other regions of the country. Scientifically, a description of the Northwest would begin with a description of American civilization and how this civilization compares with those in other times and places. The next step would be to compare civilization within the Northwest—Oregon, Washington, and part of Idaho—with that in other regions in the United States and with comparable nonregional populations elsewhere in the world. The latter comparisons should highlight the problems of small American regions that are swallowed up in a mass society of over two hundred million people.

Compared with other regions in the United States, the Pacific Northwest is very sparsely populated, and it is blessed with a high natural resources to population ratio. It is a recently settled region, and its people are predominantly Protestant and of northern European or upper Midwestern origin. There is a relative absence of extremes of class, culture, or political viewpoints, and religious affiliation is low. In two comparative studies of the fifty states, the states of Oregon and Washington fell into the most desirable groupings (Liu, 1973; Smith, 1973), yet characteristically, not because of any outstanding features. They simply score uniformly well on indicators such as income, education, and crime.

My own impression is that there is a balance in Northwestern life that is sadly lacking in what is generally regarded as the centers of civilization. Returning to the Northwest from the Northeast or even California, one is struck by its cleanliness and the even temper of the people. To a large extent, this seems to result from a more even distribution of goods—a land of fewer Cadillacs and fewer jalopies. But more important than the patterns of distribution are the egalitarian attitudes of respect and self-worth that mean a greater attention to justice and reverence for man in day-to-day life than is common elsewhere. It is indicative that in Elazar's (1972) study of political differences in the United States, the Northwest is described as an area with moralistic politics, that is, a political pattern in which everyone is expected to take part, public interest is expected to be placed above private, and government is run by public-spirited amateurs. Only the upper Midwest and the central Rocky Mountain states compete with the Northwest in this regard.

What is deficient in the regional civilization of the Pacific Northwest are those kinds of transcendence most often associated with high civilization. While productive utilities are stressed by a creative minority, emphasis in the Northwest is on affective utilities —the family, the boat, and backpacking—rather than secular or religious transcendence. It can be argued that a humanistically superior society is one that seems to be making or to have made a positive contribution to the story of man. The ideal is, of course, fifth-century Athens, seventeenth-century Holland, and late nineteenth century Vienna. The fact that two hundred thousand people, the majority of whom were uneducated (most slaves, farmers, and women), could accomplish as much spiritually as fifth-century Athens sets an experiential outer limit on what societies can accomplish. (Of course, Athens was the intellectual center of a larger world, but this larger world had fewer than six million inhabitants.)

One of the best ways of analyzing the Northwest's potential as a center of transcendence in the United States is to consider the education of its people. The region is at or near the top in terms of popular education as measured by median years of school completed, percentage going to college, or the percentage of draftees passing the selective-service mental tests. But when measured in terms of the excellence of it schools, particularly the ability of the institutions of higher education to attract National Merit Scholars, the intellectual cream of our next generation, the Northwest seriously lags. In 1970–1971, the region had 3.0 percent of the national population, 3.8 percent of all students in higher education, but only 2.0 percent of all Merit Scholars attending school (National Merit Scholarship Corporation, 1970, 1970–1971; U.S. Department of Commerce, 1973). In the 1960s Macalester College in Minnesota attracted more Merit Scholars than all the Northwestern institutions put together. We must remember that there is a relationship between where a person goes to college and where he decides to live. Looking at the performance of Northwestern graduate schools, it may be discouraging to Northwesterners that only a school of nursing and two forestry schools rank among the top professional schools in the nation, and studies of graduate departments in the arts and sciences show there are no really outstanding departments in Northwestern universities (Roose and Andersen, 1970; Margulies and Blau, 1973), although there are, of course, outstanding individuals and special programs.

How far the Northwest is from the level of spiritual transcendence of California in relation to the ideal standard is suggested by the comparison of two books. The first is Starr's *Americans and the California Dream, 1850–1915* (1973). This well-organized recital of the intellectual life centered in San Francisco during this period details the vision of California as a promised land. Almost immediately after its statehood, men came to California to build a new world. The following two decades were the days in California of Mark Twain, Bret Harte, Ambrose Bierce, and Henry George. H. H. Bancroft's remarkable series of histories of the West, a unique experiment in historical collection, printing, and sales, began in the 1870s. In the 1880s, a native Californian who was to become one of Harvard's leading philosophers published a study of Calfornia. It was a critical intellectual and social history meant to incite Californians and, by extension, all Americans to make a greater effort to achieve the promise that so many had felt. Around the turn of the century, California experienced another period of intellectual and artistic ferment. This was the period of Frank Norris, Jack London, Mary Austin, Gertrude Atherton, and Luther Burbank; of John Muir, the naturalist; of Isadora Duncan, the dancer; and of Thorstein Veblen, the economist. It was also the period when the railroad millions of Leland Stanford were put at the disposal of David Starr Jordan in the noble experiment to build a great private university without tuition, catering to the poor as well as the well-off, dispensing practical knowledge as well as theoretical.

California never quite fulfilled the dreams, but still it went on to great achievements. Hollywood ruled the entertainment world, California beaches determined life styles, and the University of California has become the most outstanding university in the country, at least in terms of the international reputation of its top faculty.

Let us then look at the other book. In 1972, Cantwell published a rambling but significant review of the Northwest experience entitled *The Hidden Northwest*. Cantwell asks why, with such an environment and such promising people at the beginning, the region's civilization has remained so sparse and undistinctive. His discussion actually explains very little, but his wrestling with the problem displays a sensitivity and sense of the issues that is unfortunately seldom found in discussions of the area. Cantwell is a Northwesterner related to the original settlers. Having spent much of his life as an editor in the East, he is a cosmopolitan literary critic; yet he remains more attracted to the outdoors, to what is the glory of the Northwest, than to his writing. But here is his dilemma—he cannot find an intellectual message "out there" in the woods. There must be *purpose* in the scenery. Yet, since the scenery does not actually exist on an intellectual plane, the attempt to explain this purpose too often lets the writer slide into foolish rhapsody. Cantwell is often in danger, yet he stays on the high ground, unable to accept easy answers.

Like many writers on the Northwest, Cantwell is on the defensive. The title suggests that the purpose of his book is to correct the image of the Northwest as a dark, gloomy, wild, and desolate region. Cantwell developed his thesis around the work of Theodore Winthrop, an enthusiastic young man who wrote about his wanderings in the region in the mid nineteenth century. Winthrop promised that a great civilization would emerge from this beauty. Yet this image keeps sliding away, for what Winthrop meant does not seem specifically Northwestern; he refers to a sense of wilderness, of being away from it all that gave perspective, or of a newness that allowed man to start over again. In spite of this ambiguity and the paradox that development must destroy the wilderness, Cantwell tests the Winthrop proposition by examining the Northwest one century later. He finds the promise unfulfilled in the cities and towns and in the thousands of miles of slash left by the lumbermen. The art, music, literature, and architecture of the Northwest is largely commonplace. And strangely, Cantwell finds the promise of a highly developed civilization to be right where Winthrop left it—in what is left of the wilderness. After examining the literary product, he notes that Northwestern writers, in the words of H. L. Davis, "failed to establish a unity between it [the regional past] and the world out of which they wrote" (Cantwell, 1972, p. 283), because they relied on derivative forms. They created a rip-roaring frontier past that had hardly existed. At its best, Northwest literature is personal reminiscence rather than history, new thought, or art.

Cantwell (p. 285) concludes a discussion of Northwestern writings with these observations:

> *If they do not add up to a distinct regional character, they may imply something more valuable. It may be that the deepest wisdom of the Northwest consisted in not developing a unique regional society to set it apart from the rest of the country. . . . No other part of the country has so little to live down.*

Thus the quest comes to a dead end, and Cantwell falls back upon middle America's horror of being different and its penchant to relax in the bland. It is also a Northwestern ending.

If we compare the six million people of the Pacific Northwest to the six million people of Switzerland,[5] we will note that the Swiss are jammed in an area one tenth the size of the Northwest, although they are equally proud of their land's natural beauty. There seems to be less emphasis on enjoyment and more on production in Switzerland. The Swiss are far more religious and in every way more strict in their attitudes toward proper behavior.

On paper, the Swiss are much less educated than the people of the Northwest, especially in the percentage of those who receive higher education. Yet newspaper readership is about the same, and the quality of the Swiss newspapers is much higher. This is true for two reasons. First, the best Zurich paper is of international reputation and can reach anywhere in the country in a few hours. Second, one can only conclude from examination of the press in most of the smaller Swiss cities that the editors maintain the standards of the top third of their readership rather than the middle third. This may make it possible to support the excellent bookshops of the country and the 125 major publishers, compared with one in the Northwest (Saur, 1969).

The churches of Switzerland are well supported and often beautiful. Old buildings are kept up, and to them the best of modern architecture has been added. Of course, the Northwest is not like that; it does not have much past, and religion is lightly treated. Its great architecture is in banks, colleges, and research centers. This is good enough, but it is not just a matter of time. The art museums of Switzerland are far superior to those in the Northwest, not because there is so much history in Switzerland, but because Northwestern money simply has not been used for civilization of this type. Winterthur, an industrial city of 100,000, has three large museums; to add its collections to the Northwest's would greatly aid the people there to appreciate ninteenth- and early twentieth-century art. The difference in the congeniality of the two lands for artists is symbolized by the fact that Seattle's most famous artist chose to live in Basel for his last years.

In making these comparisons, we have, of course, emphasized only a portion of literary, educational, and artistic factors. There has been a small but important school of creative artists in the Northwest, and the area has recently produced some excellent poets. The Northwest has had a considerable record in the development of theatre, both in Seattle and in Ashland, and in the mid 1970s Seattle seemed to be establishing itself as a center for Wagnerian opera. But these successes are fragile, hothouse developments. However, there has certainly been transcendence in business: Boeing has succeeded in the aerospace industry in spite of an unfavorable location almost devoid of supportive industry, while Tektronix's dominance of the field of quality oscilloscopes also developed in an unlikely location, both technologically and industrially. Yet by and large the region remains dominated by agriculture and lumbering. In 1975, six of the ten largest Northwestern corporations were involved with forest products, and two more were partially dependent on the industry (Cohn, 1954; *Fortune,* 1976).

Many people who come to the Northwest, hoping to take part in building a new civilization, leave disappointed. Its greatest artists and writers have generally ended up leaving the area to carry on their work elsewhere, at least until recently. There has not been much transcendence outside of practical areas, nor does there seem to be an atmosphere for it. As Carolyn Kizer, an astringent, exiled poet of impeccable Northwestern lineage says, "We don't lack people here on the Northern coast. / But they are people one meets, not people one cares for" (Kizer, 1964, p. 64). There are, of course, other regions of six million people with poorer prospects in terms of the standard we have used. But between the Pacific Northwest and areas with more transcendence, whether historical or modern, there is a gap. The challenge is to find what can close that gap.

There is not space to do more than suggest the direction in which the analysis must now proceed. For we must explain scientifically why we believe there is a gap in regional transcendence, and in the course of this explanation start to develop the ways in which it may be reduced. Part of the explanation is a time lag between economic and humanistic growth, and another part is the civilizational background of the people who settled the region (the feedback of a civilizational level tends to maintain that level). Neither argument explains as much as we would hope. For either to be true, we must establish whether there has been relative progress or regression in the

last hundred years. More is explained by the observation that the
Northwest is a small region submerged in a large country; unlike
many similar regions, it had little recorded history before its incorporation into the nation. Biosocially, its problem is that of the European provinces compounded. In addition, there has developed in
much of the United States, particularly in the Northwest, a regional,
populist, egalitarian tradition of living that is pleasant but not chal-
lenging, that enshrines mass culture and the easy way. Everyone in
the Northwest is touched by the tradition (including the author, who
finds it rather comfortable and to his taste).

Humanistically, we must also face certain conundrums that go
to the heart of our analysis. For example, is not the civilization of the
Northwest more balanced than that of Florence or Athens? Were they
balanced at all? Does great achievement in any realm require a lack of
civilizational balance? If so, why should we wish the Northwest to
accord to the ideal standard we have set?

But if we do stay with this standard, what could be done to
move the Northwest closer to it? To lift the weight of a civilizational
tradition and to solve the problem of regional submergence in a large
nation is no small order. But we notice that one difference between the
Northwest and some other regions of the country has been the Northwesterners' lower level of seriousness, of the sense that they as a
regional people can make a difference in the world. There is no way to
create this belief except for Northwesterners to take their civilization
seriously. Sometimes this means negative criticism, the type of tear-
ing down that is an aspect of comparison. But it also means building
up, taking inventory of what is best, what has been accomplished, and
the obstacles that have been overcome. Most Northwesterners know
very little about the region's many creative and industrious business-
men, educators, and political reformers. They are like students in a
colonial land still memorizing lists of British or French kings. Transcendence cannot be willed into being, but perhaps the people of the
region can in these ways and by studying preferred models lay the
groundwork for a more significant regional life.

The social humanist must, of course, also consider the costs of
change in transcendence. As Griffith (1959, pp. 61–62), a former
Seattlite, pointed out in comparing New York and Seattle, the New
Yorker knows the difference between the best and second rate, and he

doesn't mind telling you. As the Northwest changes, criticism will become more caustic, feelings will be hurt more often, relaxation will become a luxury, and no longer will the people beam with an easy fellowship. Neither Swiss nor New Yorkers are known for their friendliness. It is also historically true that in areas of greater transcendence, there is also a larger gap between the classes, with the deterioration in human relations this usually implies. If scientific analysis cannot show a way to change without these losses, perhaps Northwesterners would be well advised not to make the effort.

Problem of Social Responsibility in Business

The argument is frequently made that American culture has produced a business culture that overemphasizes utility values, especially material production and consumption. The argument is put forth that this should (or must) change, because the pattern has produced a surfeit of goods and a revulsion with materialism that have affected the culture and changed the thinking of younger employees. Even if this were not so, continued adherence to past humanistic values is said to threaten the splitting of society through revolution or the destruction of the resources on which production is based.

Proposals to change normative patterns cover all areas of concern, but for simplicity, let us consider only the proposal that both status and income should be distributed more equitably within the organization as a means of increasing social responsibility (see the journal *Economy and Society;* also Steiner, 1971; Dierkes, 1974). In our terms, the suggestion is to reduce the weight given to productivity and increase the weight given to equality. Many might argue that greater productivity would result from these changes (Argyris, 1964). If so, then according to the general decision rule of benevolence (such that if all gain by a policy, that policy should not be controversial), the humanistic argument becomes a technical one of cost-effectiveness. The difficult question is what the choice of emphasis should be when there are real costs of a decision either to the organization or an individual in it.

As an example of this kind, let us consider what is likely to happen if a major egalitarian shift is made in one firm alone. First, because of numbers, the greatest changes must be made at the top of the salary scale, for without significantly reducing the power and income of those at the top, there will be few goods or little status to distribute at the bottom of the pyramid. The result, then, would be a more desirable income and status situation for the beginner or the less skilled but progressively less attractive opportunities in higher positions, until, toward the top, employees or potential employees will find jobs more desirable elsewhere. If the system functions, this is likely to mean a younger staff, less turnover among new employees, and more than average turnover in later years. The executives of the egalitarian firm would, then, eventually be below average in ability. One argument against this conclusion is that the democratic struc- ture of power would make good executives unnecessary (although the reverse seems more plausible). Or one could argue that there are excel- lent leaders who would thrive at all levels in such an organization and prefer this environment to one offering more money and status. Indi- vidually, this is no doubt true, but our model of man suggests that this is unlikely to be true in general, and our assumption is that we are developing a policy that would be generally applicable to indi- vidual businesses. The final rejoinder by the advocates of egalitarian- ism is that because of general cultural trends, the more equitable busi- nesses would be copied, influencing through their example both the general culture and the culture of competing businesses. In the end, opportunities would vanish for the old-fashioned executive in search of power and wealth.

But will they? While change in some areas is largely through sheer imitation and social trends, in competitive businesses consid- eration of business outcomes must count heavily, with the most important outcome being the continuing competitiveness of the busi- ness in a continually evolving context. There are five ways of looking at the likelihood that an egalitarian practice introduced in one busi- ness will spread throughout an industry. The first is to assume that the present allocation of status and income in the business represents the most cost-effective allocation, for it has been produced by trial and error over a long period. If this assumption is correct, the introduc- tion of a great deal more equality is bound to reduce the material pro- ductivity of the firm and eventually its size, ability to employ, and so on. Therefore, the egalitarian approach will not catch on except in a few special cases. The second possibility is to assume that the advantages and disadvantages of the new dispensation will roughly balance out, and the issue will then become whether people involved, or potentially involved, prefer the new cultural institution to the old. A third possibility is that the new style has always been potentially as productive or more productive, but that human nature operates both within and outside firms to create or re-create status systems, even if these status systems hamper productivity. (Since individuals are the directing social units, it is not surprising that they should systematically misuse their positions to establish organizational status hierarchies that favor their interests.) The fourth possibility is that the new styles result in lower productivity but will nevertheless spread widely and rapidly because of their inherent attractiveness or deeper cultural trends. The same result might occur (and in Europe already has) because unions have demanded such changes. However, all nations are unlikely to follow the new mode. As a result, the productivity of our society as a whole will fall compared with others, with eventual economic failure and unemployment. The fifth possibility that all nations change more or less in phase with the fourth alternative is unlikely.

Up to this point, the argument suggests that the important issue is the technical one: Will the introduction of more internal equality negatively affect productivity? Surely minor tampering will have little effect, but beyond that we must refer to comparative studies of ongoing, real-life experiments over time to see whether major changes are feasible.

Even if we answered the technical question, we would still have important humanistic issues to consider. First, is flattening status and income hierarchies an acceptable way to improve equality or to distribute justice? It may be wrong to accept the market verdict that a top executive should receive $200,000, while a harder working foreman receives $15,000, but will not the flattening also reduce the difference between the steady worker's income and that of the lazy and indifferent? Evidence suggests that there are differences in this "effort dimension" that are not due to genetic or environmental factors. Of course, if we believe everything is determined, inequalities can only be accepted for practical reasons. But this denies even the limited assumption of choice and freedom on which we based social humanities in Chapters Two and Four. If the worker cannot choose to exert more or less effort, his boss equally cannot choose to improve the worker's status. Both simply do what they must.

An equally important humanistic issue is raised when we ask whether the increase in equalization suggested by this particular approach to social responsibility would not entail certain losses of liberty that would not be made up by other gains. For example, Rawls (1971) tells us that men have the right to choose alternative life plans freely except in cases of dire necessity or when exercising this right would interfere with other critical rights. To equalize status and income will narrow choices for the person who wants to just get by at work and concentrate on avocational activities, because he will be compelled by others to work harder, while those who would strive very hard to rise will likewise tend to be discouraged by a system of equal rewards. One can hypothesize on the basis of a rational theory of man that in the successful egalitarian business there will tend to be a standard pattern of endeavor: Workers will perform their tasks, but not very industriously. (We have returned, of course, to a scientific, biosocial question that affects but does not decide the humanistic issue.)

Finally, we ask the question concerning the relative weight that should be put on transcendence as opposed to equity. If we believe that lack of transcendence rather than inequity is the problem of our society, then we should be interested in egalitarian reforms of business only insofar as they do not affect transcendence. For example, we might believe that high culture is very important to support, and we might note the unwillingness of the majority to support it in the United States. If this seems to be true, and if we accept Rawls' (1971, p. 332) moral limit that majorities should not be misled into supporting high culture that they really do not want, then we would want to avoid institutional equalization that either took away management's right to support high culture with corporate funds or diminished the wealth that enables managers to support high culture privately (see De Jouvenal, 1951).

Personal Decision Within an Institutional Framework

The elitist statement you have just read brings us to realize the impossibility of judging organizational performance without judging individual performance. It is nonsense to assert that an organization should be structured so that wealthy managers or owners can provide special services to civilization if they do not do so. Likewise, organizations must be judged in terms of their relation to individuals within and without the organizations. Seen from the outside, an organization exists to provide services or goods to those outside the organization; secondarily it exists to provide employment to those within it so that they in turn may buy the goods and services of others, either directly or through taxes. Seen from the inside, an organization exists to support its owners or administrators and its employees; secondarily it exists to provide goods and services to others. An organization is created to achieve the private or public goals of its founders, and to a large extent it must be assessed on the basis of the humanistic legitimacy of its goals, how well the organization achieves them, and how well it achieves legitimate and desirable goals for those who later become associated with the organization as sponsors, staff, suppliers, or recipients. Humanistically, a legitimate organization must contribute to the achievement of an acceptable balance of goods by all the people that are affected by it.

We must, then, examine the quality of individual response to an institutional situation and the quality of the institutional environment in which the individual must resolve his situational problems. We touched on this situation in looking at Magruder's dilemma. To illustrate here, let us imagine an individual who has been told by his superior not to reveal business deception to people outside the organization. He is being asked, in other words, to discriminate in favor of organizational interests over the general interests of society. In terms of productive utility, the superior assumes that there is a short-term advantage in honoring the request. The situation of the individual will improve and his long-term advantage will be considerable because he will have leverage with his boss that he did not have before. This would not, of course, be true if the deception were found out by those who would have an interest in making it an issue. The importance of this consideration would be determined by how much chance there was for the deception to get out and the extent to which illegality was involved. But even here, future success would depend on how the relevant subcultures generally weighed such moral transgressions, particularly how the individual's business-related significant others would judge him were they to find out. If the individual was single and living among thieves, there would be little loss of status, but in another part of town or in another group, disclosure of such activities might make him an outcast. (In this case, a defensive policy would be to change one's friends before possible disclosure.) Finally, the individual is likely to have aspects of his life, known to his superiors, that he does not want revealed. It may be, of course, that the superior has misjudged the situation to the extent that it is to the immediate advantage of the individual to reveal the deception, because he will gain more by appealing for support to a new audience than by playing to the narrower organizational audience. However, this will not usually be the case.

Opposed to the high bureaucratic value on the utility of silence may be a personal, extrabureaucratic desire to satisfy a nonmaterial utility, or, in our terms, to satisfy nonutilitarian criteria, by going against the superior's order. The internalized culture of the individual and of significant others (but a different network of significant others) will make a person feel better about himself and therefore lead to more satisfaction if the deception is revealed. Obviously, the weight of this consideration against job success will be a critical influence on the individual's internal evaluation.

In real life, the individual will often feel that he is doing more good or less harm in this job than in any other readily available job, and that this particular deception only detracts somewhat from his overall favorable balance of social good; thus, he is morally justified in committing individual sins to avoid greater losses. This calculation may be right, yet in general such analyses erode an individual's standards; ultimately, the man who started out applying this analysis would not recognize the man it eventually creates. (In this sense, all cultural traditions are eroded or strengthened by each bearer, for himself and for those who observe him.)

Looked at externally, the analyst might first note empirically that men do not always go along with their superiors. Some do risk their positions and take the consequences. They may be lucky, they may lose economically but win psychologically, or they may lose out and end up bitter and disappointed. Since it is possible to make a choice, and since there are economic, moral, and psychological risks, this is, then, a humanistic issue. In terms of the pluralistic framework, since in the absence of moral limits people may be led astray by the calculation of offsetting benefits, one suspects that those who go against their superiors are irrationally obeying personal moral limits they cannot go beyond. If they do provide rational justifications, these are probably in terms of justice, perhaps based on the argument that silence would not be fair to those hurt by the deception.

However, the moral questions of balanced extension, that is, of loyalty and dependence, must also be considered. The superior trusted the individual to support the deception. The superior may well have hired him as a favor. Unless there is trust within the office or organization, the organization will not have an atmosphere acceptable to either the individual or his superior, and both the public and the organization will suffer. (For a discussion of the importance of trust and its relation to freedom and privacy, see Fried, 1968.) In addition, the individual may have a family dependent on him or associates who will rise and fall with him. What right has he to satisfy his personal moral scruples at their expense? For these reasons, when we consider individuals who reveal deceptions, our external judgment might be to condemn them for betraying loyalty to those closest to them in favor of personal and selfish concerns. By definition, we cannot make this argument when the individual reveals his superior's deception by following otherwise appropriate moral limits in a particular case. But did he have an obligation to make his limits clear to those who were dependent on him both before and after taking the position?

Let us step back a moment, and note again that the organizational and the personal levels of analysis continually interact. One's judgment of an organization's prospects and social responsibility must reflect judgments of the purposes and prospects of individuals within it, while personal moral calculations must be seen to some extent in terms of organizational survival and its desirability. Part of our personal culture is our understanding of role definitions within the multitude of organizations with which we intersect. The analyst may be asked to make his analysis as though one or the other focus is critical, but this must lead to partial distortion. In particular, the institutional changes will result because people in a variety of roles are seen as having changed their view of what is desirable or necessary. The resulting analysis may become impenetrable because of the subtle interplay between positive knowledge, prophecy, abstract humanistic judgment of what is desirable, and concrete judgments that reflect shifting balances in the real world.

If the guiding objective is the achievement of balance, those responsible for or employed by an organization must create organizational forms that will make possible a balanced community life as well as a variety of humanistically acceptable balances for the individuals connected with the organization. For the individual, the goal is the achievement of a balance that is fundamentally acceptable to oneself in terms of one's life plan, or how one conceives of oneself. Generally, the elements selected must be sufficiently compatible to avoid dissolution of the organization or personality. Yet the analysis cannot be so relativistic as to endorse balance merely for the sake of balance, or to place goals such as survival or adaptation above all other humanistic values.

Evaluating a Proposal to Exert Pressure on Internal Soviet Policy

In August and September of 1973, a controversy developed over the extent to which the United States Government should link offers of arms reduction and improved trade relations—that is, the detente policy—to the willingness of the Soviet regime to liberalize its treatment of Soviet intellectuals and to allow the free emigration of Soviet citizens. The exacerbating events had been the difficulty experienced by Russian Jews in getting permission to go to Israel—not a new issue—and warnings by the Soviet physicist Sakharov and the novelist Solzhenitsyn that the Soviet Union was becoming more repressive as a result of detente (*New York Times*, 1973; Shabad, 1973; Jackson, 1973; Solzhenitsyn, 1973; *AFL/CIO Free Trade Union News*, 1973). The argument was that the detente policy was not serving our interests and was failing to liberalize the U.S.S.R. Instead of relying on international friendship bringing liberalization and peace, it was proposed that we should use whatever leverage we had to achieve internal liberalization in the U.S.S.R. while maintaining our military strength. When this point of view was expressed by Americans, both liberal and conservative, the future Secretary of State, Henry Kissinger, replied that although at times the United States Government makes protests against Soviet repression through diplomatic channels (Gwertzman, 1973a):

we [should] ask ourselves whether it should be the principal

*goal of American foreign policy to transform the domestic
structure of societies with which we deal, or whether the principal exercise of our foreign policy should be directed toward
affecting the foreign policy of those societies. . . . If we adopt
. . . the view that we must transform the domestic structure of
all countries with which we deal, even if the foreign policy of
those countries is otherwise moving in a more acceptable
direction, then we will find ourselves massively involved in
every country in the world. [Gwertzman, 1973b, p. 1]*

In this case, the social unit is the Soviet Union. Internally it
was characterized by a repression of dissidents, and externally by an
expected (biosocial), conservative, self-interested policy, but one with
important ideological (activist and cultural) interests. Situationally,
it operated this foreign policy in an environment in which the actions
of the United States were taken very seriously, which had varied from
determined hostility to detente. After the death of Stalin, Soviet
repression eased. It was soft at times in the 1960s, but under detente,
instead of further relaxation, it has tightened in some respects. So far
there is little dispute in the matter; no one likes the continued repression. The questions are:

1. Scientifically, if United States policy relaxes, will there be a positive or negative feedback relationship with Soviet liberalization?
2. Are we increasing the chances of peace or other gains through
detente?
3. What would be the outcome if the United States tried to tie Soviet
internal liberalization directly to the continuation and development of an extended American detente policy?[7]

The primary humanistic questions are:

4. What interest do we have in a liberal Soviet internal policy, good
trade relations, or world peace? What is the balance of these
interests?
5. Should we place a moral limit on official United States noninterference with internal Soviet policy?

Kissinger evidently had several beliefs about the biosocial pressures involved. He accepted the realist view that it is better for the nation if international relations are confined to external relations. In particular, he believed that achieving detente with the Soviet Union improves the long-range chance for world peace. More generally, if a country's actions can be reciprocated by another so that there will be short-term international gains (for example, lowered defense costs or increased trade), then there will be long-term gains in the chance for world peace and freedom. Interference in the internal affairs of the U.S.S.R. is seen as involving unacceptable risks of damage to more general world interests. Kissinger obviously judged both the monetary costs (arms) and the nonmonetary costs (risks of war) of policy before detente to be unacceptably high. He would have added that the best chance for internal liberty and plenty in all nations in the long run is improved by detente, for gradually our lack of interference in the internal affairs of the Soviet Union (or other nations, such as China) will lead to the more relaxed international situation, including liberalization, that accompanies peace.

Humanistically, the Kissinger argument emphasized the achievement of the highest overall social utility. This was seen to lie in reducing chances for war, with the added benefit of economic gains. Kissinger also implied a rule of extension that made a clear distinction between the intensity of normative concerns within and beyond national borders, insofar as these concerns do not relate to the external relations of nations. This could be carried so far as to place a practical prohibition on United States interference beyond its own boundaries. If so, this was not a rule deriving from a reverent concern for nations; it was a utilitarian rule that was thought ultimately to be to the United States' advantage and that gave the highest probability of avoiding war.

In Kissinger's thinking, there may also have been a distributive consideration that reduced the significance of Soviet dissenters. Even successful interference in the U.S.S.R. would have initially benefited only a small group of Soviet citizens. In a descriptive analysis, the actual size of this group should have been determined, but in any case it would have been a small percentage of the whole population.

Turning to the criticisms that may be advanced against the Kissinger point of view, the first argument would be a biosocial argument that unless balanced by communist liberalization, the measures of accommodation associated with detente will unbalance international relations. While detente rapidly erodes both the psychological and material defense capability of liberal societies, the more controlled communist societies are little affected. The paradox is that communist societies in this view are unable to liberalize very much without communist leaders losing power. Since leaders strive to maintain power, communist leaders generally will not liberalize, and the few liberalizers who do arise will be checked by other communist leaders. The result is a growing disparity in power between communist and noncommunist states. It might be that if detente preserved peace for a long enough time, changing power relationships would cease to be significant, because there would have developed a sense of common interest that rules out violence, as in relations between the United States and Canada. But power relations are apt to change too rapidly, and as a result, the more general situation in which power leads to domination will inevitably occur, especially in regard to the Soviet presence in Europe and the Middle East.

A second argument begins by accepting the Kissinger thesis that detente is the best guarantee of world peace, as well as the modern liberal belief that communist expansion is not likely, but it denies that detente will lead to liberalization within communist states. This approach accepts, then, only that part of the first critique that points out the self-serving opposition of communist leaders to liberalization. In this view, the liberalization that did occur at certain periods in the past in the U.S.S.R. was due to a desire to compete more effectively with noncommunist states, to improve the image of communism in the West, and to raise internal morale at a time of worldwide ideological struggle. If this struggle becomes less intense under detente, internally Soviet leaders will be able to concentrate on survival, which for them means repression. It is apparently from this point of view that critics argue that the Soviets have needs that we can exploit to obtain goals beyond simple detente. We can use what international leverage we have, for example, wheat deals or arms reduction, to improve the degree of freedom within the U.S.S.R. (These critics may be right in their initial arguments but wrong concerning international leverage.)

While the first argument, which emphasizes the international dangers of detente, is essentially utilitarian, emphasizing only the

action of a different group of biosocial factors than Kissinger does, the
second argument raises humanistic as well as scientific issues by ques-
tioning the morality of "trading with the devil." Should we endorse
through detente a state that consistently denies elementary liberties,
such as freedom of speech or movement? The critic is apt to state that
individual liberty is a rule of reverence with universal extension that
should not be traded off against changing probabilities of war and
relaxation, at least until the differences in probabilities with and
without United States interference are much starker than most analysts assume today. Men like Kissinger may hold to the same rules of
reverence in internal affairs, but they evidently accept different rules
of social extension in order to make it possible for them to advance the
practical argument for the principle of noninterference. (That subgroup of American Jews that is particularly incensed by the question
of restricted emigration suggests a third doctrine of extension that is
supernational but not universal.)

It is also fair to remark that the critics of Kissinger's relative,
humanistic inattention may well be moved by elitist rather than egalitarian concerns. They value the artists and intellectuals of the Soviet
Union and their products very highly and take a particular interest in
their future. Since most people in noncommunist countries are not
particularly concerned with intellectuals, the elitism of this concern
is further evidenced by the willingness of its advocates to risk the
future of their own people for the benefit of a few foreign intellectuals.
In general, Kissinger emphasizes the materialist values of utility and
distribution in stressing the prevention of war and arms reduction,
while his critics emphasize those of transcendence and reverence. The
critics place a transcendental value on the interests of the affected
creative minority, and they see all repression in light of a reverential
concern for human dignity that is not fungible like the goods of a
utilitarian calculus. They believe in a morality of universal extension, while in fact deemphasizing egalitarian considerations. In this
case, the evidence for the likely results in preserving individual liberty or in changing the probability of war that may stem from the suggested policy change is too indeterminate for scientific analysis to
decide the question without careful specification. The details of how
either the present or changed detente policy would be carried out
would probably be more determinative than the general considera-

tions, although all would agree that we could intervene too often or too strongly, particularly in the U.S.S.R. The critics of the detente policy must describe what new set of limits on intervention they would prefer before we can evaluate dangers and opportunities. We should also take into account the limits of the proposition that unless we stand for something in the world beyond narrow United States interests, we will eventually lose the will to defend ourselves, and thus ultimately lose the ability to discourage in others the "adventurism" that leads to war.

Moving to a broader overview, in social humanistic terms there is a clash between those who view proper policy as confined largely to achieving widely distributed utilities, such as peace or economic development, and those who view international policy as equally concerned with the promotion of a better world in spiritual terms, such as liberty or self-determination. Each group emphasizes a different set of facts that relate to the utilitarian and distributional aspects of their case from a scientific viewpoint (compare Huntington, 1968; Dahl, 1971; Packenham, 1973; Gastil, 1971c). Those taking the first position accept an evolutionary and materialistic view of history. In this view, most people must have material needs satisfied before spiritual. They believe that it is only a small group of people or those in highly advanced societies that are really interested in more than peace and material plenty. Even Rawls (1971), who builds a case for liberty as the highest social principle in his *A Theory of Justice*, values liberty primarily for the well-off. Liberty, he says, may be constrained, "if it is necessary to enhance the quality of civilization so that in due course the equal freedoms can be enjoyed by all" (p. 542). Those taking the second position emphasize evidence that men at all levels of social development willingly sacrifice economic plenty for symbolic values. They see little evidence for a biosocial hypothesis that economic progress increases interest in fundamental freedoms, an observation that Kissinger (1961) himself made in an earlier work. Concepts of political development or mobilization are useful in a descriptive analysis but are not in themselves predictive of the effect of freedom. So in the end, the second group sees a larger gulf between science and value and a more indeterminate social evaluation. On this basis, they propose that the United States should interfere in the affairs of other nations to attain humanistic goals.[8]

Analysis and Recommendation

The foregoing examples are definable as discussion analyses or preliminary evaluations. Figure 3 suggests the steps that must be taken next if the analyst wishes to arrive at a judgment preparatory to action. A judgment might be one of satisfaction or dissatisfaction with the output of a social unit as it performs in relation to the particulars at issue. We should remember that satisfaction or dissatisfaction in the first cycle of analysis is only hypothetical, for it has not yet been reality tested by a thorough review of the alternatives. The reality level of satisfaction will be discovered only after we have gone through, in Cycle 2, disciplined reflections (or actual experiments where possible and appropriate) that allow a test of the particular case against the past experience of men and society. This should help us to know whether the solutions we devise are apt to improve the output according to our standards of humanistic evaluation. After test-

Figure 3. The Process of Analysis, Evaluation, and Recommendation.

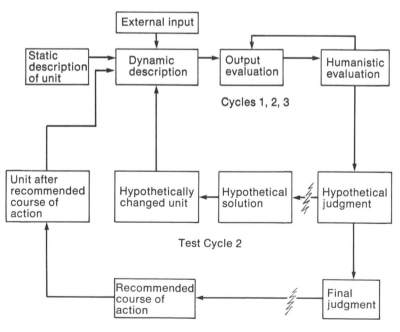

Change Cycle 3

ing several solutions at this level, we can reasonably come to a final judgment and recommend a course of action that will be beneficial (including, of course, no action at all). If the humanistic evaluation at the end of Cycle 3 is not the most desirable practically attainable at the time, other cycles of analysis will be required.

As an example of the process, let us consider a middle-aged, alcoholic woman as a unit of social analysis. She has considerable ability, but every time she runs up against stress (external input), she drinks. The result is a short-term utility of relieved stress, but long-term disutilities. She has reduced productivity after drinking and is difficult to be around. The output of her drinking is directly negative, and it has the additional feedback of changing her interests to make her less able to withstand the temptation to drink and less interested in anything else. Humanistically, this person is not adding much; the drinking is harming her children, so that she is unjustly denying them their part of the family bargain, she is going beyond the limits she herself accepts, and she adds nothing to the transcendence of man. She may have an alter ego that is telling her all of these things. But if it is too weak, she may wish for an outside evaluation and recommendation, or a court or doctor may make these irrespective of her wishes.

The hypothetical judgment is that she should stop drinking to excess. This could mean cutting down a little. But experience with similar cases suggests that total abstinence is likely to be the only solution. How should this be achieved? We note that others in her situation have improved their evaluations by joining Alcoholics Anonymous. But this is a general answer, and there may be characteristics of this particular unit that make it undesirable. For example, it might be that an analysis of this woman suggests that the social support or quasi-religious nature of Alcoholics Anonymous is unlikely to work, or it might suggest that in her environment she is apt to turn to even stronger drugs if denied alcohol. For these or other reasons, we might choose to work on the stress rather than the alcohol, hoping for an indirect effect. This is, of course, a more complicated path. First, the alcoholic problem has probably now become self-reinforcing, creating as well as alleviating stress. Second, the complexity of trying to change the nature of a problem rather than the response to it is extreme; often, the stress on an afflicted person is objectively no more than that provided in the average cycle of life.

Nevertheless, in many cases changing the external input should be seriously considered.

In this case, however, we find no special circumstances and as a result come to a final judgment against alcohol and for Alcoholics Anonymous, which we strongly recommend she join. This is no more than organized common sense, but common sense open to the disciplined inputs of the social sciences and humanities, where these are appropriate.

Concluding Note

In this chapter, the reader has been offered the outline of one methodology for applying social humanities. The material presented demonstrates the range of subjects and concerns that might be addressed within this framework. But these were only illustrative sketches. In Chapters Six, Seven, and Eight, we will look in more detail and with increasing methodological rigor at three problems of interpretation and recommendation. In particular, by pointing out in each case the assumptions of scientific fact and theory and the principles of humanistic justice essential to the argument, the presentations should both explain my views and lay the basis for their refutation.

Notes

1. I find it useful to refer to personal or social utilities as a subset of personal or social goods that includes only those goods relating to material utility.

2. The terms *positive feedback* and *negative feedback* are used in the systems sense; this is approximately equivalent to that of reward and punishment, or behavior-reinforcing and behavior-extinguishing input from previous behavior. This usage seems quite different from the thermostat model, in which negative feedback turns off a system that would otherwise run away. One can equate the two models if he assumes that maintaining any pattern of behavior requires a mixture of positive and negative feedback in order to avoid the pattern's overuse, because of immediately rewarding experiences, or its inappropriate disuse, because of negative short-run experiences.

3. The following account is taken in part from Gastil (1975a). The three cultures described are real cultures, but the accounts given are greatly simplified and may be controversial. Hopefully, for at least some of the people in each cultural area, these summaries are not indefensible. Some sources

are Holmberg (1969), Spencer and Gillen (1966), Radin (1957), Jenness (1959), and Rasmussen (1948). All accounts are meant to be representative of precontact conditions.

4. The reader may wonder why the Siriono do not work harder. The record of the primitive world indicates, however, that poor and even starving peoples may work very little (see Honigmann, 1973). Apparently, human beings can accept and enjoy almost any level of life, as long as it meets the expectations they have grown up with.

5. The Swiss-Northwest comparison is based on personal observation both by the author and by others. A beginning analysis might be made by consulting the Statistical Yearbook of Switzerland and impressionistic works such as Weigl's *Lern dieses Volk der Hirten Kennen* (1962). The Michelin Guide to Switzerland may also be compared with the AAA Tourbook for the Northwest. A good comparison with Starr (1973) and Cantwell (1972) would be Sorell's *The Swiss* (1972).

6. For the background of these views, see Graubard (1973) and Kissinger (1961). The latter book suggests that Kissinger would not always reject interference in internal affairs. However, the following discussion is based on what seemed to be Kissinger's policy in the early 1970s.

7. Robert Jervis, in a personal communication, points out two other types of questions that would affect judgment of these three: What second-order effects would follow from a particular policy, for example, the setting of dangerous precedents; and what are the opportunity costs of a particular policy, that is, what other valued goals do we forgo by choosing it?

8. For an additional example of the application of the methodology, this time to a technological and future-oriented problem, see Gastil (1976d). The analysis uses interactive diagrams as an aid to the application of systems thinking. In addition, the social scientific assumptions behind the analysis are explicitly listed and referenced, a necessary procedure when a study must be presented without an understood background, such as that provided by Chapters Two and Three.

SIX

Marriage Commitment in Modern Society: The Case for the Traditional Ideal

The Problem

In the course of their lives, men and women move through a variety of roles, and they play these roles in ways that bring greater or lesser satisfaction to themselves and others. Since for many people accepting particular roles is onerous, or in retrospect unfulfilling, or because there are changes in the extent to which a particular institution is observed, the continuing desirability of inherited institutions and roles is questioned by every generation. Currently an institution under pressure is marriage. The problem has become whether ordinary people and societal sponsors should continue to support, through their actions and statements, the traditional American ideal pattern of commitment to one lifelong marriage.

The ideal pattern is questioned, on the one hand, because of the increasing number of middle-class persons who live together at all ages without either legal or religious authorization, a trend reflected in a growing disinclination to marry. On the other hand, marriage is threatened as a stable institution by the growing tendency of marriages to end in divorce (Glick and Norton, 1973). It is often argued, of course, that the statistical increase in divorce means less a breakdown of the family than a legitimization of the breakdowns that formerly ended in separation or "facade marriage" (see De Wolf, 1973). Although there is no doubt a great deal in this, one cannot help but feel that an accepted divorce pattern reduces the inclination of partners to compromise differences and to consider their contract of long-term marriage seriously, and it increases the temptation of less dependent partners to exploit more dependent partners with the threat of divorce, an attempt that, in many cases, is bound to make divorce inevitable.

A Biosocial Model for Marriage

The social units at issue are human beings, particularly adults in modern societies. The analysis of marriage in their lives should begin with several biological facts we know about man that set him off from his mammalian ancestors. First, unlike most animals, he is sexually active throughout the year. Second, the human infant is helpless at birth, totally dependent on his parents for at least a year, and matures slowly over a period of fifteen or more years. Third, only one child is usually born to a mother at a time. Taken together, these facts imply that adult males and females will live together nearly all of the time and that they must take care of children for a significant part of their adult lives. One solution is to establish a pattern whereby males and females establish exclusive, stable sexual relationships and care for the children produced by these relationships. This is not, however, the only possibility, and the obvious unity of the primitive band led early anthropologists to assume that group marriage had been an accepted cultural solution before the evolution of exclusive marriage. However, further study demonstrated that group marriage has been exceedingly rare, and most people have lived their adult lives in married couples. In spite of a great deal of group care for children in primitive bands (see Leslie, 1967; Goode, 1971), children in all historical societies have been found to be the responsibility of particular adults, and these have usually been their biological parents or grandparents. Why?

In social science, there are three main ways to establish why a particular institution has come into being and spread widely. First is to assume that there is a biological determinant either in the genes or in the inevitable interplay of typical genotypes with typical environments that predisposes human beings to a particular type of pattern or indeed forces them to develop it. Second, we may imagine that present social patterns are the result of historical selection from a wide variety of past experiments. In this case, we would assume by analogy with biological selection that those societies with a societal pattern of exclusive marriage survived while others died out. A final approach is to adopt something like the self-interest model guiding the social science of this study and to ask whether the patterns found are not the result of repeated codifications of the best bargains that individuals could strike.

In most cases, the alternative explanations all play a part and indeed are dependent on one another. But the lability of social institutions over time suggests that the functional explanation of cultural selectivity plays the lesser role; the more significant cause of marriage universals must be the necessity to strike a salient bargain among rational self-interests developed from a genetic base. The basis of this picture becomes complete when we add two other less distinctive human biological tendencies, those of jealousy and love (this latter developed perhaps out of dependency relations as children).

Let us illustrate the biosocial pressures in the situation by resorting to a myth on the origin of marriage. The mythological quality suggests that the process described below did not actually happen, but our information leads us to expect that over time the pressures reflected by the myth led to the development and the repeated rationalization of historical marriage patterns (see Nozick's discussion of the value of a "fundamental potential explanation" of this type; Nozick, 1974). The myth begins with a community of young adults with recurrent desires for sexual access, a need for love and affection, and jealousy towards the sexual and love attachments of others. Let us imagine, too, a brutal society in which the strongest young adult males make the decisions. Let us also imagine that the members of the group dimly perceive that they attain benefits from the group, indeed, cannot survive without it. It is easy to imagine that such a society might find itself in constant uproar, with men who actually need one another to survive engaged in recurrent, bitter, and disruptive fights. We can also imagine that the strongest individual has the most desirable women and that he takes whomever he chooses when he chooses. But he is also in danger, for if the weaker individuals strike a bargain and pool their strengths, they can kill him; the more successful he is, the more likely is his demise. In this situation, we can imagine someone suggesting a major bargain by which each young man gets what he deserves in terms of his physical (or mental) strength, and by which jealousies may be reduced. By the terms of the bargain, the more numerous weaker males will collectively get more than the stronger, but individually they will receive less. (The social psychology of bargaining has found that, in triads, the weaker two will tend to form an alliance to redress the balance; Rubin and Brown, 1975.) In most primitive societies, the terms are enduring exclusive rights to particular women, all adult males get women, the more powerful males get the more desirable women (usually more than one), and a surplus of women is created by requiring young males to wait several years longer than young females before marriage. The problem of achieving this solution is one of communication, for in Kuhn's (1974) terms, the potential deal has always been implicitly present.

The exclusivity of the one-to-one mating pattern will lead to a community of common interest within married pairs (or trios, and so on), including some form of love, and this community will be extended to the children. Since each man has been forced to limit his attention to one woman (or a definite few) and has transferred over time some of his love-dependency relations to her (or them), he will also feel closer to her children than to other children. As they grow, the children will also feel closer to their parents than to other adults. A family has been born.

Of course, it is also true that, with age, young adults will displace the older generation. But unless there is an exceptional scarcity of women, the abler young men will not be especially attracted to the wives of older and weaker men, and they will also be conditioned by their experience in the family in which they grew up not to look for sexual satisfaction from a woman their mothers' age. It is also true that most older men will have confederates who will help them defend their wives, for it is in the interest of all with wives to defend the system against those without wives. Historically, older, physically weaker men have usually been able to deny young women to young adult males by invoking a variety of traditional rights (in the primitive world, the extreme example has been the Australian aborigines). Monopolization of women, however, has always been fraught with danger, most particularly the danger of breaking down the exclusivity of the marriage relation in general. Polygyny fosters adultery when it becomes excessive (see Dorjahn, 1958).

The result of the operation of these universals has been to develop in every known society marriage patterns with exclusivity that each individual accepts once he is granted rights in his society as an adult. This major bargain of individual with society then usually leads to a complementary major bargain between sexual partners. To this picture we must add the fact that sexual relations lead to the birth of children, and adults have an inborn ability to respond to young children protectively and affectionately. Since the child's first experience is with the mother, generally there is a much closer relation between the recently pregnant female and child than between the not-so-recently fathering male and child. As a result, women inevitably become associated with children more than men, unless conditions become highly artificial.

At the simplest level, women take care of young children because the love relation of mother and child pleases the former, and fathers take care of their wives because they are valuable sexual property. Since the father also has a biological ability to protect the very young, and since he is necessarily put into contact with his wife's children, he also takes on the role of protector and provider for her children directly. He becomes a father in the sociological sense, whether or not he is already one biologically.

However, these biological relationships provide an insecure basis for children: Mothers may lose interest in children; fathers may lose interest in providing for either wives or children. In a stable society, the children will be protected by other relationships that appear to be biosocially human, no matter what their biological ground. In particular, a woman continues, after pregnancy and giving birth, to preserve nurturant (love) relationships with her parents and siblings. They remain generously interested in her and through contact develop generous relationships with her children. Therefore, at the time of marriage, her parents insist, explicitly or implicitly, on adding to the agreement of sexual exclusivity the agreement that the man will care for his wife and her children (which, in most cases, are presumed to be his children) as long as the marriage relationship lasts. In other words, in return for the sexual access of marriage and the assumption of adult status that this major bargain implies (in primitive society), the young man agrees both to give up trespassing on the sexual rights of others and to care for a particular woman and her children. Generally, her family guarantees this relation by its threat of sanctions if he fails to live up to the bargain. These sanctions include, at the very least, support for termination of the marriage and spreading talk against him that will reduce his status and his chance of making other marriage transactions. To a lesser degree, the husband's family also exacts reciprocal agreement from the wife. She must also agree to exclusivity and to care diligently for the children produced (especially in a partilineal society).

It will be noted that this has so far been a male-oriented story, with the women largely passive. To a degree, this represents a genetic difference in aggression and interests between men and women (Chapter Three). In any event, male dominance was necessarily the case in the basic society, for males are stronger and less encumbered by biological demands. The woman's more intense relation with the children means that the family stability is initially more important to her, and this differential bargaining power further increases her dependency in marriage. Her husband can fight off other males more effectively than she can prevent her husband from going to other women. The woman's family, thus, has more need to protect her interests in the marriage relationship than the man's family has to protect his.

With the development of human symbolic life, complications in male-female relations occur in most cultures. The first is that the sexes specialize in terms of their biological endowment; the specialties then become cultural expectations or expected economic roles; each person agrees, in his major bargain with society, to also play the expected economic roles within the familial context. In nearly all societies, the more active roles of hunting and warfare, the roles that carry the person furthest from home, are reserved for males, while those of home care, child care, and food gathering are assigned to females (with exceptions, such as the West African market women).

As this specialization increases and symbolic values of maleness and femaleness become attached to these activities, each sex comes to need the other for additional, extrabiological reasons. Specifically, it means that a man requires a wife as much for economic as sexual reasons if he is to establish independence from the generation of his parents. Therefore, in marriage, the wife comes to agree to take care of the husband as much as vice versa, and we have emerged with the marriage pattern of most societies up to now.

Cultures, however, have generally made further additions to the marriage equation for apparently biosocial reasons. With symbolic development, individuals tended to develop a sense of group identity that went beyond the habituation of being together in a common group at the family and band level. When disputes arose, it was quickly noticed that the largest groups or the individuals with the most allies were generally victorious. Once the survival value of allies was noticed (either actually or metaphorically through selection), the most obvious way to develop allies was seen to be through extension of the biological relations that depend upon attachment in either the original family of orientation or the later family of procreation. This could be done in three ways—emphasizing all relationships equally, emphasizing the ties of mothers to children, or emphasizing the ties of fathers to children. The first is the most obvious, but it tends to be limited to a small group living in one place, and the danger of a marriage breakup or the death of a spouse makes it a less reliable source of extra strength than emphasis on a particular biological line. It is obvious that with frequent marriage breakups and poorly enforced exclusivity the matrilineal arrangement for extending reliable loyalties is preferable to the patrilineal. But this approach tends to split the loyalties of fathers who, through the procreative family situation, naturally come to favor their own children over their sisters' children. Since the loyalty of men is more essential to group strength than that of women, with stable marriage (and, for other reasons, with polygyny) the patrilineal form of extending reliable kin relations became dominant. This was particularly so where the demands of maintaining sexual peace in the band and the desirability of developing stable relations with neighboring groups led to interband marriage, with the necessity of one partner moving to live among strangers. Because outside males are also outside warriors and potential opponents, it was harder for them to be accepted into a strange group; therefore, patrilo-cal residence became more common, and with it, of course, a further emphasis on the position of the males in relation to females, many of whom were outsiders. But this is anthropological history, and this aspect of the marriage relationship has largely faded today.

Marriage, then, is a relation that began in biosocial necessities, and those societies that worked out the more successful rules were his-torically more enduring. But times change and we are faced with the necessity of reexamining the marriage relation, because today many are avoiding its assumptions in whole or in part. Specifically, we wish to examine two questions: The desirability of confining sexual relations to marriage and the desirability of encouraging permanence by restricting divorce.

As pointed out above, the reason for exclusivity was to main-tain sexual peace, particularly after an early period of experimenta-tion. However, uncontested identification of the father became more important along with growth in the importance of patrilineages. This was necessary to establish male responsibility for child support and to identify clearly lineage relationships within the group. Finally, as the transactional value of women was increased by the growing ability of men (or patrilineages) to pay for the right to marry, exclusivity came ideally to apply to the sexual relations of women before marriage. The early marriage of men was then institutional-ized to defend the institution of exclusivity (by allying most men in its defense) and to protect the right of powerful but aging males over their young wives.

Limiting sexual relations to marriage was also supported by other biosocial pressures. One of these was the inevitable conflict between sex and other activities in lives that have limited time and energy.[1] This is symbolized in many primitive groups by prohibi-tions on sexual activity before war or the hunt. Generally, spiritual activity has been seen as the antithesis of sexual activity, a relation-ship that receives its extreme expression in the monastery or nunnery but, again, has many primitive parallels. Clearly, a society ambiva-lent about diverting its energies to sexual activity will be inclined to restrict sexual activity outside of a stable marriage. A second reason to restrict sexual activity is to enlist the maximum number of persons in stable marriage relationships that are best able to produce and raise

children. For leaders of a kin group, the number of kin was always a
critical issue in economics and war. One of the best ways to increase
the number was to imply that marriage incurred the responsibility
for having children; making this tacit agreement was essentially the
only way to have sexual relations with any regularity.

After years of living together, two people may be so attached to
or dependent on one another that separation is unlikely. Yet separation occurs because marriage partners change in many ways, but especially in their relative sexual or affectional interests. Dissolution of a
marriage may satisfy the desires at the time of one or both partners,
but it is seldom in the interests of their children or of either parental
family. For the economic and affectional unit established by a marriage consists of a complementarity of roles, roles that after breakup
will have to be filled by others with conflicting responsibilities. The
problem is less acute in unilineal systems, for then the responsibility
and interest of the kin is clear. It is most acute in bilateral and neolo-
cal systems, such as our own, in which there is often no responsible
party to which the child can revert. With development beyond the
familial society, it is especially in this type of culture that social scientists note that family disintegration places responsibility on the general society that would otherwise be borne by individuals.

A family disintegrates because of the problems of adjustment
within the family, but also because of the availability of alternatives
to adjustment. Dissatisfied members of any organization have the
alternatives of exiting the organization or of attempting to improve
the organization through their vocal efforts. But, as Hirschman
(1970) suggests, there is a bias in favor of exit such that this alternative, when present, will tend "to atrophy the development of the art of
voice [dissent]" (p. 43). Intuitively sensing this, many societies have
developed conventions or laws making divorce very difficult. Apparently their sponsors have realized, as Hirschman does, that the more
the exit alternative is closed, the more likely a person is to stay within
an organization and work for its improvement. The man and the
woman on the desert island will learn to get along.

Moreover, we have to remember that the sponsors of any
society prefer order to disorder. When to this general consideration is
added a bourgeois ethic that sees sex as a mixed and limited good and
that teaches the necessity of the individual to control his individual

desires for the benefit of the group or spiritual goods beyond the group, the basis is laid for declaring the marriage contract to be unbreakable, except when one partner flagrantly ignores its basic sexual, generative, or economic expectations.

Preliminary Humanistic Evaluation

We have, then, sketched the main reasons for the development of the traditional pattern of marriage commitment accepted as the ideal by the last generation, especially the society-maintaining middle class (see Chapter Three). We have seen the biosocial and historical development of the ideal, but what have been the social and individual outputs of trying to adhere to it?

Drawing up a balance sheet for the attempt to preserve the ideal of lifelong commitment in marriage is more difficult than it might appear. It depends to a great extent on the observer's expectations of life and of the people who live it. Polls and questionnaires indicate that most persons report themselves reasonably satisfied with their marriages, and most people consider, in retrospect, that their family life was the most rewarding aspect of their lives (Leslie, 1967, pp. 497, 576). On the other hand, social scientists probing deeper believe they have evidence that most marriages quickly become hollow exercises in conformity, stunting one or both partners, with eventual damage to the children as well (Leslie, pp. 490–496). The result is often a search for satisfaction outside of marriage (particularly sexual), separation, or finally divorce. Divorce in this view frees the partners from an impossible situation, which in many instances is to the advantage of the children as well (Leslie, pp. 583–624). Acquaintance with world literature, however, suggests how hard it might be to discover the extent to which such apparently facade marriages preserve redeeming values.

Comparative information on divorce is hard to evaluate. Although divorce has been very common in many societies throughout history without great loss, this was in part because these societies had strong kin groups or families of orientation. In other words, where the adult and his siblings, parents, and grandchildren (or nieces and nephews) form a stable block of interrelated commitments, marriage bonds may be brittle without social instability. But in mobile modern societies, commitment to the marriage relation is one of the few restrictions on unlimited freedom (and unlimited insecurity) that the average individual maintains after he leaves home, usually between 17 and 25 years of age. What does divorce mean in this world?

In a perceptive treatment of the meaning of marriage and divorce today, Epstein (1974) concludes that a crisis has arisen from the explosive growth of high expectations in both sex and career that are simply impossible to fulfill for most people, whether within or without marriage. The media culture has, in effect, developed a national cult of personal growth, expansion, and instant pleasure in which the "dream of the family" has been replaced by the "dream of the self," until " 'everyone for himself' has become the truly potent revolutionary slogan of our day" (Epstein, p. 317). To Epstein, the success of this revolution would mean a national lapse into immaturity, and it would cheat most of us of the opportunity of living in an environment of full commitment to something beyond ourselves. In any event, since it will be harder for marriage to work in this context than in the past, Epstein concludes, "Good marriages will depend, even more than they do now, on selflessness, character, and love. They could well become our rarest works of art" (p. 318).

A recent collection of essays, *Philosophy and Sex*, offers insight into some current philosophical judgments of the traditional ideal (Baker and Elliston, 1975). Although historically philosophers have been traditional and rather puritanical in their attitudes toward sexual relations (Baker and Elliston, pp. 1–30), the last few years have produced a variety of new arguments, both as a reflection of current sexual attitudes and as an outgrowth of women's liberation. In this collection, the key question relevant to our concern is whether and to what extent sexual relations should be demystified. Should sexual pleasures, in other words, be "like eating a good meal, listening to good music . . . or getting a pleasant back rub" (Wasserstrom, 1975, p. 212)? Although the collection is slanted toward the libertarian views of its editors, the discussions of marriage-related issues are useful. They bring out the complexity of the contrast between marital and extramarital relations, and carefully develop the definition and argument for promiscuity (Wasserstrom, 1975; Elliston, 1975). One author asserts that marriage is simply a form of private property (McMurtry,

1975) but another refutes this notion by pointing out that a person or right is not property if the owner has no right to dispose of it (Palmer, 1975), and one cannot, in our society, legally sell a spouse or a spouse's services. Arguing for the traditional ideal of marriage, two contributors consider the desirability of intensifying human relationships by creating a protected, intimate state of theoretically permanent duration; they also point out that by tying together sexual intercourse and marriage, the possibility of total commitment is heightened in a way impossible with the assumptions of the hedonistic ideal (Bayles, 1975; Wasserstrom, 1975). Certainly, it is true that until the last generation, sexual intimacy and emotional concern for another person (outside of consanguinal relations) were closely related for the majority of adults. Finally, the philosophers include but fail to address themselves to the traditional philosophical and Catholic position that monogamy is good for man because it favors mastery of self, which is a humanistic good in itself (Pope Paul VI, 1975). This is a thought the editors of *Philosophy and Sex* only seem to understand as an espousal of prudery.

Analysis and Recommendation

To this point, our discussion and preliminary humanistic evaluation of modern marriage and divorce indicate that there are both costs and benefits to preserving the traditional ideal of one life-long marriage. Let us, then, run two hypothetical reformulations of the ideal pattern through the analysis and recommendation process suggested in Figure 3 of Chapter Five.

Rational-Traditional Ideal. Sex is a positive good. However, ideally it should be used to support rather than detract from other social and personal goods. These are, in particular, stable interpersonal relationships and the provision to each child of a stable set of parents for his care. Therefore, young people should be encouraged to limit sexual experience before marriage or to marry early where this is impossible. A marriage should be seen as a high point in life, and its continuation as a major subsequent goal. To prevent pressures from poisoning marriage, sexual relations should be restricted to marriage, as should other flirtations likely to lead to sexual relations.

Divorce or separation should not be seen as approved escape, although there should be legal means of divorce for those who feel that a relationship has become impossible. Divorce should always proceed with the awareness that it is both a personal and a social failure.

   Hedonistic Ideal.   Sexual pleasure is a positive good that may be legitimately pursued for its own sake. Young people should be encouraged to engage in sexual behavior as they develop (although pressures to rapidly begin sexual activity are played down in some versions of this ideal). Marriage is a relationship that exists alongside of, and may be reinforced by, sexual attachment, but it should not be treated as a sexual prison. The value of a marriage is in the pleasure that the persons in the marriage obtain from it. When either finds it stultifying, that person should work for its termination providing he strives to avoid damage to the other partner and the children. He has a responsibility to his own personal development, and in the end this must be decisive. No one should feel guilty about a divorce in and of itself.

   The first solution is a modernized or rationalized version of the traditional model, or status quo, while the second may be considered the radical or change-oriented alternative. Our common sense models (Chapters Two and Three) would lead us to predict that a society that generally supported the first alternative would have fewer popularly accepted divorces, which would therefore make divorce a less acceptable personal choice. On the other hand, societies adopting the second ideal would set up a positive feedback for divorce that would lead to its rapid extension. As divorces became an acceptable part of the culture, they would increase in frequency until marriage either became irrelevant or the cumulative negative feedback from operation of the solution led the society's sponsors to shift their support to another ideal. It is, of course, frequently the case in our society that attempts to escape marriage re-create the form under more informal rules (see Ramey, 1975). Note that in our discussion of marriage, we suggested that it was biosocially rather than biologically determined and that it has a variety of forms and degrees of permanence. Human beings who are not compelled to work out differences because of strict divorce laws will not naturally develop stable monogamy.

   But how might one judge the two alternative ideals in terms of our framework of humanistic evaluation (see Chapter Four)? In terms of productive utility, the sexual deemphasis and stability supported by the traditional solution may make it superior to alternatives, which indeed is the reason that the U.S.S.R. and the People's Republic of China stress conventional morality. The leaders of these societies are obviously attracted by the strictness of the puritan ethic and the productivity of that ethic—two sides of the same coin. Although the comparatively dry, gray lives produced by the uniform enforcement of the ideal pattern reduces the productivity of some people, this is not a general result. For example, marital regularity among Mormons, who live by this creed more than others, certainly does not decrease productivity or joy (Gastil, 1975b, pp. 126–136, 237–243). The desirability of a stable marriage from both the personal point of view (because of jealousy, security needs, or the desire for privacy) and the society's larger needs is illustrated by Leslie (1967, pp. 125–156) in his discussion of the radical kibbutzes of Israel, the Soviet Union between the world wars, and the Oneida community. Recent experiments in communal living seem to reinforce the point.

In affective utility, the outcome of the evaluation of the two solutions is mixed. Almost by definition, in the short run the utility of a freer system for sexual marriage would be desirable. The teenager yearning for a sexual partner can have one without the inhibitions of larger concerns. In divorce, at least one partner and often both desire the divorce—that is, see their utility to be improved by it—or it would not occur. On the other side, of course, childbirth out of marriage has often been disastrous for those involved. Even when thoroughly accepted, it has often meant loading an extra responsibility on a partner, a parent, or the society, for which they would not have freely contracted. With improved methods of birth control and easy abortion, this concern is greatly lessened. Moreover, the actual (as opposed to apparent) affective utility of unattached sexual relationships may be disputed. For example, the carefree world of the teenager is restricted by the easy availability of sex at the same time as it is expanded. Intense relations are readily entered by such teenagers; but without the sanction of codified access, they are always threatened by loss.

It may be that contrary to the adolescent dreams of all ages, the emancipated attitude toward sex does not offer more affective utility even in a strictly sexual sense. The Freudian anthropologist

Gorer certainly believed it should. But when he studied a Himalayan people, the Lepchas of Sikkim, who had very permissive attitudes toward sex, he found a declining people, a people with homosexual and child rape, with a surprising amount of suicide and threats of suicide (especially among children), and what to Gorer was a curious obsession with sex—a subject of continuous, open, and "obscene" discussion (Gorer, 1967). The Lepchas had taken the love and passion out of sex, made it as much a daily necessity as food, trained the young, in the now official Swedish manner, in its practice at an early age, and had gained nothing but immediate sensual gratification. Beyond perhaps considerable achievement in distribution, Lepcha society did little to promote the attainment of either material or spiritual values.

The instability that leads to a continual emotional strain under pressure of premarital or extramarital relations is also the chief affective loss in those societies with an easy and accepted availability of divorce. The outstanding sociologist of the family, William Goode, argues that adult love requires "1) many exchanges based on custom, 2) limitations on the kinds of freedom that expose one to the temptation of potential alternative mates, and 3) mutual dependencies that mean that life is less rich and satisfying when one is absent from one's mate" (1972, p. 442). The second, or hedonistic, ideal causes marriage to be devalued, because it no longer caps a developing relationship of intimacy. The effort expended in making a marriage work is devalued by the fact that it can be terminated at will when the pleasures of either party seem threatened. It is sometimes claimed that this keeps the partners more sensitive to the affective preferences of each other. But it also increases the leverage of the partner who is most willing to terminate the relationship and weakens the struggle for a mutually acceptable compromise that is the mark of adult life.

When we turn our gaze to the concept of justice, this suggests that sexual freedom operates to undermine commitment and thus encourages selfish abandonment irrespective of the feelings of others. The sad story of the forty-year-old male who marries the twenty-year-old after divorcing his wife is repeated twenty years later when she abandons him for another forty-year-old, and then ten years later this mate leaves her stranded at fifty. In this game, some do very well and others poorly. But it seems likely that greater freedom from convention gives the more exploitative and fickle persons, those less inclined to long-term relationships, the advantages, while greatly reducing the lifetime returns for those more desirous of stability.

This chapter does not emphasize the effect of divorce and separation on children, because this is a subject in itself. Some marriages are so unpromising that divorce may help the children. Yet there is little reason to doubt the general worth of popular sociology's theory on the deleterious effects of broken homes on children. As one recent discussion of stepchildren points out, parents are not simply replaceable (Maddox, 1976). If the children are unhappy, the happiness of their adult guardians turns sour.

Moving beyond the material side of life, the humanistic framework suggests that the alternative ideals be judged by their contribution to maintaining moral limits. Clearly, a person attempting to establish limits for his behavior is apt to emphasize the rational-traditional ideal. Its principles fit the definition of desirable limits, that is, the avoidance of an action in every instance because it is generally wrong, even though in a particular instance it may seem to be in the best interests of those concerned. However, avoiding extramarital sexual behavior or divorce does not fit this wisdom as well as the moral limit on taking human life for private benefit. Adhering to strict marital principles requires prohibitions that are not lightly set aside, although they may be waived if there are sufficiently serious justifications affecting all concerned—justifications that should be clearly spelled out in advance.

Equally critical, it seems to me, is the issue of the degree to which the individual transcends the pursuit of short-term personal satisfaction so that he might establish a model for the lives of others. In sexual and marital life, each person is a carrier of the lessons of civilization and should transmit, as much as possible, the best of that inheritance to his family and the society about him. It can be argued that a lasting marriage is an achievement, even though it is partly an emotional facade. For many it is perhaps the only form of transcendence that is attainable in their lives. Of course, such a marriage may block growth in other respects, and if an individual believes that he has an extraordinary but suppressed potential, he will want to escape from whatever he believes confines his abilities. But for most, premarital sex and divorce are carried out in the pursuit of personal, momentary pleasure, with no thought of transcendence; for these cases, premarital sex and divorce may reasonably be condemned as a materialistic shortcoming.

Is not breaking through convention a form of transcendence, while lamely following it is spiritual defeat? It depends on the attitude. If there really is a higher purpose than merely breaking convention, then this is an argument for transcending conventional morality. But too often there is little more than righteous cant. For the average person, the harder achievement is living up to tough social ideals of behavior, responsibility, persistence, and playing a role in all of its ramifications. The "honest Swiss" is honest because he follows a local convention, but in following it he declines to accept the short-term advantage of dishonesty every day and thus maintains the spiritual achievement of both himself and his neighbors. He may, of course, follow some conventions out of little more than fear and mental laziness. Yet my impression is that conformity on important issues, such as honesty, is often inner- or alter-directed rather than other-directed.

In making these judgments, we are speaking of the general rule. The individual may, indeed, achieve more through allowing himself the freedom of early premarital relations, casual sex, and divorce. He or she must judge this. But since everyone, in his own life, sets patterns for all, both in this generation and in those that follow, the individual must make the judgment acknowledging that transitory individual pleasure is not sufficient justification for either opinion or action. Moreover, for citizens who must decide on the rules and codes of society that will establish the framework for future life, the general reasons for premarital sex and divorce, and not the transcendent exception, must be considered foremost.

Our final judgment, then, is that the sponsors of a society should strive to maintain the rational-traditional ideal of the marriage commitment. This judgment is scientifically acceptable because an alternative has not been widely institutionalized in spite of much experimentation, because in terms of biosocial theory this seems the most salient compromise given apparent human biology, and because the affectional gains of the hedonistic ideal appear transitory. The rational-traditional ideal is humanistically preferable because it establishes a moral limit in a world with few salient limits, and it makes more possible the transcendent achievement of marriage for the average person, thereby drawing the person out of a narrow responsibility to himself alone.

Note

1.   As one study of marriage alternatives points out, "Maintaining or developing one intimate relationship is time-consuming enough, and maintaining several at once is almost impossible for most people, not just because of the psychic complexities, but because there are not enough hours in the day" (Ramey, 1975, p. 518).

SEVEN

American Indians in American Society: The Case for the Commonwealth Solution

A problem that confounds the American sense of justice, particularly in the less populous western states, is the continued material and spiritual dislocation of the American Indian.[1] Injustice to the Indian is morally more urgent and potentially more understandable by Americans than the inequalities suffered by other minorities, for the Indian not only suffers from an unequal distribution of goods, but is also entitled to rectification in Nozick's (1974) terms because of the injustice of the white man's acquisition that often denied the Indian both land and a way of life.[2] However, although historically the Indian has been unfairly treated by other Americans, this does not give the present generation a sure direction in deciding what the policy should be in the 1970s in regard to specific Indians and Indian groups that may or may not have been unjustly treated, and who must often be compensated at the expense of specific white groups. To try to obtain a better perspective on the problem, I will briefly trace how the Indian came to be dislocated and the scientific and humanistic constants involved. This will be followed by the description and evaluation of a possible solution.

The History of the Indian Question

Before contact with Western civilization, the Indians of North America had occupied the continent at a relatively low density for thousands of years. Although there has been a great deal of dispute recently over how many Indians were living in the present area of Canada and the United States before Columbus, there were probably little more than two million persons, who exploited technologies ranging from very small-scale farming to simple hunting and gathering, and social organizations varying from bands of a dozen, to towns of a few thousand, to leagues of perhaps twenty thousand persons (the latter was a very unusual circumstance, and probably fleeting).

North America in this period was in the situation of most of the world before the intensive and extensive agricultural systems of the Old World were introduced. Europe, China, India, and the Middle East had at one time been at the evolutionary stage at which the Pilgrims found North America, but by 1500 most of the Old World had moved beyond this stage as primitive peoples were conquered by successively more developed peoples, which resulted in either the former's destruction or assimilation. In its broadest outline, the destruction, displacement, or assimilation of the American Indians repeated the pattern that had occurred on frontiers of contact in Europe and Asia and that continued to occur. (It is still occurring today in Brazil and much of Asia and Africa.) As in America, this pattern begins with an initial period of organized contact and two-way acculturation, during which both sides feel they benefit. Such a "honeymoon" period occurred in early New England, in upper New York, and later in the Pacific Northwest; it lasted for centuries in parts of Canada. An initial contact of conquest, like that of the Spanish in New Mexico or California, was the exception. Sooner or later, however, and in the faster growing areas, such as New England, it was sooner, this period was followed by one of dispossession and bitter conflict.

Alongside the conflict over land were other more personal conflicts that exacerbated the fundamental struggle, leaving a more severe aftermath of destruction and hate than would otherwise have been the case. First, neither whites nor Indians were quite sure of the extent to which the other people should be included in their moral universe, or in our terms, whether human moral limits were applicable. Most

Indians were used to very short social extensions of their moral worlds, which seldom included more than a few hundred persons. The Europeans, on the other hand, were used to larger moral universes, such as that covering all Englishmen or all Protestants, but they were not accustomed to extending the rules to peoples as different as American Indians. This moral distance was increased by the sense of social superiority that stemmed from the obvious sophistication of European organization and technology.[3] On the other hand, for whites, the gap was lessened in many cases by the theoretical inclusiveness of Christian concepts, with their assumption that even Indians had souls worth saving.

An added difficulty was that many Indians quickly became enamored of the European way of life. Desire developed much faster than Indian ability to make or purchase European goods. As a result, Indians were pressed by desire to rationalize their right to steal and, in some cases, to kill to cover up theft. Lack of experience with white culture also led to disastrous Indian use of alcohol. As the moral validity of their own cultures weakened, alcoholism, thievery, and violence worsened; the old and wiser Indian leaders no longer controlled the young. The frontier was also often inhabited by white men with antisocial attitudes. It is not surprising that these persons often exploited, cheated, and killed Indians, teaching by their behavior the worst standards of European behavior. Unfortunately, such persons often became symbols of white society in Indian eyes.

As a result of multiple pressures, Indian populations declined severely, in some cases to a tenth of what they had been, although in the twentieth century there has been rapid recovery. Many Indians died in battle or were killed deliberately, but the largest losses were due to disease; for most extinct tribes, this was probably the decisive factor. Other contributing causes were intermarriage (occasionally simply by whites taking over Indian women—sometimes the Indian woman's way to a better life), alcoholism, and on occasion, starvation. Disease and starvation were hardly new, but after contact with the whites, they came to the Indian in new and more destructive forms.

Closely connected with the Indian population decline was the loss of cultural systems. Indian ways of life died out along with the Indians; several reasons may be specified. First, the culture of the winning side in social conflicts tends to take on the higher prestige. The conquering people often try to impress their superiority on the losers, for example, by enforcing coercive schooling. The leaders of the losing group often promote this change, for they may also believe their culture completely inferior, or inferior in important respects. This is one reason Indian leaders often complained of the lack of schools for their children, which had been promised in treaties. Equally important is the fact that the new system does win because of its superiorities. Today, in spite of the beauty of kayaks and silent canoes, Eskimos prefer snowmobiles, and lake Indians outboard motors. Growing potatoes is less work than searching for wild roots. Aspirin helps headaches more than native herbs, and surgery is only safe in white hospitals. For weak Indian groups, the United States military offered better protection against neighboring tribes than any retaliatory threats they could muster. For Indian women, white ideas of the rights of women offered more hope for dignity than did the male-dominated world of most Indian groups (including some matrilineal ones; see Josephy, 1965, p. 151).

Indian cultures also weakened because of the disruption and dislocations of contact. Indian languages fell into disuse as Indians came to have more contact with strange Indians and whites through school, intermarriage, and economic activities. Speaking English well became a positive attribute, with no necessary judgment of its superiority. By facilitating communication, such knowledge improved the possibility of successful transactions for Indians.

As a result of these forces, many surviving Indians became, for all practical purposes, ordinary white Americans, and passing into white society continues today. After several generations, the descendents of those who have entered white society have become so diluted genetically that only a vague family memory of Indian descent, or nothing at all, is left. On the other hand, some of those who were acculturated have remained with the Indian peoples as leaders or government agents, often, but not always, for the benefit of their people. Another group, the traditionalists (often the "hostiles" of the anthropological literature) have struggled to preserve as much of their native culture as possible in the face of the white onslaught. In many cases, they succeeded to an extent unimaginable a hundred years ago.

Their minimum success is having maintained in 800,000 Americans a sense of being an Indian.

Yet today perhaps half of this group of visible Indians remains caught in a twilight between cultures, more deculturated than acculturated, or perhaps enculturated into one of America's *lumpenproletariat* subcultures. Indians of this kind are well-known to whites living close to reservations; unfortunately, they are the group least likely to excite white sympathy. It is this group that makes the major contribution to the appalling social and health statistics of Indians.

Official American policy toward the Indians has gone through a variety of stages. After the Revolutionary War, the government took over the British policy of dealing with the Indian tribes as nations with which treaties might be signed. Unfortunately, not all treaties were ratified by Congress, not all affected tribes were offered treaties, most treaties were obtained under duress, and the Indians signing the treaties often were not able, in the Indian view, to sign for as many bands as the whites assumed they could. The official policy increasingly diverged from practice. Therefore, in 1871, Congress decided that the government should no longer make treaties with tribes as though they were protected independent states. Congress soon followed with a policy of forced assimilation. First, the Indians were to be taught white culture (generally including religious training) through compulsory education, often in boarding schools, and made into farmers through agricultural training. Second, most Indian tribes were to have their reservations allocated to individual Indians before their eventual emergence as fully autonomous Americans. The result should not have been surprising. Unused to farming, improvident as individuals, and discriminated against by neighboring people, many Indians found allocation to be little more than another preliminary to the complete loss of their claim to ancestral land.

By the 1920s, few Indians had made an effective transition to modern American life, and the condition of many Indians had become worse than in 1870. Curiously, the fathers seemed to have been able to make the transition to the new world more successfully than their sons (see Stern, 1965; Smith, 1940). For this reason, the government asked for an extensive study by the Brookings Institute. In the resulting "Meriam Report," a new approach was adopted and then extended into the 1930s. Under the Indian Reorganization Act of

1934, the Indians were to be encouraged in self-government, while their greatest possible development in both white and tribal ways was to be promoted. In addition, the Indians had become citizens in the 1920s, and by 1950 they all had voting rights.

In the early 1950s, the desire to end the continuing Bureau of Indian Affairs role and to end wardship led to a second major attempt to do away with "the Indian problem" through the termination of reservations. Since the Indian Claims Commission established in 1946 was to settle the outstanding claims of Indian groups, it was hoped that the termination policy and the commission's awards would relieve the collective American conscience of the burden of past wrongs and solve a costly twentieth-century problem. However, opposition to termination was quickly raised; although some reservations were wholly or partially terminated, the process was stopped and in some cases reversed (for example, in the case of the Menominee of Wisconsin). While many Indian claims were granted, new claims continued to be voiced (a process which continues, most recently in New England).

Since 1959, there has been a swing back to the policy of the 1930s. In addition, new Indian militancy and aroused white guilt have either blocked the resolution that was to be accomplished by the claims commission or have made it possible for the Indians to obtain large amounts of money, increased reservation size, or both. In the 1960s, new poverty and public health programs supplemented the ability of the Bureau of Indian Affairs to support Indians both in cities and on reservations. The conditions of the Indians have improved, and there is more self-help, but the living standard of the Indian remains depressed.

As disturbing is the fact that the present status of Indian affairs is built on sand. Although the Indians have finally been granted all the rights of citizens, they have managed to hold on to their historical special privileges, especially their right to tax-free and inalienable land. Therefore, in many cases, they continue to be a drain on the larger community without being fully responsible to it. The special benefits of being an Indian or enrolled in a tribe, including the possibility of taking part in large settlements for past wrongs, induces many persons to adopt a false Indian identity, reactivates dead affiliations among persons with very little Indian heritage, and even leads some white males to marry Indians for the benefits (just as nineteenth-century white homesteaders took "land brides"). The possibility of continued exploitation of Indian rights is bound to cause renewed Congressional interest in termination, while confirming the Indian's belief that he should concentrate on old wrongs and unreal traditions in order to justify his preferred position. In some cases, manufactured Indian bitterness exists even when objectively a group has been treated favorably (see Colson, 1953).

The chief proponent of termination in the 1950s was Senator Watkins of Utah, who believed, understandably, that Indians cannot be citizens who are granted all the rights of other citizens and still expect special privileges (Trosper, 1976). Watkins' solution was to do away with the special rights, as had been attempted in the allotment period. But the Indians are historically a special people, and this fact makes Watkins' cold calculation just as unstable a solution as the liberal left's generosity.

Scientific Analysis of the Present Situation

Our model of man and society and our understanding of American Indians lead to several conclusions. First, it is important to realize that the depressed position of Indians in American society is comparable to that of depressed minorities everywhere, especially those that have resulted from the conquest of a small, primitive population by a larger and more advanced group (compare Gastil, 1973a). The specifics are always different, but the outcome is generally the same. Today we read of Paraguayan or Brazilian Indians, but before that there were the Tasmanians (now extinct) and the Australian aborigines (reduced in numbers, dependent, and apathetic). On a different level, we can consider the analogous relations of the Irish and Welsh to the English, the Bretons to the French (Wenner, 1976), or the Tadzhiks to the Russians (Allworth, 1973, especially pp. 64, 98).

Why the difference in the economic and social indicators between these groups and the majority populations? In part, these depressed populations are remnants; the most effective and adaptable descendants of the original minority groups have moved into the larger society over the generations, becoming culturally and eventually biologically indistinguishable from its other members. In part, the depressed living standards of these groups are due to the fact that primitive cultures are not as productive, and therefore what their bearers produce is not competitive. Those who stay in minority societies may fail to adopt new methods or fail to adopt them effectively. Most primitive cultures do not inculcate the attitudes and habits that are appropriate to more advanced technologies or organizational forms. Low living standards also result from the fact that primitive groups have little bargaining power to advance their interests, and this is reduced even further by the relative inability of their members to cooperate in bargaining encounters with the outside world. Of course, poor, less competent, or different people are generally treated prejudicially by ruling majorities, so that even those individuals who could succeed often do not because of the group label.

Less advanced peoples faced with this situation generally lose a sense of group worth and ultimately of personal worth. Temporary solutions such as alcohol or gambling exacerbate the problem. Loss of distinctive characteristics, including language, rituals, or inherited skills, results from the apathy and changing needs of successive generations; but these losses depress the collective sense of group worth even further. Hatred and dislike of the majority, stemming from the minority's historical and current position, further lessen the group's chance of successful adaptation. Indeed, often those who adapt leave the group because their adaptation offends their neighbors.

In this situation, the comparative poverty of the primitive minority may excite private or public generosity. Soon the people are being given a living just for existing. (Cash or "in kind" settlements wrung from majorities sometimes give more psychological benefit.) Unearned income deepens the sense of personal and group worthlessness at the same time that it reduces the needs for self-reliance and disciplined activity. The latter are easily abandoned by primitive minorities in favor of dependency, because their chance to make an independent living that will satisfy the new material needs they have learned from their conquerors is at best marginal. Why work for such a little increment in benefits over what can be obtained without work?

Scientifically, then, there are few surprises in the condition of the American Indian, nor is it likely that their condition will change very much in the foreseeable future—certainly not on the basis of outside aid as it has been given in the past. Long-term, intensive efforts combining coercion and aid might work a transformation, but they are not consistently acceptable in a democracy. Without this option, the best chance for improving the situation of the Indians would be (1) to emphasize opportunities for Indians, as individuals or groups, to become essentially indistinguishable from other Americans or (2) to improve opportunities for those Indians who do not want complete assimilation to restructure their lives in terms of expanded group rights and concomitant self-reliance. In either case, fairer treatment in law and society should help to increase their material resources and reestablish their shattered self-confidence.

Humanistic Evaluation

The humanistic evaluation of the output of Indians in the United States and of their lives relative to other Americans is disquieting in terms of cultural transcendence, utility, and moral limitation. A decultured population is not an admirable one. However, the key humanistic concern for most Americans must be justice. In this area, the conflicts of non-Indians between their immediate self-interests, their individualistic definitions of justice, and their group definitions of entitlement have led to a vacillating policy that has done little to help the Indian. Only if we reach an acceptable consensus on a solution that is just to both Indian and white in both historical and contemporary terms, can we make possible a relocation of the Indian within American society with which our collective alter egos can live comfortably. Let us, then, consider the primary humanistic arena of discussion that will guide us toward a solution.

Right of Self-Determination. The American Indian question should be viewed as one aspect of the more general international question of the right of self-determination. Group self-determination is now accepted as a general right of all peoples, although its application has been spotty. The United Nations has promoted the right of self-determination, yet it has inconsistently held that the right applies only to former European colonies that are separated by oceans from the imperial state (Sureda, 1973). Paradoxically, the United Nations has also endorsed the principle in international law that all states have the right of self-defense, including that of defense against internal threats of secession (Sureda, 1973; see also Osgood and Tucker,

1967; O'Connell, 1970; Connor, 1967). In taking this latter position, it is accepting a tradition of the colonialist era that rights to territory are confirmed by effective occupation and control over a period of time. This is the argument of Burke, who believed that since the origin of all states was in violence, we must protect legitimacy by respecting the veil of time (O'Connell, 1970; Burke, 1885; Lucas, 1968). (This origin for states and its acceptance in law are congruent with the model developed in Chapters Two and Three.)

The theoretical United Nations doctrine of self-determination is based upon Mill's classic statement of the rights of peoples to govern themselves (Mill, 1951, pp. 455-456; see also Emerson, 1960):

> *A portion of mankind may be said to constitute a nationality if they are united among themselves by common sympathies which do not exist between them and any others— which make them co-operate with each other more willingly than with other people, desire to be under the same government, and desire that it should be government by themselves or a portion of themselves exclusively. . . . Where the sentiment of nationality exists in any force, there is a prima facie case for uniting all the members of the nationality under the same government, and a government to themselves apart. This is merely saying that the question of government ought to be decided by the governed. One hardly knows what any division of the human race should be free to do if not to determine with which of the various collective bodies of human beings they choose to associate themselves.*

This seems to be an extreme doctrine. However, Mill himself qualified the doctrine in terms of utilitarianism and his scaling of peoples according to their stage of social evolution. Since he felt the right to self-determination for advanced people, whether in a minority or majority, was superior to that for less advanced, it was advantageous that the Basques or Welsh become assimilated to the English or French rather than emphasize their distinctiveness. Mill felt that the British in India had a responsibility to raise the Indian people to a level at which they should determine their own affairs, and as long as the British were so engaged, this responsibility overruled the Indian desire for self-determination. For Mill, the rights of small communities, such as Gibraltar, were also nullified by the defense requirements of the large state that controlled them. The right of self-determination through independence or federal arrangement was, then, limited through Mill's utilitarian calculus to that of large communities at an equivalent level of civilization and capable of free, democratic government.

Mill's justifications for exceptions to the principle are so out of harmony with modern liberal thinking that his doctrine remains meaningful to our generation only in its extreme form. In this form, the rights of heterogeneous states over their several peoples are restricted to those granted by the affirmation of these rights by each of their peoples. With regard to its peoples, the legitimacy of a state is, then, contingent upon the continued relative satisfaction of the peoples involved. Since a state can legitimately preserve itself only when and to the extent that its constituent peoples want it to, it is contradictory for a state to attempt to preserve jurisdiction over a people that does not want it. It has no right to prevent the escape of persons not wanting its control (except for ordinary crimes), just as it has no right to control peoples living in territory that it took possession of by force or that are forced onto its territory.

But how do we know what a particular self-conscious people want? One can distinguish three types of situations. In the first, there is a tight state control over the territory and people and a lack of reasonably democratic procedures. In this case, a small disaffected elite may temporarily be regarded as representing the desires of the people, because the people for whom the disaffected speak may not have been given substantial opportunity to know what they want. The second situation is where there are or have been democratic procedures that give us a good idea that a people wish to enhance self-determination. This offers the best case for enhanced self-determination. Finally, there are situations, such as that of Puerto Rico, where the majority has repeatedly expressed disinterest in further self-determination, but the world continues to hear from a dissaffected minority. This is an illegitimate case for self-determination; its advocates must change the judgment of their own people and not appeal to the conscience of mankind for further support.

Considerations such as these suggest that the ideal of self-determination need not always imply that a balancing of the rights of states and their peoples will lead to complete independence. As in the

Aaland Islands decision of the League of Nations (Sureda, 1973), if a state meets its obligations to its people in terms of economic, cultural, and political equality under democracy, other factors may place a legitimate limit on a potential demand for self-determination, or, as Cobban (1945, p. 174) put it, "Although in [some] cases independent statehood may be out of the question, all nations or subnations should exercise self-determination within the limits of what is practicable, in the form of regional autonomy."

Commonwealth Solution

Accepting the right of self-determination as tempered by Cobban's (1945) advice and premises derived from Chapters Two through Four, and understanding the present situation of Indian groups, let us suggest the following hypothetical solution: The United States should strive to establish new major bargains with Indian groups (now largely reservation groups) that reaffirm the rights and duties of United States citizenship in certain regards (national defense, foreign relations, some aspects of transportation, and postal services), but that grant Indians the choice of group independence and responsibility in most other affairs. The complexity of economic and social relationships that have developed between Indian and white communities would make the details of such bargains far from simple. As the bargains are worked out, the result should be in terms of historical entitlement and avoiding the establishment of new privileges. For example, depending on the local situation, special privileges in sales of otherwise illegal or taxed goods (such as cigarettes or firecrackers) on Indian lands to non-Indians should be restricted. On the other hand, the new bargain must be responsive to historical Indian rights off reservations when the major Indian rights protected by treaty were fishing or hunting rights rather than land.[4]

The new major bargains would include legal review, but the emphasis would be put on restoring directly what they had lost—land and hunting or fishing rights—and not on cash settlement unless it is the only solution. Restoring land lost to a reservation is preferable to cash settlement for the easy dissipation of cash settlements granted in this fashion is legend. An extreme example is that of the Puyallup Indians near Tacoma, Washington, that were destroyed both physically and socially by large cash settlements for land in the late nineteenth century (Smith, 1940). However, many Indians, particularly off-reservation Indians, prefer to sell their Indian identities for ready cash, since the older values of the primitive economy are no longer attractive.

The potential for restoration may be suggested by considering the dispute over the Treaty of Ruby Valley between the government and the traditionalists among the Western Shoshoni. In 1863, the Treaty demarcated a very large area of northeastern Nevada as belonging to the Western Shoshoni, particularly the band headed by a leader called Timoak.[5] The Shoshoni in return gave the whites a number of rights in the territory, in particular the right of free passage. But the government also was granted the right to give the Shoshoni a reservation within the area. However, under the influence of another band leader, the government failed to establish a reservation within Timoak's boundaries, and as a result, Timoak's band refused to settle on any reservation. Because of the sparseness of white settlement, many of the descendants of the band's members have managed to stay in the original area. Characteristically, the Indians today demand the whole territory demarcated by the treaty (less that small portion privately owned), while their ancestors in the nineteenth century had demanded only a reservation within this area. Nevertheless, since the area described is public domain, there is an unusually good chance for a satisfactory compromise by returning substantial portions of the original territory of the Western Shoshoni back to the Indians, with transitional guarantees for whites now leasing from the Bureau of Land Management.

In many other cases of tribes broken by repeated treaty changes, inexpensive federal land exists that could do much to recompense the Indians. For example, in the nineteenth century, the Flatheads were forced onto a small area and compelled to accept other Indian peoples with whom they did not wish to live. Then, without further reducing the official reservation size, reservation lands were opened for sale and homesteading to whites until most of the best land was taken. At this late date, these whites should not be dispossessed, but ancient Flathead claims to other lands in the area should be restudied (Trosper, 1976; Fahey, 1974). It would not be a tragedy if the management of 10 percent or so of our federal and state land was gradually turned over to Indians by such readjustments. Since few Indian tribes could afford to leave new lands unused for long, they would either put the land to use themselves or lease it as managers of public lands do today. Incidentally, since conservationists probably have more to fear than developers from this policy, they should be consulted about projected revisions.

The question of Indian lands confronts us with the issue of group rights versus individual rights. The allocation and termination policies stressed the latter, while reorganization and nativist approaches are based on the former. Should we protect the rights of individuals or act to ensure the continuance of groups? As usual, the best solution is a compromise. For reasons of equity, we must devise a policy that will give equal treatment to every individual in the terms he desires (although we should regard children as part of the families to which they belong, with adults deciding for them). For reasons of utility, we must try to satisfy the preferences of as large a number of those affected as we can. On the other hand, it should never be government policy to help eradicate a group's identity, as long as some members want to preserve it. This is also reinforced by the transcendence that many Indians are likely to achieve only in terms of their own tradition. Therefore, since most Indians have their inherited capital primarily in their land, they should have a right to either cash in their interest or retain it in common, with individual Indian rights on Indian lands determined by Indian customs rather than white.

According to this plan, at specified intervals after a legal decision as to what a group of Indians really owns, any Indian may sell to the government his share of the total reservation property. The time intervals should be on the order of ten or twenty years, and time lags and counseling by both Indians and whites should be used to prevent hasty decisions. Individual Indians who cash in their property and the descendants of these Indians should be considered for purposes of public policy the same as non-Indians, although they may form group-sustaining organizations like other ethnic groups and may, under special regulations (and with the repayment of their cash settlement plus interest), rejoin their people. Those who do not choose to sell their property shall enjoy their people's special lands and rights in accordance with legal review and be responsible for their own affairs on a semiautonomous basis.

The size of group lands will vary somewhat with the number of original shares that have been sold, especially those lands adjacent to public domain. These areas, to be known as *commonwealths* rather than the now pejorative *reservations*, shall have agreed degrees of independence from outside law, but also from outside welfare and other programs. The commonwealth status of Puerto Rico is well-known and accepted, and recently the Northern Marianas have also chosen this status. Federal taxes will be paid for specified services, such as national defense, but beyond this there will only be local Indian taxes. There should then be initial grants to get the commonwealths under way, but there should not be an automatic outside responsibility for their welfare. If additional members wish to sell their property they may, but the commonwealths will remain, although smaller, as long as any Indians want special status. A compromise formula might be the following: Every twenty years there should be a review of the commonwealth, and if at this time the population has fallen by more than 20 percent, 10 percent of the commonwealth shall be transferred to federal lands, with the choice of land decided by the remaining Indians.

The commonwealth form would not suddenly diverge from the reservation form, but would gradually become more self-sufficient. (In many cases, the evolution would be no more than a stronger institutionalization of trends already underway.) Law on reservations today is, in effect, a mixture of federal, state, and Indian statutes, customs, and administration. This situation would be regularized for each commonwealth, with the exact balance varying from place to place. Some commonwealths would be so small that they would probably take on little more than symbolic functions. There would still be an area of federal responsibility that would require a bureau of commonwealth affairs equivalent to a small Bureau of Indian Affairs. The commonwealth concept is specifically meant to avoid the mistakes of allotment and termination such as occurred with the Menominee. This tribe, well-known for its self-sufficiency, was badly hurt by replacing reservation status with two new statuses simultaneously: as a new county in the state of Wisconsin and as a corporation. In particular, the land taxes levied by Wisconsin placed a new burden which quickly led toward land alienation reminiscent of the allocation period. State regulation of timber and the strange corporate forms, while not ill intentioned, added unnecessarily to Indian bitterness. The result was the loss of the Indian's independence that had been tenaciously built up earlier in the century (with an independent hospital, utilities, and sawmill; see Lurie, 1972).

Many traditionalists and many well-meaning Americans would welcome the commonwealth solution (and perhaps extend it to the Spanish Americans of northern New Mexico, to the Amish, and others), but they must also be prepared for its costs. While some Indian groups or individuals would thrive with the new group freedom, habits of dependence would be hard to break, and habits of group cooperation often hard to form. The Indian record in managing reservation affairs has not been encouraging. Perhaps new democratic forms that incorporate both modern and traditional features or explicit education in the operation of political parties would help (see Lurie, 1976). In any event, the result of increased self-determination in some commonwealths is likely to be the collapse of schools, increased violence, and even poorer health conditions than are found today.

Yet it would destroy the purpose of establishing more autonomous Indian personalities and societies to step in authoritatively and paternalistically at this point.[6] Some commonwealth Indian families will leave and become residents in neighboring counties, but as long as they do not renounce their affiliations to the people of the commonwealth, the services given them may be charged against their commonwealth. There is no right in distributive justice to tax some communities to pay for those in other communities that do not pay taxes to support these services. Paternalism must be limited: The child who grows up is expected to take care of his own needs. If the Indian cultures are to mean anything, they must be treated as adult cultures.

The suggested approach is obviously most easily applied to the relatively large and distinct Indian reservations of the Southwest. The situation is much more difficult where, partially as a result of the allotment period, many Indian reservations have large numbers of white residents; in some cases, the majority of persons within reservation boundaries are non-Indians. Somewhat different is the situation, found especially in southern California and Washington State, of the minireservations (originally preferred to grouping in large reservations by some Indians because of their localized sense of place and unfamiliarity with the meaning of land ownership). In these cases, nonland perquisites such as fishing rights may be the basis of the commonwealth. As long as there are bona fide Indians in groups, they should be given a chance to live by their own standards.

Evaluation of the Commonwealth Solution

Current government policy toward the American Indian has many elements of the commonwealth solution. However, unless the basis of this policy is explicitly institutionalized, recent changes will be open to reversal at any time. For a solution of this type to become a long-term national policy, both its justification as the product of accepting a universal right to group self-determination and the limited reach of its expected material accomplishments must be understood. Let us then examine what the output of the commonwealth approach suggested here would be compared with the alternative of inaction. The experience of trying to help Indians has been frustrating; almost every type of education, training, and poverty program has been used in attempts to improve the lot of American Indians at one time or the other, and with little success. The cultures that have been infringed upon the least, especially in New Mexico, have been the most persistent. But even here, social welfare indicators are well below those for neighboring white Americans. Even those Alaskan Eskimos that have never been dispossessed have often been badly scarred by contact.

At the least, the suggested approach is based on the experience that what the Indians have done for themselves, whether as individuals or groups (for example, the Fox or the San Carlos and White Mountain Apache), has had more lasting benefit than what others have done for them (see Linton, 1940; Spicer, 1961). Our model would suggest that the Indian is helped most by giving him the opportunity to make it on his own. This has the corollary that if he does not make it in our sense, he will suffer the consequences.

From the point of view of humanistic evaluation, the Indian has many claims on our attention. Most important is his claim that he is entitled, under justice, to live in his own way on his own land, which, in many cases, was taken from him through the use of violence or fraud. The commonwealth solution helps to satisfy this claim by seeking to reestablish group rights. Yet it suggests adjustments or errors in law rather than payment with interest on white guilt; allaying guilt helps whites, not Indians. In trying to create more justice, the commonwealth solution does not ask individual non-Indians today to sacrifice significantly for past errors. We have no reason from the principles of the framework to extend either our moral limits or our sense of justice in this way. Certainly there must be millions of poor, working-class, non-Indian Americans who have gotten less out of life for more work than have many Indians. We also cannot effectively extend our obligation, for we do not know in terms of justice or utility what is best. If we turned the whole country over to the Indians we might all starve, including the Indians.

It will be objected that many Indian commonwealths will not provide sufficient access to jobs or resources to support their people. In some cases, the major bargain must take this fact into account. But in most, it will not be true if the members of the reservation make sufficient effort and if they are willing to accept a lower standard of living than the average American. In fact, a lower standard is implicit in the bargains accepted by groups such as the Amish and Hutterites. Others will object that it is wrong to thrust Indian children back into primitive ways of life, often based on the crudest superstition. One can only reply that we allow a great deal of life at this level for other Americans on the basis that people have a right to their idiosyncrasies. The moral rationale of the state is to provide a basis for achieving the interests of individuals and groups as they see them, and not as the staff of the state sees them. One can also argue on a utilitarian basis that it is better for all of us to have Indians believing in Indian verities than in nothing. Too often culture contact has destroyed rather than built; for deculturated families, reaffirmation of traditional ways may be preferable to more modern or "scientific" ways of life. Of course, individual Indian children may grow up to reject their cultures. If so, they should be welcomed into the general society to live by its laws unless or until they decide to return to their former group. The commonwealth solution should offer individual Indians two authentic and self-confident ways of life from which to choose.

As Berger (1974, pp. xiii–xiv) concludes in a study of those people of the underdeveloped world who find themselves caught between the twin forces of capitalist modernism and Marxist revolutionism:

> *Human beings have the right to live in a meaningful world. An assessment of the costs of policy must also include a calculus of meaning. Modernity exacts a high price on the level of meaning. Those who are unwilling to pay this price must be taken with utmost seriousness, and not be dismissed as "backward" or "irrational." The viability of modern societies, be it in the West or in the Third World, will largely hinge on their capacity to create institutional arrangements that take account of the counter-modernizing resistances. A key area for such institutional innovation will be in the creation of intermediate structures—intermediate, that is, between the modern state and the undifferentiated mass of uprooted individuals typical of modern societies.[7]*

My final judgment is that the commonwealth solution is a desirable innovation. It is the best available means of meeting the valid claims of both justice and absolute law against the body politic on the part of the descendants of the original owners of the land. This implies a right to a significant degree of self-determination, and this in turn implies accepting a risk of economic and social failure. In addition, Americans feel called upon for distributional reasons to concern themselves with the quality of life of American Indians, and yet at the same time, justice requires that this not be at an unreasonable expense to other Americans. In this regard, the commonwealth solution promises more than the continuation of the struggle of incompatible policies that has been witnessed for the past century and a half. There are also spiritual and material advantages that subgroups sometimes gain when they are given a satisfactory legal or social environment in which to maintain their traditions. Finally, the solution represents an attempt to live with the fact that, at least outside of totalitarian societies, neither force nor charity has succeeded in improving the lot of minority peoples from primitive backgrounds.

Notes

1. The discussion is based on years of study of American Indians and other primitive peoples, particularly the Indians of the American Southwest and Northwest. The author also went to school with and later did a small

amount of field work with the Digueno of southern California. References particularly used were Spencer, Jennings, and others (1965), Colson (1953), Stern (1965), Taylor (1963), Josephy (1965), Kluckhohn and Leighton (1946), Kroeber (1939), Spicer (1961), Colden (1958), and Meriam (1928). Also very useful were Indian biographies, such as *Son of Old Man Hat* (Dyk, 1938), *Sun Chief* (Simmons, 1942), and *Crashing Thunder* (Radin, 1926).

2. Of course, blacks were also deprived as individuals. But their ancestors were enslaved in Africa, and their people now control those lands. Ultimately, Americans do not have the bad conscience about slavery that they have about the unavoidable fact that they live on someone else's land.

3. No doubt in some frontier situations (see Trosper, 1976) the superiority of whites to Indians was not stressed until Indian land was wanted. However, from the beginning, middle- and upper-class whites saw Indians as inferior for a variety of reasons, of which religion was often the most important. After defeat, most Indians tended for their own reasons to accept this white judgment at some level of consciousness. When this occurs, a people and its culture collapse.

4. In some areas of the country, notably western Washington, the Indians agreed to treaties in which their rights to fishing and hunting were judged more important than land. The very small reservations they received cannot now be judged their main claim upon the area (see Swan, 1857; American Friends Service Committee, 1970). Since this time, there have been a number of decisions reaffirming the natives' rights (see Raymond, 1976).

5. The current status of the dispute was presented in a recent ABC television documentary called "Dispute at Battle Mountain." The account here, however, is based on Harris (1940).

6. However, as Nathan Glazer points out in a personal communication, this is precisely the weakest point in the approach. How we can justify not stepping in to help at points such as this needs to be worked out in convincing detail.

7. This is, of course, reminiscent of Nozick's (1974) concept of the state as a framework for utopias.

EIGHT

Problems of War: The Case for a Restrictive Doctrine for Initiation and Conduct

The effective but noncatastrophic control of force to achieve social objectives is the most critical requirement of our civilization. The existence of nuclear weapons intensifies our need to work toward better solutions than we have found in the past; yet as we have seen in Korea, Vietnam, the Middle East, or even Angola, the problem is far more general than that of nuclear holocaust. It is also a problem we cannot exorcise by wishful thinking, for social orders are ultimately built on the use or threat of violence; in the bargaining process that establishes the framework of civil life, those who are unwilling to threaten life must ultimately lose out to those who are.

We have defined society as a state in which recourse to violence will always be an alternative, and the existence of this alternative will always require the capability of counterviolence, even by those who would avoid violence. Among states, we established in Chapter Three that this fact has universally led to the development of military forces and generally to recurrent wars whenever the cost/benefit balance of war seemed favorable to the leaders of nations who found themselves at critical decision points. Larger and better organized societies have

218

meant more intense wars, an effect steadily heightened by technological change.

This rationality of violence is also supplemented and reinforced by irrational personal and cultural aggressiveness and maliciousness; indeed, in most times and places, this dark side of humanity has led a minority to choose violence as a preferred method of achieving their interests.

Wilson's Declaration of War

The first problem of war is to define the conditions under which it is justifiable to go to war. In order to examine this, I will consider the decision of President Wilson to bring the United States into World War One, for it exemplifies many of the issues of war initiation. I choose World War One in order to avoid more recent and still emotionally charged events, and because the issues involved are sufficiently unclear to approximate the kind of problem that is most likely to confound us in the future. I also choose Wilson's declaration of war because Devlin's *Too Proud to Fight* (1975) offers us a recent, detailed examination of the factors that went into the decision, combined with the ethical interests of the social humanist.

Provisionally accepting Devlin's text as a definitive account of what happened, we will formulate the discussion in terms of the analytical outline suggested in Chapter Five. The social units of the analysis are the United States in 1914 to 1918, President Wilson, and, at certain times, other persons and nations. (The middle or bureaucratic level of Allison's [1971] decision trichotomy discussed in Chapter Three is largely ignored by Devlin, although this level is necessarily reflected in the role playing of the participants.) The problem is the declaration of war, which appears in four guises: Why did Wilson do it? What were the alternatives before, during, and after the time of decision? Given answers to these, should he have declared war? Finally, what do we think of Wilson or other actors as a result of considering the behavior that occurred in the situation?

The reader is surely aware of the context of World War One and of America's entry into it. Nevertheless, it is appropriate to review briefly the most important facets of the situation as seen by Devlin, for it is in terms of this summary that we will later offer a judgment. Both the allies and their opponents were disparate groups. On the one side, Great Britain and France were democracies, although they held a great part of the world in colonial bonds, and they were allied with Russia, a nation just emerging from feudalism. On the other side, Germany, a nation of rising strength, with a modern and partly democratic system, was allied with the Austro-Hungarian Empire, an evolving state of the *ancien regime*, fearful of dismemberment by the growing nationalism of its subject peoples.

Out of a series of alliances, as well as military plans, fears, and ambitions, World War One suddenly burst upon the world. Yet it soon was stalemated into a prolonged bloodletting in which the Germans maintained initial gains without being able to break through the trenches in the West. In this situation, the critical question became which side would be exhausted first. As a supplement to the battlefield activity, the Germans hoped to bring England to its knees with submarine warfare, while the British hoped that a general blockade of direct and indirect sources of overseas supply would eventually choke the Germans. The Germans used submarines because the British controlled the ocean surface. The British had been the traditional sea power; indeed, breaking this monopoly was one of the goals of the development of German power, and it represented at least one cause of the war.

In 1914, the United States was part of an international system in which neutrality was the expected response of countries not directly affected by a war. The United States had also developed a supplementary historical doctrine that it should not involve itself in European wars. The loyalty and identification of American leaders along the eastern seaboard were with England and France because of past history, language, and a general feeling that these were the more advanced countries in terms of democracy and liberality. However, there were also many Americans of German and Irish background with the opposing loyalty, and a large number of Americans were pacifists except when their direct interests were involved. In particular, America's Secretary of State at the beginning of the war, William Jennings Bryan, took a strong, religious, pacifist position. It should also be remembered that the United States did not have a significant army to field even if it had wanted to affect the war in its early stages.

As the war went on, Americans became increasingly irritated

by the effects of the German submarine war and the British blockade on American shipping. Although both belligerents proceeded with some care and there were frequent changes of policy, neither side strictly abided by previous understandings of what was permissible action in time of war against neutrals and noncombatants. However, the submarine campaign sank vessels with loss of life, while the British blockade chiefly involved infringement on rights and the loss of money. The callous disregard of the Germans for the rights of the Belgians also confirmed the picture of the Germans as barbarians, while the British attempt to starve a whole nation was a vague, indefinite form of barbarity that did not have an impact equivalent to the German atrocities. America, therefore, tilted in favor of the Allies, especially on elite levels, but as a nation it continued until 1917 to want no part of the war.

Wilson understood and accepted the nation's attitude. However, until the United States entry into the war, he represented the nation's ideological antiwar feeling, as it had been expressed in the beginning by Bryan. At this time, Wilson did not see the war as a crusade against evil but as an essentially foolish struggle that the United States should stay out of until it could pull the belligerents apart. Wilson saw the United States mediation of the conflict as the basis upon which a world order to defend peace and freedom might be established. To achieve these ends, Wilson directed appeals both to the leaders of the opposing sides and directly to their peoples (in the hope that they might influence the leaders).

Wilson made two major attempts to stop the war. The first was in the form of a tentative agreement worked out in 1916 by his main emissary, Colonel House. Wilson pledged, in effect, that if England and France went along with his call for a peace conference and Germany either refused or agreed to a conference but subsequently refused to accept reasonable terms, the Americans would go to war against the Central Powers. Viewing Wilson's plan as an election ploy, allied leaders never took it seriously, even though objectively it was certainly in their favor. After his reelection in late 1916, Wilson strove to achieve peace more evenhandedly by delivering notes to both sides asking that they state their war objectives or peace terms. He tried to generate popular support for this approach by bringing it to public attention in his "peace without victory" speech in January

1917. Although the official reception by both sides was cold, this second attempt did get the two sides to outline their aims more clearly; it also placed the United States in a more objective stance than the first effort. Yet the parties were still too far apart for the conference table, and by January 1917, the Germans had desperately and mistakenly concluded that a few months of unrestricted submarine war would allow them to dictate peace terms no matter what the United States did. German leaders had always warned the United States that if Britain continued to try to starve them, Germany would return to unrestricted submarine war. When they announced its resumption in the midst of Wilson's second attempt to bring the sides together, the shock was devasting. Many could only see this as further proof that the Germans were unreliable and that peace could only come with the United States entry into the conflict.

In the first flush of disappointment, Wilson broke diplomatic relations with Germany and then, more reluctantly, with Austria. But after these moves he hesitated, still hoping to save his peace policy. Yet the slide to war seemed irresistible. Wilson had said that America would not go to war without overt warlike acts. They were slow in coming, but in mid March three ships with Americans aboard were ruthlessly sunk. The intercepted Zimmerman telegram heightened the war fever by revealing an attempt by Germany to enlist Mexico and Japan in an alliance that would open a southern front against the United States. The Mexicans were promised several American states in the Southwest as their reward. Although it was a wild scheme and would only be implemented in case of war, the fact that Germany would attempt to raise such hopes in Mexico seemed to confirm their perfidy, and it brought the importance of the war to the heart of the country. At the same time, Wilson's alternative to war, "armed neutrality," consisting largely of putting guns on freighters, did not interest other neutrals or appear workable. Finally, on March 20, a meeting showed Wilson's entire cabinet to be in favor of war, even those who had previously been considered pro-German. Irresistibly propelled, on April 2 Wilson asked Congress to bring the country into war, and within a month Wilson had become the apostle of a war to the finish, of a war to make the world "safe for democracy." The United States was to lose at least 100,000 men as a result of the war and more than twice that number were wounded. The results were a failed peace treaty that drove Europe into another war twenty years later and no direct gains for the United States. On the other hand, without the United States entry, the imminent but unsuspected collapse of the Russian armies might well have led to a British and French acceptance of modified German terms, a peace that would have had unforeseeable effects.

Devlin (1975) accepts Wilson's moral seriousness but is puzzled by the contradictions exhibited in his decision for war. Discussing several reasons for Wilson's decision, only to reject them, Devlin concludes that Wilson did not go to war because he thought Germany was in the wrong, or for economic and financial interests, or to vindicate the rights of neutrals. In part, he went to war both to maintain national dignity and to avoid the appearance of personal error or cowardice. But in the end, Devlin rejects these as major causes and declares that the primary reason for Wilson's declaration of war was the "conviction that an order of things erected on a German victory would not be safe for America or the world" (Devlin, p. 674). This conviction was acceptable to the nation because it encompassed both the idealist argument that emphasized Germany's threat to the peace and justice that Wilson hoped to bring to the world (and therefore to the United States) and the realist argument that saw Germany as an aggressor that ultimately would threaten the integrity of the United States.

It is significant that Wilson and his Secretaries of State, Lansing and Bryan, were idealists. Wilson himself did not see a direct danger to the United States, indeed, he was fully aware of the greater dangers to the country from the death, destruction, and moral callousness that would result from American involvement in the war. But when his attempt to achieve peace fell apart because of Allied disinterest and the German return to all-out war, Wilson saw the only hope for a better world to be in United States participation in the war on the Allied side, so that through its domination of the peace conference, a stable peace might be constructed (Devlin, pp. 679–680). However, in Devlin's opinion, the average American went to war because he had concluded or had been led to believe that Germany was an evil nation whose victory would present a clear danger.

Wilson meant his words when, at the high point of American idealism, he announced:

But the right is more precious than peace, and we shall fight for the things which we have always carried nearest our hearts—for democracy, for the right of those who submit to authority to have a voice in their own governments, for the rights and liberties of small nations, for a universal dominion of right by such a concert of free peoples as shall bring peace and safety to all nations and make the world itself at last free. To such a task we can dedicate our lives and our fortunes, everything that we are and everything that we have, with the pride of those who know that the day has come when America is privileged to spend her blood and her might for the principles that gave her birth and happiness and the peace which she has treasured. God helping her, she can do no other. [Devlin, 1975, pp. 687–688]

Wilson expended American blood in a war that unfortunately was fought on the false premises that Germany was both a criminal nation and a direct threat to the United States.[1]

In turning to a humanistic evaluation of Wilson's decision, we must understand something of the traditional moral doctrine of the *just war*. The doctrine asks us to examine the acceptability of both means and ends, but we shall be concerned here primarily with ends. The just war may be fought for any good purpose if there is a probable proportionality between the expected costs of the war to all concerned and the benefits expected to come from it. Some now believe a just war is limited to self-defense, in which there is a reasonable chance of victory by the defending country. Self-defense also includes a right of collective self-defense, or coming to the defense of a nation whose independence is threatened (Osgood and Tucker, 1967). In modern terms, we might say that since it is distributionally unfair for one people to force their rule on another, any proportional or reasonable response to attempts at conquest are justified. As such, the just-war doctrine offers a basis for balancing the claims of all of those potentially involved, and especially those attacked, to reasonable shares of probable utilities. I would argue that there are exceptional circumstances in which a country can legitimately go to war for reasons other than self-defense, for example, as we might have in 1941 before Pearl Harbor. The attempt of a poor nation to achieve a more equitable share of the goods of the world through war might also be justified if there were no other means of redress, if the prewar distribution of goods had been brought about by grossly unfair means, and if the redress achieved by war would be of greater value than the expected costs of the war.

However, many wars, including Wilson's, have been fought for transcendent purposes. This is true, on the simplest level, because only a strong social extension going beyond the family group can motivate individuals to sacrifice their lives by accepting the role of a soldier.[2] This sacrifice of the individual for the group is the fundamental act in the morality of responsibility in Gehlen's (1969) terms. But Wilson went beyond this level of responsibility. His actions and statements lead us to conclude that he implicity believed that he, as the leader of the United States, had the right to send Americans off to die because it was in the interest of the world that American ideals triumph everywhere.

This raises the moral question of what a leader of a democratic polity has a right to do (for the institutional differences between democracies and other polities, see Chapter Three). Leaders are selected because the group needs a center of authority that will decide in the interests of the group, and it is with this reciprocal understanding that the responsible person accepts the commands of his leaders. The leader has no right in such a compact to be more universalistic than those he commands. It is their survival and their interests that he represents. In this sense, it is wrong for such commentators as Osgood and Tucker to be surprised that calculations of the costs of war seldom include the costs inflicted on the enemy (Osgood and Tucker, 1967, pp. 202–203). In his public acts, a leader should include these costs only to the extent that his people are also acutely concerned. If, as we assume, Wilson used Americans convinced of the realist argument of German danger to achieve his minority, idealist vision of American interests, he walked on questionable moral ground. Still, in a Nietzschean sense, this was a form of transcendence—transcendence of the small-minded, collective self-interest that he would normally have been expected to represent. (In the end, his reaching beyond destroyed him politically, and probably psychologically as well.)

Turning to the question of moral limits, by their nature wars overcome the interpersonal rule that "thou shalt not kill" by transforming individuals into tools of their societies. As tools, they kill and are killed (compare Osgood and Tucker, p. 241). The traditional

justification of this transformation of the meaning of life is an appeal
to necessity, and necessity implies that when one group has trans-
formed its members into tools and threatened the existence of another
group on this basis, there is no effective choice for that group but to do
likewise. When Germany attacked France in 1914, this was a sufficient
reason for conscription to be put before the French peasant. But
Wilson had no easy justification in these terms, and according to
Devlin (1975), he did not believe that America even indirectly had a
self-defense case for going to war.

It is important at this point that we reaffirm the distinction
between utilitarian and spiritual arguments. Certainly Wilson felt
that what he did was in the long-run interest of Americans. He looked
at the costs, projected the benefits, and declared war. But arguments
for war or peace are not always reducible to quantitative calculation
(Osgood and Tucker, p. 234). There are absolute norms, and the point
of an absolute is that it is affirmed even when in the specific case its
utility value is negative. If this were not so, homicide would not
always be a serious offense, for some murders are undoubtedly of positive utility to society. The world after a German victory might not
have looked as pleasant as a world dominated by England, but this
was a result Americans could have lived with; indeed, as history developed, it would perhaps have been preferable to the world produced by
Allied victory.

Idealists around Wilson, as well as many Englishmen,
thought America should have gone to war before 1917 for the sake of
democracy, for only democracy fit the spiritual nature of man, offered
what Rawls would call the "priority of liberty"—that absolute reverence for the individual that had been achieved in a few countries
since the eighteenth century. Hans Morgenthau echoed this argument in 1960 when he wrote that if the United States failed in its international purposes:

> *The nations of the world will look elsewhere for mod-*
> *els of social organization and political institutions to emu-*
> *late. . . . Alone in a hostile world, we would no longer be able*
> *to renew our sense of purpose through the experience of terri-*
> *torial expansion and universal emulation. At best, equality in*
> *freedom would still have a home in America. Yet, thus muti-*
> *lated, could the national purpose survive in America itself?*

> *And if it should not survive, could America survive without its purpose? [Osgood and Tucker, 1967, p. 272]*

This is a real concern; it might be real enough to justify the most distant war. But Wilson did not believe it, and indeed Devlin (1975) points out that Wilson continued to doubt the degree to which even Great Britain and France were democracies.

In fact, World War One was not a war between tyranny and democracy. One of the unfortunate blind spots in our understanding of our democratic system and its place in the world has been a continuing inability to concern ourselves with the "grays" of freedom, the possibilities that lie between absolute tyranny and pure democracy (for an attempt to remedy this deficiency, see Gastil, 1973c; 1977). Most countries fall in between, and it was inexcusable that the British and Americans continued to be unwilling to acknowledge the extent to which the rule of law and free institutions had developed in both Germany and Austria-Hungary by World War One. Although Devlin himself skirts the issue, his text indicated that during the war there was perhaps as much freedom in Germany as in England. Devlin (p. 557) writes of Karl Liebknecht:

> *[He] combined his activities as a socialist deputy at the furthest extremity of the left with underground pamphleteering under the name of Spartacus. He was notorious in the Reichstag for his interpellations: how many Belgian civilians had been shot, he would ask; and when would the government publish the foreign documents on the responsibility for the war.*

Liebknecht was arrested in 1916. But there still remained in parliament Independent Socialists, who continued to demand negotiations for a peace without victors or vanquished. Of course, the German parliament was not very powerful, but the fact that it functioned in this way during the war suggests more similarities between the contestants than differences, a reflection that in no way could have been made in an analysis of World War Two.

In terms of the overall destructiveness of the war, Wilson might have argued that by coming in when he did he would save lives, because only America could shorten the war. However, since these were not American lives he was saving, and he had distinctly less responsibility as President for non-Americans, this would not have been a strong argument. Moreover, with Russia's dropping out of the war, the Allies might well have collapsed before the end of 1917 without the material and spiritual lift of the United States entry. Such a collapse would have saved perhaps a million men that were still to die. But this calculation was not Wilson's, and it is easier done with hindsight.

The analysis may be completed by looking at Wilson's alternatives. Admittedly, alternatives were more available before 1917. Had Wilson developed his 1917 world consciousness by 1914, he might have brought the country into the war because of Germany's wanton attack on Belgium. Since this was one reason for British entry, United States entry at this point would have served to directly support a developing international understanding against aggression of this sort, and it would have been at least indirectly supported by the doctrine of collective defense. However, without the American people behind him, a declaration of war in 1914 would have been infeasible and as doubtful a moral act as his final decision in 1917.

A more agreeable alternative for most Americans might have been to respond directly to the German challenge at sea through the development of an aggressive and strong navy that could break both English and German blockades. This would have given us a role in the subsequent establishment of peace without the great loss of lives suffered by our subsequent expeditionary force. Even in 1917 this remained an alternative, although our naval forces were inadequate. In any event, Wilson did not seem to have the imagination to develop what would have been a truly aggressive neutrality.

To sum up, Wilson brought the country into World War One through an act of social extension that transcended previous definitions of the role of a national leader in a democracy. In terms of his purpose—the construction of a world order that would guarantee peace and democracy—there was certainly a proportionality between expected losses and expected gains if we accept the transformation of people into tools of the state in times of war. Wilson's vision was one of internal and international justice. However, in pursuing his vision, Wilson probably went beyond the understanding of his people concerning the conditions under which they would sacrifice themselves and others in war. Because Wilson identified his personal role with his role as leader, his transcendence broke a moral barrier, and this fact considerably tempers Devlin's (1975) enthusiasm for Wilson's creativity and courage. However, to come to a clearer understanding of Wilson's culpability, we must develop a firmer doctrine on the legitimate relation between moral limits, democratic leadership, social extension, and creative transcendence. This we leave to the future.

But we should not drop the issue of the relation of war to national necessity that has been raised by the discussion. Osgood and Tucker (1967) frequently point to the fact that men evidently regard the state they live in as an end in itself, deriving their self-worth in part from its existence. Placing an absolute value on the state makes it possible for the state to justify the revocation in war of the absolute requirement that men must be treated as ends in themselves. According to Devlin's account, it was the concept of the absolute value of the state, tied up with that of honor, that made Wilson's appeals to leaders of Germany, England, and France fall on deaf ears; even though in pursuit of the maintenance of the honor of their respective states, the warring leaders were sacrificing the lives of millions.

What is this patriotic value? It is neither simply utilitarian nor institutional. While nations may achieve material benefits through war, they very often fight without a reasonable hope of recompensing their losses through victory or even a belief that defeat would result in greater losses than continued war. Neither is the state an absolute value, because only some form of state is required to preserve the protective shell within which civilized life exists. Even a conquering state will soon provide a state shell for the vanquished. Evidently, then, the state becomes an absolute because states are invested with mystical significance, with which many of their subjects identify their past and future. In this sense, the state is a transcendent or holy object for which men may reasonably fight and die. The Japanese soldier of World War Two was only more explicit than most in this identification, and his death in war was justly regarded as a most transcendent act, albeit on a different level of social extension than that vicariously attempted by Wilson.

We may abhor the spiritual transcendence achieved by persons in a nation at war, but we cannot deny its moral significance. Neither

will it be sufficient to try to talk men out of such antimaterialism. A
preferable approach would be to enclose the human capability to sacrifice self for ideals within absolute moral limits of what man may
permit himself to do in a balanced life, placing the most severe limits
on the conditions of recourse to war, especially as these involve the
lives of others, and on the means threatened or employed in war, once
it is begun.

Rejecting Assured Destruction as the Basis of Strategic Deterrence

The other side of the war issue is the manner in which war once
begun may be legitimately fought. The question of limits in war has
been most severely forced on us by the invention and large-scale production of nuclear weapons. Since the 1950s, most of our leaders have
been satisfied with the doctrine that the use of these weapons is to
deter through massive threat. But is the threatened use of nuclear
weapons as a last resort against opponent cities an acceptable national posture? This remains a critical problem for our generation.

Before we analyze this issue in depth, let us be sure where we
are. Since the 1950s, our doctrine on nuclear war has been both unreliable and unclear, in part for rationally acceptable reasons (compare
Rosencrance, 1975). At times, United States leaders have spoken as if
we would launch nuclear weapons against Soviet cities if the U.S.S.R.
attacked anywhere along the line. At other times, we have spoken of
confining our objectives in nuclear war to attacks on opponent weapons, to the use of tactical nuclear weapons, or to second-strike
responses. Indeed, complex new lines or weaponry have been introduced to make these alternatives possible. However, again and again
we have come back to the position that it is America's ability to
destroy the opponent's society that must be maintained. This is our
so-called *retaliatory* capacity, or *assured destruction* capability, and
is what leaders most often mean when they speak of "the deterrent."
Its strength is generally calculated be reference to the millions of
Soviet citizens that we can hold hostage after a Soviet first strike
against our forces. Our Polaris and now Trident submarine forces
have been developed primarily for this assured destruction mission
because of their relative invulnerability. The goal of *mutual assured
destruction* (MAD), which makes it irrational for either the United

States or the U.S.S.R. to strike first, is favored by most of those concerned with stopping the arms race or reducing budgets. This is, indeed, the "balance of terror."

In this section, then, the social unit is the United States (although our NATO allies might be equally included), and the problem is the acceptability of basing our security on the deterrent intention implied by the doctrine of assured destruction.

Wars have generally been fought with certain rules. In part, this was because wars have often had a gamelike aspect. Games without rules are nonsense, and games ending in unlimited destruction would defeat even the victors. For the leaders of nations at war, long-term outcomes are never predictable, and it is in the interest of all leaders to follow rules that place a limit on the extent of their losses in case of defeat. Therefore, only exceptionally confident leaders or those from foreign civilizations are apt to ignore accepted constraints. In part, wars have been fought within rules because they are always fought in a state of tension between the demands of personal morality that would make them impossible and the offensive or defensive "necessities" that make them societally acceptable. Rules codify this compromise. As pointed out in the last section, one codification of the rules is the Christian just-war doctrine, which echoes in international agreements and national laws covering legitimate behavior in war (Osgood and Tucker, 1967; Ramsey, 1968).

Reviewing the record of war, it is important to counter the widely held belief that typically no holds are barred in war, that combatants simply do anything they feel like while making hypocritical comments on the "crimes" of opponents. As Devlin (1975) records, the American movement into World War One was strongly conditioned by the extent to which one side or the other broke the rules in regard to both neutrals and opponents. World War Two ended with fires in Dresden and Tokyo and with nuclear explosions. Yet as Quester (1966) points out in a careful study of the escalation of violence to this level, raids of this kind became possible only after a steady breakdown of the fairly high standards of avoiding direct countercivilian attacks earlier in the war. Public discussion of the My Lai tragedy showed the lack of appreciation of these rules by the American people, but it demonstrated how seriously many of the people at the front took the rules. Reading over the early exposés of the event shows that neither the Americans nor Vietnamese involved saw the behavior of Captain Medina's men as a "just part of war" (see Hammer, 1970).

The rule observed most often in modern war is that attacks shall be against military targets. However, this rule was explicitly renounced by the British early in World War Two when they found no other way to carry the war to Germany than by high altitude, inaccurate night air raids (Quester, 1966; Frankland, 1970).[3] This rule continued to be acknowledged by Americans; unfortunately, by the time of Hiroshima, the allies had become accustomed to considering whole cities as military targets in spite of the large number of civilians involved (Batchelder, 1961). The residual assumption that military actions must be against military targets soon changed to a more realistic but ultimately more dangerous one. For a few years after World War Two, nuclear weapons continued to be seen as simply very large bombs for use in war. But soon the Soviets obtained nuclear weapons as well, and then fission weapons were replaced by the even more powerful hydrogen bombs. As a result, it came to be widely believed in the 1950s that a war between two well-armed nuclear powers would be too destructive to achieve any goals that the combatants might have. This judgment was made, in part, because atomic bombs had been used against cities at the end of a war in which cities had come to be defined as military targets. Therefore, even with military targeting, a future nuclear war was seen as directed against the urban societies of the combatants. With these assumptions, a large war would inevitably destroy both sides.

If this belief was justified, it meant that neither the United States nor the U.S.S.R. possessed nuclear weapons for actual use in war, but only to threaten opponents with annihilation if war broke out. They were deterrent rather than war-fighting weapons. In the minds of the strategists, this meant that they were to be used to punish an opponent for breaking the peace, or in the later revision, to punish the opponent for using nuclear weapons against us. The strategists spoke of "tit-for-tat" responses; we would "exchange cities," destroying his only to the extent that the opponent destroyed ours. There were efforts to escape this view of deterrence by shifting targeting to enemy weapons instead of cities and the development of defense, including civilian defense. (This was the point of view argued most eloquently by Kahn, 1961.) But today it remains the prevailing view that, in the last analysis, nuclear weapons are an apocalyptic deterrent threat against populations. (It is no accident that since this approach is also one that saves money, it appeals to politicians from the far right to the far left.)

Scientifically, the calculation of behavior that makes sense of the deterrent approach rests on the model of enlightened self-interest we have used to develop our model of man, and on the idea that bureaucratic rulers will play their roles with due caution. Indeed, as the experience of the last few years has shown, most leaders, most of the time, will keep their countries very far indeed from nuclear war because of its possible costs. But there are countervailing facts. In Chapter Three, we criticized Allison's (1971) suggestion of the importance in decision-making of personal or bureaucratic interests, but to the extent lower levels of organizational interest can determine crisis responses, the rational extrapolation of deterrent strategy becomes less reliable. More important, we must not forget the footnotes that go with the model. On the one hand, these footnotes might cause us to increase our reliance on rational deterrence theory. The prudent leader, knowing how much can go wrong in war, will be most reluctant to risk nuclear war, even if the calculations of his experts show an expected gain. On the other hand, there are footnotes that should reduce our reliance on deterrence. History shows that nations sometimes slip into war when they are least expecting it, and events often outrun rational decision, as they surely did at the beginning of World War One. Occasionally, moreover, irrational individuals or factions achieve so much power in a state that they cannot be controlled by men of reason.

Therefore, it is not morally irrelevant that the United States and its allies persist year after year with a declared policy of retaliation that would incinerate tens of millions of noncombatants if our bluff was ever called. We can claim that rationally United States leaders would not follow their declared policy in a nuclear war. Indeed, in discussing the recent arms control talks (SALT), a commentator writes:

> *In pressing to limit* ABM's *and accepting a hold on its biggest missiles, the Soviet Union may be a convert to the macabre doctrine of assured destruction, even though there is no equivalent Soviet term, not yet anyway. What needs next to be said is that nuclear-force planning is one thing, nuclear-*

war planning quite another. Assured destruction is really
just a tool for modeling forces and isolating the heresy of out-
right nuclear superiority. America's strategic forces are built
around a capability to destroy some given part of Soviet urban
society and industry; yet perhaps the most intriguing of the
ironies of SALT—certainly the most reassuring—is that while
assured destruction appears to have become the solemn
dogma of strategy, it is unthinkable that (short of a massive
nuclear attack) an American president actually would retali-
ate instantly against the aggressor's cities, thereby inviting the
destruction of his own. And there is no reason to assume that
Soviet leadership is less rational on this point than American.
Like most of what passes for strategic doctrine in the nuclear
age, assured destruction is an abstraction, not reality. Reality
lies closer to the endless scenarios devised by planners, in
which the accidental or limited use of nuclear weapons
against the United States (or Western Europe) would presum-
ably be met with a selective and limited response that would
seek to avoid population centers and rapid escalation. [New-
house, 1973, pp. 266-267]

I am not entirely reassured. The general populace and thousands of military commanders have been taught that assured destruction is what the forces are for, although the phrase "to destroy some
given part of Soviet urban society and industry" euphemistically
masks the destruction they are intending. America and its allies have
not developed the civil defense or ABM capabilities that are appropriate for limited wars (see Holst and Schneider, 1969; Knorr and Read,
1962). Those "endless scenarios" may not work, and to rely on them
to cushion our consciences is an intellectual evil only too common
today. Crisis anxiety leads to tunnel vision and a dangerous polariza-
tion of judgment. For example, it has been suggested that the Kaiser
entered World War One even though he thought the outcome would
be disastrous for Germany; fear and hostility had become so great
that only war could relieve the strain.[4] Under some conditions, the
strain of a nuclear crisis or attack is likely to lead to a narrowing of
view, especially if decision times are short and the fact that we are
being selective is not clear, or clear soon enough to opponents. There
is certainly a wealth of social psychological evidence on the effects of
anxiety and frustration on rational behavior (Stegner, 1965).
    Turning to the humanistic evulation, let us consider a recent

formulation of the just-war doctrine (Purtill, 1975). In addition to the requirement that it be a defensive war, Purtill gives six additional conditions: (1) A just war must be legally declared; (2) defense must be limited to repelling the attack and achieving a just peace; (3) there must be reasonable hope for success; (4) war must be a last resort; (5) the good expected to come from the war must outweigh the evil; and (6) no immoral acts are likely to be necessary in carrying out the war. In this last category, just-war theorists particularly consider as immoral the avoidable killing of innocent persons. Unfortunately, executing the deterrent threat violates this condition, and is likely to violate the second, third, and fifth conditions as well.

It might appear that if the last condition (6) was rigorously applied, most war would be condemned. Because just-war theorists do not reach this conclusion, some of their critics assert that the just-war doctrine is useless, at least when applied to modern conditions (for example, Wells, 1975). However, since we cannot ignore the existence of intergroup violence, it is important to try to contain it as much as possible within a framework of limits. To do this, the just-war theorist, faced with unavoidable civilian death in war, evokes the principle of *double effect*. According to this principle, a noncombatant cannot justly be targeted directly, but he may be harmed justly if this is a secondary effect of a purely military action. Traditionally, if a city was defended by military forces it might be shelled, but not if it was abandoned and declared an open city (as Paris was in World War Two). As a result of this line of thought, United States leaders apparently thought of Hiroshima as a military target, with the civilian casualties secondary. We can regard this as a monstrous piece of hypocrisy or self-deception, but it is important to note that it was morally distinct from the more recent postnuclear intention to hold hostage tens of millions of an opponent's population. Attacking cities in a nuclear war to kill hostages is a clear violation of the just-war doctrine. However, such attacks would not necessarily violate military law and custom, where retaliation and "necessity" figure more prominently (Osgood and Tucker, 1967, pp. 320–321). Indeed, reprisal is essential to the structure of military custom, because it is the final sanction against rule breaking by an opponent.

Those who view the just-war doctrine as little more than an elaborate justification for immorality fail to distinguish between the moral rules that govern interpersonal behavior and those that govern the behavior between individuals serving the impersonal purposes of groups. The "rule books" of humanity, such as the Ten Commandments, were meant to apply to individuals treated as human beings and not as social tools. When a human being becomes a tool directly used by another person or society in a self-defense situation, then he is killed when and as he operates as a tool.

A flagrant and yet almost universal mistake of the ethicist is to imagine that war can be seen in interpersonal terms. For example, Nagel (1974) justifies the distinction of combatants and noncombatants on the basis of hypothetical personal relationships, in which one can rationally explain to a combatant but not to a noncombatant why he is being attacked.[5] One can, in Nagel's view, bayonet an opponent on the line because one could satisfactorily explain to him that, "It's either you or me." However, this is to misapply personal standards to the behavior appropriate to the role of soldier. Indeed, if it were only a personal matter, the soldier would have every right to decide to be a pacifist and let himself be killed. Neither is the question of guilt and innocence relevant to most situations in which persons are killed in war (see Fullinwider, 1975).[6] A soldier bayonets another because both are acting as tools of opposing groups or whole societies. The crucial act of the soldier is putting himself in the service of his society and thus accepting the need to kill when necessary to obtain his society's goals. Killing is part of a soldier's role only because there is often no alternate way to fulfill the role.

But if persons on the other side are not tools in a direct sense (for example, the people of Kiev would not be tools in this sense in a war between the United States and the U.S.S.R.), then they can never be the objects of attack. They remain individual human beings to which the morality of peacetime, of guilt and innocence, or of personal self-defense applies. (Distance and large numbers do not depersonalize the citizens of Kiev morally, although unfortunately they do psychologically.) In general, mistreatment of prisoners can also never be justified by the laws of war, for once they are prisoners, persons no longer operate as effective tools of the other side.

If we accept the concept of a different morality for wars in which some people must be treated as tools, then we may wish to choose between the two bodies of thought that have been developed to prevent the breakdown of limits: the just-war doctrine and the laws of war. Many, including the political scientists Osgood and Tucker (1967), object to the attempt to resurrect the just-war doctrine. They believe it is unrealistic and that the advances in the control of war in the last two centuries have come primarily through refining the laws of war. However, it seems to me that the reliance on these laws, based ultimately on reciprocal response, puts an insufficient intellectual brake on the escalation to all-out nuclear war, which has become the nightmare of our generation. We must adopt a doctrine that cuts off the Armageddon scenario, or that at least gives us a firm intellectual basis to block its development. We must fortify the intuition that certain kinds of actions are simply not justifiable, and laws of war constructed on the principle of reprisal cannot offer such an insurmountable intellectual barrier.

The current revivification of the just-war doctrine is to a significant extent due to the work of the theologian Ramsey (1968). In developing his analysis, he correctly believes that the first problem of humanistic or ethical judgment is to convince the potential actors that there can be moral limits, that the issue is not simply one of tooth and claw. He believes that the tendency to exclude war from the moral universe and thus to leave no boundaries around it except quantitative cost/benefit analysis is typically American, especially civilian American, and it is his job to educate us to the many hard choices required by responsible morality. Not believing in an imminent millenium, Ramsey believes that political action will always involve the controlled use of force, the use of the lesser evil to avoid the greater.

Against this background, Ramsey emphasizes in his interpretation of the just-war doctrine the distinction between intending civilian death and its occurrence as a side effect. In these terms, Ramsey rejects the countercity deterrent as clearly immoral. He compares such deterrence to an attempt to prevent auto accidents by strapping babies to the front bumpers of automobiles. No matter how successful and no matter how many babies would be indirectly saved by the practice, the means would simply be wrong. Ramsey finds it more difficult to reject the argument that we might say we will retaliate against attack by wiping out enemy cities without intending to do so. But he generally rejects this view, partly on the practical ground derived from Kahn (1961) that the lack of intention would show through. I would also point to the evil training that such a position would give to the world, including many Americans who would not be aware of the moral intention behind the deterrent bluff.

In these terms, Ramsey develops a strategic option that would emphasize conventional force, counterforce attacks, and no first use of nuclear weapons except over one's own territory. He rejects in this approach even consciously holding in mind the idea that in extreme instances after enemy attacks on our cities, we would destroy enemy cities. But Ramsey adds that the very existence of nuclear weapons involves the possibility of city retaliation and that this would constitute a useful deterrent even if we publicly disavowed an intention to make such an attack. He also points to the fact that there would be great destruction in any nuclear war and that this fact should be sufficiently deterring, even if we abandon the countervalue option of attacking enemy cities. Of course, by qualifying his position on deterrence, Ramsey has opened himself to the criticism of sophistry.

Hypothetical Solution and Reexamination

The beginning of wisdom is to achieve an acceptable balance between the utility calculation that led to deterrence in the first place and the absolute limits of the just-war doctrine. This is the distinction between the absolutism and utilitarianism of Nagel (1974)—between looking at expected outcomes and looking at acceptable means to the outcomes. The shift toward emphasizing limits and reverence for human life—wherever we can grant it this meaning—would mean an absolute decision never to target populations and never to use weapons where the expected effect against civilians is out of proportion to military effects. This might mean, for example, never using nuclear weapons larger then 5 kilotons (about half the power of the Nagasaki bomb) in populated areas, and then only when there is a clear and significant military advantage in such use.[7] The attempt to preserve double-effect limits for larger weapons in population centers is too perilous and encourages leaders to the self-justification that destroyed Hiroshima and Nagasaki.

The practical problems of maintaining these limits were not overwhelming when the United States had a great lead in nuclear firepower over the Soviets. Instead of deterrent forces, we could have seen our forces as essentially counterforce, strengthened by a developing support of active and passive defenses. One of the arguments that blocked that choice was that it would cause the Soviets to launch us into a never-ending arms race. However, the Soviets still continued the arms race; they now have forces more powerful than ours, and the margin seems to be getting even greater (see Nitze, 1976; Iklé, 1973). We seem increasingly forced into the position of saying that we will maintain an assured destruction (that is, countercity) capability, no matter how much the Russians try for supremacy. But since our humanistic evaluation rejects this choice, we should seek an alternative strategy.

This begins, like Ramsey's, by emphasizing nonnuclear war. In fact, since Nagasaki there has only been conventional war, even though we have gone through periods of nuclear monopoly or near monopoly. China successfully stands up to the U.S.S.R. with a small nuclear force. We do not yet know how the Kremlin will operate against the United States and its allies if it attains clear strategic superiority—a superiority that would give it a reasonable probability of destroying 90 percent of our nuclear capability on a first strike while holding considerable force in reserve. However, it is not unreasonably optimistic to hope that the Soviets do not engage in such an attack or even seriously threaten it, because of the unforeseeable dangers such a war might create. In this view, it is the conventional balance at points of tension (such as Cuba, Angola, the Middle East, and Korea) that is decisive and not nuclear potential, especially in the absence of nuclear monopoly.

In regard to nuclear war, the United States should accept the stance that we will never hold hostage the civilians of another power or attack them in retaliation. The declared and operational objective of our forces at all times shall be to repel or destroy opponent forces (tools), whether these be human or material, and that in any war we can be expected to persist in this purpose until our goals are achieved. To make more meaningful the distinction of combatants and noncombatants, we will strive for highly accurate, low-yield weapons. To reduce the necessity for rapid, careless response, we will continually improve force survivability and communication.

To make this posture more credible in peacetime and workable in wartime, we should emphasize civil defense, especially the ability to rapidly develop a civil-defense capability in crisis, and we should strive to renegotiate the anti-ABM treaty (see Gastil, 1969a, 1969b; Burns, 1970; Russett, 1974). Renegotiation can be achieved on three bases. First, the Soviets were sold the approach when our forces were superior. As they attain superiority, the argument that they have something to fear from our defenses will hardly be compelling. Second, as nuclear weapons proliferate, the chance that they will be used foolishly increases. The world, including the United States and the Soviet Union, must prepare for this danger. In addition, the relative ineffectiveness of modest defense expenditures against Soviet- or American-sized forces is balanced by the great effectiveness of these expenditures against the present and projected nuclear forces of other states. Third, since the anti-ABM treaty, technology has evolved and new approaches, such as the laser, may greatly increase the cost-effectiveness of defensive systems. Internally, active defense may be more saleable to those with deep suspicions of the Pentagon when the United States has clearly accepted parity or inferiority in its nuclear forces, for the United States is less likely to contribute to an arms race after we allow the Soviets an offensive lead.

In adopting this policy, we would essentially accept the principles of the just-war doctrine as summarized by Purtill (1975). Unfortunately, in a future engagement with a much stronger U.S.S.R., we might not be able to satisfy the criterion that there be reasonable hope of success. Therefore, for the purposes of deterrence, we should propound the doctrine of the value of hopeless struggle, even though in a really hopeless situation the struggle would, and probably should, be abandoned. We are again faced with Ramsey's countercity deterrence dilemma (discussed above) of claiming to have an intention that would be immoral to carry out. Yet in this case, the immorality is less disturbing. The results would generally be less calamitous, and fighting in a hopeless cause has a balancing element of transcendence that I do not find in countercity retaliation.

We are also justified in striving to strengthen deterrence by revising Purtill's principle of repelling attack. As we pointed out in the discussion of Wilson's policy, the just-war doctrine does not say that war can be used only in defense. The cause of justice can be served by armed intervention, and this right is only conditioned by the law of proportionality that requires that the costs to all be considered (particularly in the nuclear age; Ramsey, 1968). Neither justice nor utility nor moral limits require that war, once begun, simply be defensive. While it has been argued that World War Two should not have been fought to unconditional surrender (Kecskemeti, 1958; Iklé, 1971), this is open to question. In fact, unconditional surrender probably improved the subsequent lives of Germans, Italians, and Japanese, at least in noncommunist areas. If the claims are correct of dissidents such as Solzhenitsyn and Sakharov that the Soviet system is a danger to mankind, then if the Soviets did plunge the world into war, reestablishing the status quo in the U.S.S.R. should not be our preferred war aim unless other outcomes could only be achieved at an exorbitant cost. In order to avoid war, one form of deterrence we wish to maintain is the possibility that a war, once begun, leads to disaster for the leaders that began it. Communist leaders have traditionally feared disruption or revolution in their homelands, and this fear should never be allowed to leave them as long as they contemplate war.

As we run the alternative strategy I have suggested through the evaluation process, there is the nagging thought that it is not enough. The hardheaded will assert that if the Soviets faced a United States so weak willed as to renounce countercity deterrence, they would simply bluff us into eventual isolation and submission. On the other hand, the softheaded will say that the approach is merely a blind for justifying huge military forces, resulting in a continuing arms race and eventual war. Our analysis here and in Chapter Three suggests that this objection stems primarily from an overly optimistic view of the nature of international relations. However, the first objection remains worrisome, especially if we do not make the detailed and eventually costly effort required to increase the alternative's realism. Without being sure of the utility balance of alternatives, this alternative is a useful way to achieve a broader humanistic balance. Human life means to strive for something, to strive to overcome events rather than to succumb to them. In this field, only establishing the impermissibility of countercivilian targeting is likely to promote a sufficiently salient limit for a long-term human victory.

Notes

1. Methodologically, Devlin (1975) has given us a scientific description of the decision to declare war, albeit an idiographic (particularizing) description. Such an idiographic description is preferable to a nomothetic (generalizing) one when we have detailed situational evidence, such as Devlin

provides. It would add little to refer to the fact that Wilson could not find an overlap between what he was willing to exchange or get the Allies to exchange and what the Germans were willing to offer until he turned to the ultimate exchange of bads in war, at which point, since he had more to offer, he achieved the major bargain of the armistice. Nomothetic scientific descriptions help us imagine what would happen in a series of abstract or insufficiently known cases, but they add little to a particular case for which the details are available.

2.   By going to war, the individual makes this extension. Once at the front, he typically fights for his fellows, that is, the members of a new "family."

3.   The fact that the British were first to initiate this type of war is also discussed in Irving (1963, p. 26). The justification for this flagrant disregard of limits has been attempted on the basis that this war had to be won, and this was the only way to do it (Walzer, 1974b). However, there were other uses for the British bombers; indeed, observing the limits might have led to a more creative and successful interdiction strategy earlier than it finally developed.

4.   I am not asserting that there is not conflicting evidence on Germany's role in beginning the war. There were surely rational, calculated aspects to its entry (see Devlin, 1975, pp. 239–242). Nevertheless, the fact that a good case is often made for the essentially irrational nature of the process indicates that the irrational elements certainly played an important part. For a study of the Kaiser's decision, see Holsti and North (1965).

5.   In fact, Nagel (1974, p. 21) implicitly accepts the man/tool distinction when he writes in regard to the use of dumdum bullets, "It is not mere casuistry to claim that such weapons attack the men, not the soldiers."

6.   Mavrodes' (1975) conclusion that we should regard the noncombatant distinction as a pure convention, such as driving on the right, is, however, wrong. While it is a fact that almost any limit is better than no limit, it is not inconsequential where the limit is placed, nor are all limits equally defensible.

7.   The large missile or bomb had its primary rationale when it was greatly inaccurate. With accuracy steadily improving, this rationale is inapplicable for most targets (see Brown, 1976; Digby, 1975). If we took 10 kilotons as a standard size for a future force of high quality weapons, we could have 5,000 weapons with a total yield of 50 megatons. With high accuracy and survivability, such a force could destroy a sufficient number of targets without the lethal long-run environmental and areal effects of the present United States force, whose megatonnage is in the thousands. (For a fairly reassuring account of these effects, see National Research Council/National Academy of Sciences, 1975.) Of course, we may not influence the Soviets to follow suit, but reciprocity can only be one aspect of a defense policy.

NINE

Meaning and Responsibility: A Doctrine for Individual Life

The Question of Meaning

Chapter One suggested that one of the areas of concern for study in social humanities should be the meaning of life. It also suggested that social humanities was particularly well adapted to deal with this, since as an integrative discipline it made possible an intellectual framework in which the pieces of our scattered intellectual life might be reassembled. In this chapter, we will at least begin to fulfill this promise. For this purpose, the social unit is the individual person and the problem is the difficulty this person has in finding purpose or meaning in his life when he has become fully conscious—a full consciousness that in the atomizing, anomic world of today is perhaps more common than ever before. Since the unit of analysis is the individual person, which was the subject of Chapter Two, we need not repeat the scientific basis for the analysis here. Moreover, meaning in life will be found primarily through humanistic analysis and in the interaction of humanistic concerns with biosocial reality, for science by itself does not address the question of human meaning.

The reader may object that I overemphasize the problem of meaning, that in fact most people live quite well with an implicit, intuitive understanding of the human condition. I doubt it. Most people seem to me to live "lives of quiet desperation," although this fact may be hidden most of the time, even from themselves. It is true that suicide remains relatively rare. But suicide is rare because of a biologically implanted and culturally sustained fear of death, reinforced by fear of pain as well as by the almost universal cultural proscription of suicide. A review of literature and religion suggests that the problem of meaning is hardly new. Indeed, religions have served both as attempts to provide answers to those who question life and as bulwarks against asking these question. Yet, so often they failed. In a world of fanatical Muslims, Omar Khayyam's eleventh-century poetry is replete with lines such as, "We leave reluctantly and still don't know / the purpose of our arrival, our stay, or our departure." However, Khayyam was an isolated astronomer in an age of faith. Perhaps only in recent years has there been both enough time to reflect on the generality of opinion makers and a sufficient decay of tradition for Khayyam's obsession to take root in the population at large.

Today, the question of the meaning of life is central to religious discussion but ignored by most professional philosophers. The reason is that only religions even attempt to offer answers to the most critical questions of meaning: the why of the universe and the apparent negation of life by death. Only on a religious basis may we say that the universe exists for the glory of God and thereby infer that the individual participates in this purpose. Only on a religious basis are we apt to accept the hypothesis of a life after death. However, belief in the reassuring dogmas of religion requires an abdication of independence of action and mind that is unlikely to be acceptable to those who consciously struggle with questions of meaning in our age.

One contemporary philosopher that has productively grappled with the question of meaning is Britton (1969). He argues that the question of the meaning of life is a practical rather than theoretical question. Since, in common with other practical questions, we need answers to get on with life, the answers are apt to require commitment to doubtful propositions, just as is true of all practical knowledge. Yet Britton would surely agree that meaning is such a serious lifelong question that the need to participate in daily life is not enough to induce the thinking individual to accept easy answers.

From his practical perspective, Britton identifies four characteristics we must see in life for it to be meaningful. First, we must have some degree of free will, the assumption we provisionally incorporated in our description of man in Chapter Two. Second, the person's life must be capable of mattering, at least to the person himself. Third, the person's life must be capable of mattering to others. Indeed, an apparent lack of meaning to others is basic to the problem of suicide. Finally, a life must be thought to matter insofar as it consists of a particular pattern of events that the individual then comes to accept. This includes the patterning of preindustrial ways of life that, as we pointed out in Chapter Seven, we have no right to destroy in the name of progress.

These are certainly characteristics of meaning, yet the latter three remain formal categories into which we have to put content; only after we have done this will our free will become significant. We must now ask: In what terms do we develop the sense in which I matter to myself, or I matter to you and you to me? And after the preindustrial patterns of life are shattered, in what way do we try to evaluate or affect our pattern of life so that it may again come to have meaning? At times, Britton deals with the concept of meaning as though we were indifferent to whether the meaning found was positive or negative. But the search must be for a positive meaning in life; a negative meaning is surely as enervating as no meaning at all.

Implicitly, Chapters Two through Five asserted that life takes on a positive meaning insofar as we strive to live in the light of an ego ideal. Since only humans have the ability to reflect upon their actions, only humans can imagine free will and act as though they controlled their lives. Therefore, there is at least intuitive sense in maximizing the degree to which we live reflexively in terms of apparent freedom.

The preferred content of the ego ideal was sketched in Chapters Four and Five in terms of a framework for humanistic evaluation. Looked at from the vantage point of self-judgment, individuals live by the framework insofar as they strive to balance pleasure, respect, achievement, and reverence responsibly. *Responsibility* is the basic transcendent commitment to care about the rightness of one's actions, particularly by a social extension into ethical action. The responsible man does not deny human self-interest in himself or those he serves, but he balances these interests against other standards. The responsible individual is one who takes account of the short- and long-term consequence of actions for himself and others; in the absence of other criteria, it is the preservation of a favorable pleasure-to-pain balance that he must think through. *Respect* for the rights of others is the key component of the pursuit of justice, for it means that the interests of others as they perceive them are respectfully taken into account. A second goal, then, is to improve access to goods (or utilities) in those terms that other individuals and groups actually desire. Likewise, respect means to accept the choice of a lack of effort as well as effort and to help fashion a world that reasonably rewards each individual's choice. Respect for others is an agapeic love of others that grants them their due regardless of how much one may like or dislike them.

Reverence is a spiritual attitude that sets aside certain values and actions (or inactions) as values in themselves, and thus as values that are not exchangeable for other ends. It preserves a distinction between the sacred and the profane. Negatively considered, one may live because of either responsibility or reverence. If he lives out of a sense of responsibility, he judges that the loss to the group to which he has extended his moral identity would be greater by his death than by his presence. If he lives out of reverence, it is because in his system of values or belief, reverence for human life defines suicide as an impossible choice. Thus, life becomes a moral endurance contest, with every day a meaningful affirmation of the faith.

The first aspect of meaning is, in sum, to strive to be a moral person within the framework. But this is too pallid. The second aspect of meaning is to see one's life as part of an endless biological chain, a chain that has produced wonders, including mankind, and a chain that continues to produce wonders. This may be seen as a collective biological continuity, so that by contributing to the eternity of the group, even the childless contribute to the biological chain. This can be raised to a third aspect of meaning by seeing our lives as part of a chain of civilizational growth, of a growth of knowledge, structures, and symbolic systems that make the possibilities of each new generation greater than the last. As pointed out in Chapter Four, the study of history is itself an important form of transcendence in search of a limited immortality. This aspect can also be seen in chains of continuity for subcivilizations (specific cultural traditions), which an individual may inherit, develop, and pass on to the next generation. While in past ages many cultures may have disappeared without a trace, the net of worldwide intercommunication is so great today that seldom is anything lost. Each of us influences others and they in turn affect others, producing a widening circle of ripples that will continue as long as humanity persists, and will persist perhaps even beyond that in the form of the artifacts we leave behind. The fourth aspect of meaning in life comes from the drive for experience, the freewheeling, generalized interest of human beings in keeping the machines of perception, cognition, memory, and physical movement operating, even if minimally. Emphasizing the direct personal utility of a life devoted to pleasure, this is the opposite of meaning through pattern. Sometimes this effort is reinforced by a drive to achieve, but just as often the interest is passive. If so, one can forgo participation and merely observe with little change in meaning, for the essential experience of human beings is within their minds.

To those who center on events, life is the sum of past memories, present experiences, and future anticipations. Life is bearable for some because they are so involved in events that they do not ask questions. But this is a fragile, unthinking understanding, one that becomes ever more impossible with advancing age. To others, life is bearable because there is always something about to happen that the person does not want to miss out on, be it another installment of a television series or a daughter's first child. Still more passive is the old person's willingness to see events primarily in retrospect, to see life primarily as an opportunity to remember past experiences. Of course, events may be so negatively valued that a life lived through events has meaning without purpose, but usually sheer curiosity makes us want to live to see how things unfold, even when the ending seems unlikely to be pleasant.

As mentioned before, an event-centered life will have more intense meaning if it is more than a simple exercising of human machinery—if it includes an aspect of achievement or transcendence. Achievement may be in the sense of self-achievement, group achievement, or even the achievement of mankind as a whole, insofar as a person can sustain such a heroic social extension. Most intense is the life that finds meaning in personal achievement. Yet too often the achieving personality continually competes with others, with him-

self, and in relation to an exalted ego ideal of what real achievement
would be. In such a life, the achievements of the day may be so dises-
teemed that the significance is drained from what others would judge
to be a successful life.

The question of the meaning of life contains two questions:
What is the meaning of human life in general, and what is the meaning of my particular life now and in the foreseeable future? A suicide
does not necessarily lack good answers to the first question. But in
attempting suicide, one is saying that he sees no satisfying answer to
the second. Apparently, he is far from living up to his own ego ideal
and the events he anticipates are not pleasant (the expected pain out-
weighs the expected pleasure from anticipations). One may also commit suicide because he sees no good answer to the riddle of existence.
But I doubt if this is common.

The problem as Koestler (1967) expressed it in the *Ghost in the
Machine* is simply that man has developed a mental ability that goes
far beyond what is needed for survival, an ability that allows for reflection, and this inevitably allows the question of meaning to arise. The
problem is acute because this mental ability developed in a biologically limited body granted only a few short years on earth. Man was
created a god, but at the moment of conception his immortality was
stripped from him. If we were immortal, we might still ask why we
exist and rebel against the endless repetitions of life. Yet illogical as
it may seem, given our mortality, when we ask for the meaning of life,
we are often asking why we have to die. The question of meaning has
become a code question for a complaint that the life of events eventually runs out. Britton (1969) suggests that there may be no real happiness possible once we are conscious of death. Ionesco wrote of the terrible burden that life became once he fully realized its finiteness, once
tomorrow was already the past. He was interested in the meaning
of death, not the meaning of life. In this sense, the question strikes at
the core of the human condition.

In the framework of Chapter Four, we have emphasized the
centrality of transcendence; the daily transcendence of the question of
the meaning of life is no small achievement for the thinking person.
To Ulich (1955), the answer to the question of meaning is the transcendence of the human condition that is only possible through faith,
which is not in a system of dogma but simply in the existence of a

meaning, of a connectedness of things, that is irretrievably beyond human intelligence. This is the ultimate spirituality, for it requires both an act of will that transcends our biological ability and a sense of reverence that limits the degree to which we will use our intellect as the measure of the right of all things to existence.

Taking Responsibility

Let us then relate this discussion of meaning to the picture we developed earlier of biosocial man. All men are animals, and no matter how friendly they may be, animals are not moral creatures. Insofar as they have some touch of morality, it is a weak and fragile growth that needs to be tended closely and defended. In humility, human beings must not expect too much of themselves or others, nor imagine that they have come very far. In Chapter Two, we selected the self-interest model for man and his interactions because it has the closest fit to our common experience. In spite of countervailing tendencies, in most situations human beings act selfishly, often when they think they are acting with the greatest unselfishness; they are sometimes churlish and irrational, even in respect to their own limited rationality. With all this, man does have a moral aspiration and hope; he can possess a divine inspiration and act upon it. The fact that you are reading this chapter reflects that fact. If human beings focus on this sliver of humanity, they can accept themselves and others, and hope to make life a little better.

From this perspective, the significance of each life lies in its example as a moral work of art and its influence on the lives of others. Each person is influencing the quality of civilization for himself, those around him, and those who will come after him by the way he lives, the decisions he makes, the leaders he chooses, the heroes he praises. Each must ask himself whether from this point of view he is producing the civilization he would want. Following this course, there are many potential patterns that may form the basis for a meaningful life. To give one example of a set of abstract patterns that would be consistent with the approach to social humanities developed in this book, three principles for a responsible life are presented below.

Responsible Moral Judgment as Justice and Reverence. Mankind must strive to think in terms of higher orders of sanity than the barest minimum and try to establish the relation of sanity to responsibility. There is a form of moral inadequacy that stems from excessive rationalism that may be considered a form of insanity. In this type of individual, the normal instincts of selfishness are restrained only by the known dangers of getting into trouble. With no social extension, the interests of such a person in a transaction do not extend beyond the self. One suspects that morally inadequate people with low IQs are frequently in trouble with the law because their ability to project the consequences of their actions is relatively poor (see Di Palma and McClosky, 1970); morally inadequate persons with high IQs are responsible for a great deal of "white-collar crime" and, in the underworld, may easily plot the murders of others. The morally inadequate are not necessarily persons who have no sentimental emotions; they simply do not empathize with others, particularly others with whom they have no direct relation. They lack alter egos that we would recognize. In addition, they learn but do not internalize the usual inhibitions associated with interpersonal life in their cultural group. Selfish and uncivilized, they may copy any life style that suits their purpose; they therefore appear high flexible.

At the opposite extreme, the thoroughly responsible person strives to live as an example that would make possible the good of others in this and later generations. He forgives himself for not living up to this standard on occasion, but he does not exonerate himself. He lives with guilt not as an overbearing burden, but as proof of his aspiring humanity and as the basis upon which he forgives others. Since each of us is by necessity an example, and the best example most of us can offer the world is that of a responsible person, we can tolerate in society very few who are irresponsible as adults. Anyone not in a mental institution must be responsible for his life patterns, if not always for his specific acts.

Beyond his own community, each person has a responsibility for the human race, for its beliefs, ideals, pain, and happiness, and for its future. Converting this responsibility into meaningful actions is of course extremely difficult and beyond most of us. Charity, education, and missionary activity have so often failed to have the desired effects in retrospect, and even to have been worse than no help at all. Yet past failure does not absolve anyone from trying. It is a dangerous course to believe that others in difficulty or danger would be better off left alone, that their problems are not ours. When people died violently in Vietnam, Nigeria, and elsewhere in the 1960s, we knew that we were failing these people, even if we did not know the right course of action. We should carry this guilt without letting it overwhelm us, until that day when we or our descendants see how we might act more usefully to correct the numerous problems that afflict the world.

In passing, we should note the difference between criminal responsibility and the concept of personal responsibility that I have described. Personal responsibility looks outward to society, and criminal responsibility looks inward from society. An individual should be punished by the law only to the extent that this might deter potential criminals, prevent further crime by removing the individual from society, or make the law-abiding feel that their continued respect for the law was the best gamble. But legal punishment is more than utilitarian calculation. It is also a matter of fairness and justice; the teen-ager who does not steal a car and take a joy ride may feel it is unfair for the joy-rider not to suffer for his transgression, much as he feels that it is unfair for a fellow student to cheat successfully on an exam. On the other hand, the degree to which the individual is personally responsible may be suggested by a particular crime, but is hardly determined by it. Penalties serve the social purposes of the majority in a democracy, whether or not a particular individual deserves the penalty. Indeed, a personally responsible act may also be a criminal act (see Rawls, 1971, pp. 363–391). Like everything else, this interpretation can be carried too far. We are concerned here with the individual judging himself for his own purposes, and not with the way in which society might judge him.

If we are to live in a moral universe, and only a moral universe is meaningful, then we must be willing to accept evaluative moral categories such as good and evil. In part, social humanities is based on the idea that the medical-treatment analogy for dealing with social and personal problems is unacceptable, because it reduces human beings to biological machines. Of course, if we are to treat a person in a mental hospital, it would be better to call the person mentally ill than to call him evil. For the average politician or neighbor, however, moral evaluation of an individual is more appropriate, for we cannot hope to change his basic nature and are more likely to suffer from an interchange in which we do not understand the extent of his intractability. There is also the question of vocation: The job of the mental hospital is to treat patients, but that is not the job of the neighborhood. The issue is perhaps clearer if we consider Hitler. He was mentally ill by many definitions, yet politicians had to understand that importance must first be placed on opposing the evil he represented, with attention being directed to his possible illness secondarily.

A man may commit a terrible act in the heat of emotion or under longer-term psychological compulsions and still show by the general tenor of his life that he is a good person. In this case, the acts are evil, but not the person. An evil person may be morally inadequate and simply do whatever he can get away with, creating a moral framework in which he imagines that everyone is equally irresponsible. Such a man lacks social extension. Or an evil person is one who, like Hitler, has strong idealistic traits, but since his idealism is not checked by appropriate moral limits, he is a danger to all. Both of these types of evil persons corrupt society by their bad example and by their works. Both are the result of that dangerous combination of animal egoism and the rationality that only man can achieve. Such evil is the opposite of what is meant by *civilized*. Unfortunately, whenever inherited civilization becomes disorganized, these types of evil become more common.

Responsibility as justice and reverence involves respecting individuality, for individual human lives have meaning to those who live them primarily insofar as they are personally unique. Therefore, the responsible action of one man may not be that of another. Men are not equal, although for certain moral purposes we threat them as if they were. At the extremes, the preservation of those irremediably crippled by physical or mental debilities may seem foolish alongside the preventable day-to-day suffering of men who fully exhibit the characteristics and possibilities that we ordinarily associate with humanity. Yet moral limits must be drawn generously. To ignore the human rights of a man, no matter how limited a man, can too easily lead to the breakdown of belief in the sacred value of each individual, the belief that ultimately protects us all.

Leaving the problem of the extremes unresolved, we must nevertheless deal with the wide range of variations among "normal" individuals. Although there is always a physical aspect to human differences, the differences that are important to us morally are intellectual and emotional. One of the most intransigent problems in society is the difficulty in establishing successful, harmonious relationships between men of average intelligence and men of very high intelligence. Generally, successful leaders have been those with IQs only moderately above average; the best of these are able to mediate between the very intelligent and the masses. But too often the intellectual elite in its impatience and irritation, in its concentration on ideas rather than things and on abstract relations rather than human relations, rejects and denigrates society without adding much to it that is permanent. Its models of the good life are too often models for a minute few. Many of the elite become actively antidemocratic, while others lapse into an irascible negativism. Yet this elite remains primarily responsible for civilization, and the world must look to it to solve the problems of the future.

The relation of the very intelligent to ordinary men should be one of mutual respect, in which each is just to the claims of the other; but how can it be other than one of jealousy, impatience, and lack of communication? Making college education available to everyone is hardly an answer, for the superficially educated may be more irritating and even antiintellectual than the uneducated. As a result, real intellectuals often prefer to associate with primitive peoples or craftsmen rather than the mass of college graduates. Nevertheless, there is the danger that universal college education will allow intellectuals to exploit their easy handling of symbols to lead others to accept their own most recent ideological fantasy. Mutual respect between people with differing intellectual abilities must not come out of a false sense of mental equality, but out of a sense that each person is doing what he can to rise above day-to-day selfishness and to work in the interest of all. Each must genuinely try to understand the other and to recognize that the other has a right to pursue a good that he alone has a right to define. Good may consist of the attachment to what appear to be the oddest beliefs and practices, but each man has a right to his beliefs. In particular, the results of mass beliefs and practices must be dire indeed for the intellectual to believe he has a right to use his tools to bring them under control.

In extending transcendence into the area of justice, acting responsibly entails an element of conformity. For example, the penchant of surburbanites to criticize their neighbors who fail to mow the grass is often scorned. Yet if one moves to a suburb with neatly cut lawns what are his responsibilities? Let us imagine that after buying his house the new resident lets his lawn go to weed. His neighbor does not seem too happy with the result and occasionally makes suggestions about what should be done. The neighbor may be a narrow-minded fool, but the new neighbor knows that those around him like neat lawns, which run right up to his weeds, and what the standards of the neighborhood were before he moved in. It is his responsibility to do something about his lawn, even if he does not care about yard-work or the appearance of his neighbors' lawns, and even if he values weeds positively. This is not a matter of personal freedom, but of responsibility to neighbors. This may be a homely and irritating example, but it makes a point that many overlook. You should not only not do what you would not want done to you, but you should also avoid doing that which those around you would not want done to them. The same point is illustrated if the neighbor allows dogs to run free or dumps his clippings in an unused lot or on public land, and others do not like these actions. The most general principle, then, is that when we act or fail to act, our concern for justice demands that we take into account the feelings and interests of those around us.

There is no doubt as wide a range in emotional ability as in intelligence. It is only natural that when we meet another person we project onto him our capacities to feel and react. Although we know rationally that these vary widely by age and sex, and probably by race and culture, it is hard to do more than judge others by ourselves. If this were only a matter of lowering efficiency in the marketplace through jagged human interactions, there would be no moral issue. But in fact we are judging one another and ourselves in terms that may not be applicable or fair. Society sets up certain standards of behavior and expects conformity to those standards in spite of wide differences in human cost for the participants. Even if we look only at the normal range and not at the extremes, the problem is still severe. (In most situations, it is unnecessary to distinguish between those differences due to the training and experience of individuals and those differences that are genetic. When we meet a person, the origin of the difference is irrelevant, but what we do about it is central.)

We need to distinguish between the crimes of emotional strength and the crimes of moral weakness, between transcendent crimes and failures of personal control. A sensitive man may dodge induction into the army because of a deep, emotional aversion to killing, an inability to stand the emotional strain of taking orders from intellectual inferiors, or a simple unwillingness to accept responsibility. Cowardice as a reason for nonparticipation is an intermediate case between true pacifism and irresponsibility. We must be careful not to simply accept what the person says; irresponsibility is so often cloaked with noble-sounding reasons. A little knowledge of the pattern of the person's life will help: Persons who commit a crime on one occasion have infringed decisively on the rights of others, but morally their crimes leave their personalities much less worthy of disrespect than those of persons who pursue lives of crime.

The emotional range of man is indicated by the classification of some as *sane* and others as *insane*. The use of these categories will depend upon the situation and the needs of society. Here, however, we are concerned with how an individual thinks about himself and others along this dimension. Paradoxically, while irrationalities suggest tendencies toward insanity, as we pointed out in Chapter Two, in human terms the completely rational man is also suffering from a kind of insanity. If, on the other hand, a person consistently plays an accepted role in the world and is of little danger to others, he should be treated as sane. He may have the oddest ideas about what his role is, how the world is organized, and so on, but if he keeps these to himself, they are of little concern to others except when they indicate a possible future danger. We must remember that the feedback from experiences is different for each of us, because each of us perceives and remembers in very personal ways. In terms of the knowledge and experience that has filtered through the mind of an individual, his perceptions and actions may be quite rational, although judged irrational by others with different abilities to know the real situation. The insane person may have insights the sane world can use (which is not to say that he cannot profit even more from opening his mind to the outside world).

Responsibility in Conflicting Roles. Each of us has a personal and a public life; these are often expressed through two quite different personalities and require two quite different modes of social extension. It is quite difficult to be successful at both kinds of life; many of us would be more than pleased if either worked out. The transitions between the two occur nearly every day; they are apt to add to the stress of living, so that those who construct three or more lives instead of the conventional two find themselves in so many complex relationships that they may not be able to hold themselves together. There is nothing immoral in having more than one life form and set of reactions, as long as one strives to live each one responsibly. Needlessly complicating the situation may, however, deemphasize consideration of one's moral role, so that the individual falls back on just getting by instead of developing the human capacity for transcendence.

The most important role conflict in life is between personal and public roles, where *public* is defined as beyond the home or circle of close friends. The conflict of the relation of a person to his parent's family and to the new family he creates may be emotionally severe, but there is a rule generally accepted in our society: Regardless of deep sentiment, a person's responsibility is to the new family and its future. On the other hand, there is no generally accepted rule governing the public-to-private relationship. Each person must work it out himself. Most people see their private worlds as more understandable and important than their public. If there are mistakes made in the private world, they are immediately apparent and reacted to by important others; public mistakes are generally impersonal and shaded with grays. The danger for all of us is that by taking our private responsibilities seriously we will develop a public life based on daily patterns of immorality and minor omissions and frauds. Eventually, these patterns will be taken over by those around us, including our children, and finally absorbed into the tradition of society. Even if it seems that all we care about is the welfare of those closest to us, in the hope of preserving a world worth living in, we must give the outside world its due and responsibly serve society as well as our family.

Responsibility in Balancing Action (Utility and Transcendence) with Control (Justice and Moral Limits).   Our biological and cultural heritage and the love that our parents gave have provided us with capacities to sense, feel, and enjoy life in an endless variety of ways. Each person will value different ways, which will change at different periods of life. Sensual pleasures are the most vivid and exciting for most of us, and of these sexual pleasure is most intense. Because of this intensity and the traditional relation between their control and the community need for organized families dedicated to raising children, sexual relations have sometimes been constricted by such an overabundance of taboos and regulations that they denied the validity of the experience and meaning of sex. This is unfortunate. Sex should be enjoyed as one of the goods that life has to offer; eventually, nearly everyone should be able to work out arrangements for his life that make this possible. Tying sex exclusively to the production of children had traditional importance, but it no longer fits the conditions of the modern world and the accomplishments of modern health care.

Pleasures, of course, go far beyond sensuality. One of the greatest pleasures of civilized man is to be able to do something for himself and do it well. More selfish, perhaps, but very human is the pleasure that comes from being able to do something better than someone else, preferably better than someone who many think is skilled in the activity. This need not be a direct competition, and it can be in the most diverse activities. For example, the joy of one man's life may be that he is more accurate than anyone else in his company; another may be proud of having made important inventions. Both achievements are for these individuals forms of transcendence. Many people receive a quiet daily pleasure just from being responsible, from playing the game of life as expected and doing a good job of it in nearly everyone's estimation. In many ways, these pleasures are replications of the rewards received as children, but this does not affect their validity. All of us to some extent become parents of ourselves as we grow older, and it is our loss if we do not learn how to be good parents.

More generally, pleasure is central to the good life as we now understand it. The good life for most people will be a life with a great deal of pleasure, intense or soft, universal or very personal. This is not to take any position on what the nature of life really is. Rationally it may seem pointless. But life is never lived humanly if it is lived merely rationally. Perhaps if we live life as though it is an idealistic romance, we will get the most out of it for ourselves and give the most to our children. Life is a game in one sense, and games are meant to be enjoyed. If the necessities of our ancestors made it hard for them to play, that was too bad; we should not feel guilty about doing what we can even if they could not have done the same thing. This is not to say life is devoted to the pursuit of pleasure, for that cannot and should not be.

Overcontrol, or too much emphasis on limits and absolutes,

can be ugly. Totalitarian states are hideous, for they make men slaves or playthings of a few, and only these few can be said to be completely human. Overcontrol is also found in excessively rigid internal-control systems that some societies have forced upon their members. It is hard to stay on the target; perhaps those who bring their children up very strictly are partially right in assuming that to give way a little is eventually to lose the game, if not in the next generation, then eventually. Control can be a good habit, but for some people it will lead to a joyless, hollow life and endless drudgery.

This takes us back to the very different possibilities of success. Since few will succeed in a general, public sense in any society, to not enliven an ordinary existence with a little joy and ecstasy is to deprive a man of his life. However, for those few who succeed, success generally comes from more-than-average control and justifies it. Such men need not be pitied for being on a treadmill; in fact, too many of the little pleasures of life would interfere with their real pleasures in their public roles. However, there is a danger, because for the man of public success to deny himself the plain pleasures of life may be dehumanizing. It sets him apart from common experience and leads to a prototylalitarian frame of mind that nurtures plans for an "average man" who cannot and will not exist.

There is another less aesthetic reason for control in life. Control promotes productivity, and there must be productivity for life to exist. There is no technological miracle that is going to eliminate this need. While much of our current production may be misapplied, the growth of needs is bound to outstrip productivitiy for individuals and communities in the future as in the past. Improved health care, pollution reduction, park expansion, better housing—the list of present American needs is endless. Even if they are only symphony orchestras in every hamlet, the future will create needs. They will be felt to be real needs at the time, and we can no more deny this right to the future than did our ancestors to our age. This, too, is justice.

The decadence in modern movements does not come from the fact that they welcome the pleasures of the senses with open arms, but rather from the lack of a matching sense of responsibility and control. To be meaningful, pleasure and control must go together, for like any good game, life should be played as an aesthetic experience, and real aesthetic experience is less personal expression than it is the creative manipulation of controlled form.

In a valuable essay, Sapir pointed out that rhyme achieves a finer expression of meaning than prose because of the limitations that it places upon the author (Sapir, 1949). Poetry is essentially highly disciplined expression, even when traditional forms have been replaced by newer ones. Sapir believed that because the poet was quite constrained by a form, he was forced to think harder, to make every word count, and thus to create an economy of meaningful expression quite beyond that attainable in prose. What is true in literature is true on a broader scale in life. Historically, great thinkers or artists have generally been very hard workers and from a very early age. They took on a subject, which their parents often forced them to study or practice, and after many years of disciplined application, they achieved those creations in science, philosophy, art, or statesmanship that make them seem great to us. At least in this sense, those who made our civilization were mostly "squares." It was the tight boundaries of their lives, socially imposed, self-imposed, or imposed by nature, that made the greatness of their lives possible.

Considering sex in this context, in Chapter Six it was suggested that the person who creates a successful marriage within the confines of monogamy has created more to be proud of than the man who makes a successful marriage only on the third try and after several side adventures. Many will point to happy couples living in the French upper-class pattern that accommodates both wives and mistresses. This may be only a form of polygamy; in a regularized, responsible form, polygamy is certainly valid, although if it is generally practiced some males are going to lose. It should be clear that the main point is not the number of spouses in a relationship, but the dedication and thus the tempering of immediate impulses with control derived from an ideal of form applied to personal life. Much the same argument might be made for rules of eating, drinking, the use of drugs, the buying of clothes, or indulging conspicuous consumption (see Barclay, 1971). It takes a lot to go on living, and the child who is not brought up to appreciate form in life is not going to see much purpose in living when his impulses and desires are thwarted by outside reality.

It is important to distinguish between the importance of limits and the importance of conformity. Many of the great men of history were not conformists. Some had little regular family life, often as the result of homosexual tendencies. Nevertheless, they scorned giving their lives away to these tendencies. They established patterns for their lives and they generally stuck to them. While too much control often leads to psychological difficulties in adjustment, the greatness in man is achieved through his ability to control himself and organize himself for action, just as on the social plane greatness stems from an ability to organize people together into working units that can achieve more than one man alone. As we saw in Chapter Three, comparing the organization of the personality to the organization of groups is more than an analogy. The capability of the one reinforces the capability of the other. Organization, or the control system, is what makes possible the creation of a life worth living, a life with meaning at least in its form, just as organization in society makes possible the achievement of creative societies.

When we turn our consideration to art and literature, this point of view implies that control and restraint produce more of lasting value than do the rather boundless and formless aesthetic standards we see operating in much of the aesthetic world today. It is significant that the work of nineteenth-century authors, who plunged at least as deeply into the nature of man and society as our contemporaries, could also be characterized by the reticence of language that was prevalent in their time. The reader might reflect on whether peppering the work of Dostoevski or Tolstoi with four-letter words and more detailed descriptions of sexual relations would have added or detracted from their achievements. If such additions add little to literature, then it is probably a combination of the pressure of the marketplace and the antisociety stance of the culture heroes of our day that have caused the movement toward the full exploitation of social shock and sexual arousal in art. Today, the artistic and literary movement that originally had as its objective the full disclosure of reality has now far overshot its mark. In addition, the clinical approach in art and literature seems a deliberate attempt to reduce man to a biological specimen in a cage, reminiscent of the "blood and soil" image of the Nazis. Literary freedom today also seems to be a part of the fad of "letting go," of "letting it all out" that runs so counter to civilization. Of course, there are occasions of revel and abandon in many societies, but they are generally patterned and controlled forms of release restricted to definite times and places. After a few hours or days, the old rules again apply. Today, the novel, the movie, and an increasingly more liberated television program are our daily fare, and a situation requiring restraint is the exception rather than the rule.

Unrestrained language has now entered the classroom and is used in essays in top national magazines. Usually used with wild imprecision, four-letter words function as symbols of allegiance to certain groups, express a willingness to shock others, or are seen as more real than traditionally proper language. This is reminiscent of the currently held assumption that one learns more about a people by seeing a movie than by reading a book. Our writers seem to feel that the only way to make words as high in feeling as reality is to make them directly reflect the emotional world of the bodily functions. The realism is dreary at best; at worst, it is neither true to life nor educative. Too often the selectivity and purposefulness of the older literature has been replaced by a flat landscape of repetitive, sensory impression.

Conclusion

Addressing the problem of the individual's attempt to create a meaningful life, we have emphasized the part that responsibility might play. Since human beings are very different and must play different roles, there will be a variety of legitimate models for a variety of roles. Life also will need to have a preservative, social function alongside the search for individual validity. Living alone in the woods may be a legitimate life form, but only if a few adopt it; if too many do, that which makes living in the woods desirable will be destroyed. Thus, in pleading for pattern, organization, and responsibility, we have not resolved the paradox of choice; hopefully, we have suggested an outline in terms of which many may find meaning.

Philosophers have often written of the tension between the ideal and the real in man's existence and of the dangers of denying man either. The Greeks thought of the perfect life as a state of balance, what they called the *golden mean*. It is difficult for societies not to go to an extreme, to fall into the traps of either sensualism or rigid spirituality, and it is equally difficult for individuals. Typical of many periods of excess have been the sensualism and materialism of the masses on the one hand, and the dedication of small, intense, religious or political elite groups on the other. We might call this a Spartan totalitarian state with circuses. It is much more difficult to create a society that expects a great deal of personal, unregulated internal control. Post-Reformation Northern Europe and Puritan New England were such societies, and we still live off their remains (see Weber, 1958; Elazar, 1970). Very different successful societies of people under internal, personal, willed control have been those of Japan and of the Jews.

Although it is impossible to judge adequately the prospects of our age, we may be entering a period of extended turmoil for which the old guidelines of action will no longer seem sufficient. Like it or not, the fortresses of religion that have helped to hold this country together are crumbling fast, and new compounds of science and irrationality are taking their place, whether under the labels of traditional cults or the new slogans of secularism. There is a good possibility that the resulting struggle of pure hedonism with movements of mystic escape and millenarianism will endanger the degree of civilization we have achieved, resulting in unnecessary and overwhelming bloodshed and finally in totalitarian systems. By themselves, most individuals can do little to avoid this outcome, no matter what their views. In a similar situation, the Stoics of the Roman and Hellenistic worlds elevated the quality of life of many individuals through teachings based on the belief that adherence to moderation and rationality is the highest achievement of man, and informed with the science and knowledge of their day. One of their last and greatest achievements was the life and thought of Marcus Aurelius, the Roman emperor. Although educated in the best sense of the word, he was not brilliant. Not successful as a parent, and unable to do more than delay the collapse of the empire and his personal values, he continued to live and rule by his ideals as best he could, and bequeathed, perhaps unknowingly, an example to a future he could not have understood. Today we cannot guess what the future of our world is; as the Durants note, "The Universe has no prejudice in favor of Christ or against Genghis Khan" (Durant and Durant, 1968, p. 46). But whatever the future holds, we can at least do our job and live our lives in the finest way we know. In so doing, we will bequeath a meritorious example of what man could be in our time. We mold our lives or must live in the faith that we do. In one aspect, this book is an attempt to help individuals mold their lives in terms of the attitudes of Marcus Aurelius and what little we have gained in the knowledge of man and nature since his time.

This is also a text on survival; modern man cannot survive as man unless he lives in a moral universe that he understands and to which he feels he can make a contribution, no matter how small. This is not a discussion of how the average person can achieve self-fulfillment, nor is it another exhortation to the pursuit of excellence. There has been far too much pressure placed on each of us to scale these pinnacles. The demand for excellence could shrink this generation as much as success did the last. Individuals can only hope for a sense that they have done fairly well and that if men did as well, they would be doing a good job of meeting the challenges of life.

This chapter has attempted to relate our scientific and humanistic models of man to the core problem of humanity—the meaning of individual lives. As always, the goal has been to achieve a balance among humanistic values that does not violate the limits of man presented in the scientific analysis. Our attempt suggests these principles. The first is accepting the social extension that implies that life is meaningful only to the extent that we go beyond an unconscious self-affirmation to ask hard ethical and aesthetic questions about our personal actions and judgments. The second principle is that for most persons the greatest transcendence that can be hoped for is to sculpture a personal life that others can use as a model. The third principle is that such a life must be lived within definite limits, which include fulfilling role expectations in an exemplary manner, except when there are stronger humanistic reasons not to do so.

There is, however, one last burden for morality, and that is optimism. As Schweitzer (1923) so correctly concludes, the task of our time is to think through a philosophy of life that is founded on both a commitment to ethical behavior and an affirmation of life and the universe. But affirmation is a task for another day. For us now, optimism must rest only on faith.

TEN

Social Humanities: Institutionalizing a Discipline

The foregoing chapters have explored the argument for social humanities, developing with examples a particular school of analysis within the proposed discipline. It was suggested that an integrative discipline of social humanities might improve research and analysis in the social sciences and humanities by more adequately dividing without divorcing the concerns of the respective fields. By carving out a serious discipline for the generalizing and integrative analyses that lie between the social sciences and humanities, social humanities should make respectable and ultimately acceptable the generalist analysis that must be used to grasp the larger issues faced by individuals and societies.

To be fully effective, social humanities must get beyond academia and become institutionalized as an applied discipline. As we do this, it may well be objected that a discipline so involved in value judgment will necessarily be overly responsive to the interests of its financial supporters. This is a danger in any applied discipline, mitigated in our pluralist society, however, by the variety of potential sponsors and the lack of a monolithic power structure (see Bunzel,

1967). Moreover, since there will be advice generated either professionally or nonprofessionally at the generalist level, the answer cannot be to eliminate the level. It must rather be to provide those working at this level with a discipline and tradition that gives them a degree of independence from their sponsors. For the social humanist, the alter ego of social humanities will take the place of the alter ego of science, law, or medicine for complementary professions. Thus, it is hoped that the suggested profession will raise generalist advice above the undisciplined sphere of pure hucksterism that is often encountered.

Need for a New Role of Social Counselor

In Chapter Five, I promised to return later to a consideration of what social changes might have prevented Magruder's acquiescence in the Liddy plan. Proposed changes in our society may either be in government or the cultural foundations of government. Changes in government might include greater reliance on the statutory departments and agencies in order to reduce the power of the dependent staffs of the President, or a reform of campaign financing that would reduce the amount of free money available for corruption. But what could be done to change the institutional foundations of government? Surely the old moral virtues or the countercultural critique of success might be inculcated at every level of education, as well as through the media and the press. Yet if such preaching remains public and general as it has in the past, it will accomplish little. This is particularly true today, when science seems to many to have destroyed the possibility of individual responsibility and when the contradictory advice of a thousand contending schools of social science and popular philosophy reduce their audience to exhaustion.

The problems of moral communication could be overcome by a forced conversion to a new orthodoxy of behavior and belief, reinforced by the self-criticism sessions of totalitarian states or the behavior modification techniques of modern psychology. It must be a forced conversion, because in our secular, complex civilization there is no organizing system of thought that could hold society together without compulsion. We are far too sophisticated a society for our most intelligent to endorse voluntarily the neat formulas of indoctrination. Therefore, this is not an acceptable answer, for we would lose more by the required compulsion than we would gain.

One way to avoid this dilemma might be to provide individuals an opportunity for periodic private discussions in a professional atmosphere of their day-to-day problems that would be directed to improving their understanding of the social situations in which they find themselves and of their moral responsibilities in those situations. This opportunity would be provided if there was a profession of social counselor that provided an institutional resort for persons with such problems as Magruder faced in Washington. Long before Watergate, Earl Warren suggested the need for a similar professional role, which he labeled "counselor in ethics" (Bracker, 1962). This would be an acceptable term except that it fails to imply the balance of science and humanistic judgment that our age requires. Although the suggested profession would have much in common with other professions, including those of law and marriage counseling, the primary models would be the psychiatrist and the priest. But for most of us who face moral decisions such as Magruder's, psychiatric advice is not critical and clerical advice is too intertwined with particular sets of beliefs to be available. Magruder was not in poor mental health before Watergate, and it would unduly confuse terminology to imagine that he was. What I am proposing is a profession closer to that of the priest confessor. Perhaps the role of social counselor would often be filled by divines. Religiously guided or not, practitioners would be trained to offer significant help to those isolated in social situations that they understand neither sociologically nor morally.

As in psychoanalysis and confession, there needs to be a background of common education and moral belief before such counseling could help. Fortunately, this is widely available in our society, even if weakened by two centuries of confusion. Magruder's education, his religious interests, and his personal contacts with Coffin had predisposed him to listen to moral argument. Yet at the time of the Watergate events, this side of his intellect was not brought to consciousness in the rush of events. When he had been so involved in moral argument, one suspects the discussion had been abstract, disconnected from the events of Magruder's day-to-day life.

The exact specification of the institutional role I am suggesting would develop with experience and vary with individuals and situations. Yet prior experience suggests certain features. For example, to discuss issues of direct relevance to an individual, the social counselor would have to be a person sworn to silence in regard to his client's activities. This would have been absolutely necessary for Magruder. The social counselor would be trained in the social sciences and humanities. On the one hand, he would help to explain to his client some of the sociological reasons behind his actions and the kinds of traps into which alternatives would be likely to lead him. Choices and their ramifications would become clearer and be related to the client's problems, rather than the general problems that must be addressed by a lecture course or a traditional discussion group. The counselor would be well advised to use a nondirective approach and to attempt to make the individual review and develop his values and moral concerns until they became relevant to the actions he was taking (Rogers, 1951). This approach would, in any event, better accord with the respect due each individual.

The counselor would have the task of strengthening the client's moral alter ego, that aspect of his consciousness that sets standards in terms of which the more humdrum, determined organism strives. While the culture provides an individual with an unconscious, often primitive superego and some conscious realization of the dangers and opportunities that face him, the assumption that man is morally responsible implies that he rework this material to create ideal images of what he or she should be like. For a moral man, subsequent life is to a degree marked by a dialogue with this spiritual alternative. The counselor's function would be to help develop, and when necessary to personify, this alter ego. Had Magruder such a relationship with a counselor in Washington, not only Watergate, but the compromises that preceded and followed it would have emerged, and Magruder's moral control over what he was doing would have been increased.

Of course, at the time, Magruder would have felt he had no time for such counseling. If he alone had been counseled, he would have lost his job, and someone else would have done it. In regard to any particular individual facing new institutions, this is bound to be true. Customs need to get started, but once accepted, there is always time for what custom prescribes. Church, regular athletic exercise, and, increasingly, psychotherapy are accepted diversions for men in public life. In a moral nation, if such a profession existed, even cynical men of power would feel it in their interest to take notice, and gradually having a social counselor might become common practice. Industries and administrations whose top people had social counselors would come to be trusted more than those without. We have a great deal of social science with which to start and powerful humanistic traditions on which to build. We need only an institutional role that would make both of these directly interact with the lives of individuals pressured by their immediate concerns.

Institution Building: Applied Social Humanities

The social counselor is only one of the opportunities social humanities offers for building a coherent intellectual basis for new institutions to replace spiritual and judgmental resources now dangerously depleted. In modern European and American societies, traditional religions play a smaller role than in the past, and this is particularly true among opinion makers (leading professors, journalists, and authors). The gap has only been partially filled by science and the arts. Neither offers institutional forms that could provide an adequate intellectual or spiritual basis for human life. As a result, there are millions of well-educated Europeans and Americans who have nowhere to turn when faced with serious questions on the nature of their personal moral responsibilities and purposes or on the kind of society that they should support or promote.

Persons with personal moral concerns can go to a clinical psychologist or psychiatrist. However, as suggested in the case of Magruder, advice on the moral purposes of life is not the primary function of these specialties, and their practitioners are not equipped for it. Their job is to help seriously disturbed individuals to function in the society in which they find themselves. Their job is to achieve a level of minimal functioning; in this situation, the great interest in drug therapies of the last few years is appropriate. But to transform problems of meaning and responsibility into psychiatric problems is to reduce them to a matter of techniques. For the functioning individual, this seriously misses the point.

Persons concerned with the best directions for social organization find themselves stranded between serious sociological work and the casual futurist fads. Unfortunately, the serious academic in social science, philosophy, or other humanities devotes his time to classes and research intended to add to a particular intellectual tradition oriented toward others in his field. He is uncomfortable with giving prescriptions for social change.

Lack of resources for coherent advice in social humanities is not only a problem for the private individual. When a politician or a businessman asks for general advice from the intellectual community, he is able to find narrow technical advice but little general advice that goes to the question of priorities. The fact that he seldom asks for general advice is based on the lack of a credible source. It does not mean that he does not need and want more than he is getting.

However, the argument for institutional insufficiency can also be made from the point of view of the needs of society, irrespective of currently felt needs. When we look at the basis of support for the great creative traditions of societies, we find that these were generally spiritual traditions. The great traditions of the past in art, literature, music, and architecture centered around belief systems, but most of our important writers, architects, and composers do not have frameworks of this kind. Looking at the past from a slightly different angle, the most successful civilizations and individuals possessed positive, self-denying motivations that implied a corresponding set of rules and restrictions. Modern life provides little basis for either. Only in highly ideological states, such as the People's Republic of China, or in states still fanatically pursuing growth do we find belief systems that effectively prevent the collapse of restrictions on human conduct.

New institutions are needed to counter emerging threats to pluralism. An outstanding heritage of Western civilization is that personal and social life are not determined by a government or ruling party. But with the decline of traditional belief systems within the West, there is a tendency either for science and technology to take the place of ideology or for government to create a new ideology of administrative efficiency (evidenced most strongly in Sweden's bureaucratic socialism; see Huntford, 1972). If these trends continue, there will be a considerable loss of freedom and flexibility, and ultimately the end of scientific advance as well. For in the absence of countervailing forces, the tension of science and government must be resolved by their fusion.

It is a commonplace among some intellectuals to say that what this society needs is a new religion, just as atheistic social scientists have often claimed that every society needs a religion. Obviously, we cannot manufacture religions. However, it is possible that we can create a basis upon which some of the integrative or advisory functions that religion has ceased to provide for most intellectuals might be available to a future society. The steps required would be the following:

1. Institutes of social humanities or departments of social humanities at universities would develop a core of research and thinking that would form a significant learning tradition.
2. Applied social humanists, educated primarily in social humanities programs, would then appear as consultants or social counselors to individuals, corporations, and governments on nontechnical problems of interest. These practitioners would develop professional ethics similar to those of priests and psychiatrists.
3. These consultants and the academic social humanists would cooperate in offering lectures and seminars for the general public in their geographical areas.
4. Groups of social humanists, their audiences, and clients would form schools of thought, provide meeting places, establish or take over colleges, and so on. These colleges would become new centers of cultural ferment and produce community leaders.

The relationships of the individuals to their communities would vary widely, but one can expect certain principles to develop. The first would be that anyone can set himself up as a social humanist; however, only certain people would be accredited by the more serious organizations. This is necessary both to keep the system open and to serve the interests of people at all social and educational levels. The leading accrediting organization would require evidence of both extensive knowledge in the social sciences and relevant humanities and the ability to relate this knowledge coherently to real problems. Consultants with this accreditation would use the latest scientific and humanistic knowledge, with traditions continuously evolving.

Lay persons would benefit from social humanists both as a passive reading and lecture audience and on a one-to-one basis. In the latter form, it would be expected that the individual would not go from consultant to consultant according to the problem, but would stay with one person or tradition. For example, among Shi'i Muslims, there are a variety of high authorities representing different insitutional interpretations of religious questions. However, each lay person is expected to choose one of these authorities for advice and not change guidance on each issue. Thereby, the religious and moral realm becomes, for the individual, more than a decorative gloss on life, and yet a certain flexibility is given to the whole society.

This, then, is the framework of social humanities as it might be developed. Of course, each reader will find some parts attractive and some repelling or unconvincing. Insofar as it does not meet the ultimate test of acceptability, I can only hope that it will encourage readers to build a firmer structure. The work must be done: Serious integration is a responsibility that intellectuals must not abdicate.

APPENDIX

Struggling with the Crisis of Incoherence

The criticism of ideals is everywhere brilliant and effective—those very ideals that gave intelligence the leisure and occasion to criticize them. Meanwhile the instincts of preservation and perpetuation become exhausted or perverted. . . . [The] spectacular and voluptuous doom of a political structure is celebrated by a bonfire on which everything is heaped which fear had kept from being consumed before. State secrets, private shames, unspoken thoughts, long repressed dreams, everything from the depths of those overexcited and joyously despairing hearts is brought out and thrown on the public mind. . . . Respect evaporates and chains melt away in the incandescent consummation of life and death. [Valéry, 1962, pp. 218–220]

At this final stage of our inquiry, with the full spectacle of the human prospect before us, the spirit quails and the will falters. We find ourselves pressed to the very limit of our personal capacities, not alone in summoning up the courage to look squarely at the dimensions of the impending predicament, but in finding words that can offer some plausible relief in a situation so bleak. . . . If, by the question "Is there hope for man?" we ask whether it is possible to meet the challenges of the future without the payment of a fearful price, the answer must be: No, there is no such hope. [Heilbroner, 1974, p. 136]

The first response of the sophisticated to proclamations such as these is a shrug of the shoulder. Our world drifts on decade after decade. There are crises and tumults, and warnings of crises and tumults, and yet it goes on. Some of us remain calm. The more we know of history, the more we remark on the similarities of recent trends with those in previous civilizations, the more we see the future as a repetition of the past. Of course, there are changes, but these are largely technological, and will be adjusted to in time. Future shock is for the young and imperfectly educated. Yet if we look again, we may perceive that underneath the placid surface of events there thrives an irresistible florescence of intellectual and spiritual goods that we no longer have the ability or will to manage. With every generation, the implications of this growth become more profound and less remediable. We no longer understand what we understand.

Philosophers of history may be divided into those who see history as progress and those who see history as repetition. To most optimists, the future holds the promise of improvement, and whether they be Marxist ideologues or modern technocrats, they look at the grand sweep of human history as justification for their views. To most pessimists, on the other hand, advances are chimerical; every bright day reminds them of the storm ahead. Looking at the records of past civilizations, history offers recurrent evidence for their forebodings.

Sorokin (1937–1941, 1950) developed the most substantial sociological version of the pessimistic, repetitive understanding of history that the world had come to know through the more intuitive works of Spengler and Toynbee. To Sorokin, the cultural histories of the great civilizations were best understood as the immanent development but ultimate failure of the major premises of the intellectual elite. In particular, Western history was the story of the successive working out of the implications of sensate and ideational premises. The ideational premise is that reality is primarily symbolic or metaphysical, of which the sensate world is only a pale reflection. It is the fundamental assumption of the great religions. At the other extreme, the sensate premise is that reality is solely what we can feel, taste, see, hear, or smell. From this viewpoint, the fundamentals of the great religions are sheer nonsense. Sorokin found, uneasily situated between these two overarching premises, a third, an idealistic synthesis epitomized by fifth-century Athens. Yet this third possibility appeared to be highly unstable and might not occur at all in the course of a fluctuation between the two primary premises.

In its age of effectiveness, each major premise brought a high civilization into being, but in the process of creation each also exhausted its potentialities. In the period of subsequent decay, the alternative took the intellectual lead and throve in the minds of men until it eventually went through the same cyclical pattern (although the process was seen as an indeterminate fluctuation by Sorokin). In the terminology of systems theory, there is a kind of thermostat in human affairs so that when the development of one alternative produces sufficient negative feedback to overcome the inertia that has accumulated, the course of history is reversed for a time. Sorokin offered evidence for this thesis from the histories of such fields as science, literature, art, philosophy, and social organization. To Sorokin, our own age is a period of decayed sensate culture, in which the originally freeing and creative forces released by the victory of the sensate premise has led inexorably to an overemphasis on transitory and superficial sensate experience. The "crisis of our age" (Sorokin, 1941) is simultaneously the death throes of the old materialism, desperately trying to maintain its equilibrium, and the birth pangs of a new and as yet indecipherable civilization that will likely be dominated by an idealistic or ideational view of reality. Sorokin failed to emphasize that although sensate culture produced an increasingly large body of knowledge and interpretation, which the computer finally had to store and relate, by its very nature the culture could produce no guiding scheme by which to evaluate the product.

On the basis of a quite different analysis from Sorokin's, Weber showed how the problems of "late sensate" cultures were indeed endemic in modern civilization. A commentator writes:

> *Increasing rationalization and intellectualization have had one decisive consequence, on which Weber laid great stress: they have disenchanted the world. With the progress of*

science and of technology, man has stopped believing in magic powers, in spirits and demons; he has lost his sense of prophecy, and above all, his sense of the sacred. Reality has become dreary, flat and utilitarian, leaving a great void in the souls of men which they seek to fill by furious activity and through various devices and substitutes. [Freund, 1968, pp. 23–24]

This is the intellectual problem that sensate culture has inevitably intensified with the passage of time. In the theological mind of Schaeffer (1968), this problem was born when St. Thomas Aquinas distinguished between a world of grace and a world of nature, and thereby allowed them to be considered separately. Since nature is easier to study, its proofs easier to come by, and its rewards more immediate and apparent, gradually from this time on nature was destined to "swallow up grace." Essential to this process was the gradual acceptance of the position, which, of course, Aquinas had not foreseen, that all that is vague, unreal, and emotional is in the area of grace, while all that is real is in the area of nature. Along with God, grace, freedom, significance, morals, and love, even the existence of persons as units dissolves under the hammer blows of the study of physics, biology, sociology, and psychology. As Musil (1953, p. 37) writes:

Who can be interested any longer in the age-old idle talk of good and evil, when it has been established that good and evil are not "constants" at all, but "functional values," so that the goodness of works depends on the historical circumstances, and the goodness of human beings on the psychotechnical skill with which their qualities are exploited.

In Schaeffer's view, the process of dissolution is only hastened by the efforts of many religious modernists to create pseudogods, "Gods behind God." He supposes, and I think correctly, that such gods have little influence on the real decisions of life, because even their inventors do not believe in them.

Writing from a naturalistic perspective, Plessner (1964, pp. 65–69) points to the implication of man's naked psychological position: The individual is conscious of both the impending future and his own inability to control that future, including even the continuation of his own existence. Historically, this led him to create a world of spirits and ultimately a god that, through identification with man, offers the possibility of coherence and control, and brings order to the kaleidoscope of events, for "without such a [spiritual realm] man cannot manage the ambivalent relationship of natural man to a fragmented world" (Plessner, p. 68). Unlike Schaeffer, Plessner believes the attempt to use the forms of the past to offer meaning today accords neither with our knowledge nor our social organization. Plessner concludes that new forms, new spiritual realities *(Gegenüber)* must be produced out of the basic requirements of man's exposed position, yet he offers no hint as to what these might be. What Plessner's analysis does offer is an understanding of the operation of Sorokin's concepts of fluctuation in human history and the principle of limits. Evidently, human beings have two contrasting requirements: to increase efficiency through openness to external reality and to increase psychological security through bending that reality to match human desires, or at least the human scale. While overemphasis on either will inevitably lead to reaction, the drive for consistency inevitably propels societies toward the limits.

Following Sorokin, Polak (1973) sees emphasis on the transient and the negative in modern culture as evidence of a general decline, and he is dismayed by the inability of the contemporary intelligentsia, including its futurists, to create an acceptable replacement. Like Plessner, he regards the Christian tradition as no longer able to carry the burden. The Middle Ages will not return. In his analysis, Polak also suggests that a critical aspect of a civilization is the way in which it conceives of the relation between day-to-day reality and another reality outside of common experience. Meaning and significant creation can only exist in life insofar as it transcends the transitory nature of day-to-day necessity. In this way, Polak has managed to relate the creative basis of ancient Greek culture to that of the medieval church, the Renaissance, and the modern utopians and futurists. Polak places the collapse of both Christian eschatology and secular utopian views in the nineteenth century. He agrees with Schumpeter, the economic historian, that capitalism has probably peaked ideologically, but Polak also finds modern socialism unrewarding. Insofar as it is acceptable, its orientation has become immediate, incapable of transcendence. He asks for a new vision.

Without this vision, what has been happening to the civilization? In *Trousered Apes*, Williams (1971) points to the long slide from the ennobling mission of literature that was generally accepted by the elite in the eighteenth century down to the decadent "antimission" accepted by the contemporary elite. In most ages, oral and written literature was accepted by the elite as of positive value only to the extent that it supported the ideals of the community. These works were not always conservative or pleasant, but they had positive purposes. The fictional worlds of Jonathan Swift, Sir Thomas More, and Shakespeare's better tragedies were meant to serve social ends. Heroes were seldom evil in classic literature, and when they were, the "godfathers" of the time were destroyed as a lesson to audiences. Western societies have always had a humorous, often scurrilous and earthy literature for entertainment and diversion rather than moral education. But only in our age is the pornographic depiction of man in literature not meant primarily as a joke that will relieve the tensions of civilization, but as a warrant that his basic biology is the most important reality of his life.

One characteristic of recent literature is its choice of the most immediately perceived sensory reality as its subject matter. This may be the stream of intellectual consciousness or the stream of emotional response to sexual stimulation. Another characteristic is the emphasis on action for its own sake. Since for many writers both purposes and standards have been destroyed by science, we are only left with the repetitive desire for action, whether on a bed or a motorcycle. As Roszak's hero Blake wrote, "Sooner murder an infant in its cradle than nurse unacted desires" (Williams, 1971, p. 11). Williams illustrates this change in sensibility by pointing to the evolution since the eighteenth century of the treatment of Shakespeare. While at the beginning of this period Shakespeare's sex and violence were often expurgated, today they are added to productions in proportion far beyond what Shakespeare intended. In this tradition, the latest *Hamlet* of Seattle's Repertory Theater (fall of 1974) offered a barroom hood who physically assaults both his mother and Ophelia. Naturally, the play opened to rave reviews.

The indistinct gods of modern theology are paralleled by the formlessness of contemporary painting, sculpture, music, and poetry (Polak, 1973; Howe, 1963). In the following words, Horgan

(1965, p. 270) juxtaposes authentic art with what he finds today:

> *In writing, garrulity, in music, electronic feedback,*
> *and in painting, the mere energy of pigment itself without*
> *ideational function, took the place of considered statement.*
> *By considered statement I mean that which has been filtered*
> *through many layers of sensibility and weighed for its mean-*
> *ing, measured for its place in a design, and enclosed in form*
> *which precisely accommodates it.*

Horgan goes on to point out that it is a poor historical sense that imagines our age is so different in its complexities that it requires such art, and he adds that never before has the artist been willing to deal only with the fragments, to abandon an all-encompassing view.

Of course, this is theater and the arts; for most people, life is much less dramatic. The masses continue to honor values the arts have long denounced. Yet there is little reassurance to be found in this perseverance. While many continue to hold a variety of high moral standards for various reasons, the intellectual underpinning for these views has collapsed, and the average parent and his surrogate, the schoolteacher, are left with very little that is convincing to teach their children. This problem hit German culture very hard after World War One. Men as different as Schweitzer (1923) and Rosenberg (1930) analyzed in almost identical terms the breakdown of the old civilization and the necessity for a radical new basis for action. Schweitzer's answer was to provide a spiritual reawakening of the individual through reaffirmation of the sacredness of life, while the Nazi Rosenberg's answer was to provide a reaffirmation of the sacredness of the community, with the results that we know. But both understood that the old underpinnings were gone, and an effort had to be made to find a new basis.

After World War Two, the industrialized noncommunist world was reconstructed on the strength of a still intellectually backward and naively self-confident America. But by the 1970s, the underpinnings of American life may be in a Weimar condition. By contrasting the moral basis of the prohibition against alcohol consumption in the 1920s with the medical basis of opposition to drugs today, Kristol (1972a, pp. 20, 29) makes our loss of values frighteningly clear.

Beyond preserving life, we no longer understand the reason for any limits.

What, then, is the intellectual answer?

It has long been acknowledged that science is not the answer. In a recent essay on the philosophical implications of biological research, Monod (1971) remarks that ideas are successful because of a favorable degree of performance value (utility) and infectivity (emotional appeal). Unfortunately, although high on performance, he finds that science as a system of ideas is apparently low on infectivity. He concludes that people need a new religion; they need a coherent story, a system of reliable explanation that a continually evolving science cannot offer. This accounts, in Monod's view, for the continuation of interest and support for traditional religions long after they have become intellectually not viable. Our leaders continue to justify their efforts in religious terms. Yet with every year, Monod feels the rot progresses; our society cannot continue to undergird its order by referring to belief systems that its intellectual leaders and many of its political (and perhaps even religious) leaders affirm hypocritically if they affirm them at all. On every side, Monod sees our lives sapped by what he regards as "the lie at the base of our culture."

In my view, the intellectual and civilizational problem we face may be viewed as a product of both science and the arts. First, the development of scientific sophistication has left us without a basis upon which we can mobilize either ourselves or those around us for sustained social or aesthetic action. Belief in religious or patriotic dogma no longer comes easily. Second, the development of the sensate arts has stripped away the inherited veils of nobility and spirituality to reveal a clever, febrile biological organism, and in the flatness of the landscape that has been revealed, there are few external tasks worth human attention. Sealed in aimless action and solipsistic dialogue, sophistication becomes a philosophy of enervation, of simply waiting for Godot.

Among the educated young of the 1970s, there is renewed conformity but little commitment to new ideas or cultural traditions. Perhaps this is because, in the words of Bell (1975), this is the first generation to face a world in which there is no longer a distinction between the sacred and the profane, in which there are no taboos. Bell finds the generation in a futile search for a society without fathers. This is not primarily a question of the speed of change, nor is it restricted to our time. What Bell identifies is the gradual culmination of the insidious growth of relativism, the belief that all truths, times, and places are in unavoidable flux. We instinctively surmise that next year we will not hold the beliefs we do today. Again Weimar and Rosenberg were ahead of us. Rosenberg decreed his work should not be translated, for no one but a German could be interested in "German truths." Today I find the college world is awash with the cultural relativism of anthropology's last generation. The oppression by the Chinese communists of their people, their total denial of free expression, even in private, does not bother the average American because "who are we to say?" "The Chinese must like to live like that." This relativistic stance is not primarily a matter of fellow-traveler praise of a communist system, as in the unfortunate encomiums of the Soviets in the 1930s, nor is it primarily the racial prejudice that breeds the suspicion that the Chinese are really robots; it is a product of the hollow feeling that all beliefs, practices, and laws are inevitable products of natural processes. Differences between systems of government become equated to differences between species, each adapted to its own ecological niche. We are "men without qualities," so overburdened with a surfeit of bits of information and points of view that events and decisions are replaced by the passive observations of the stream of consciousness, whether by Joyce or Pynchon. Enveloped by this gossamer web of scientistic insight with nothing to give the world and nothing to stand for in the world, we are naked, helpless before those on the right or left who still believe in something.

Destructive Contribution of Intellectuals to the Crisis

Abstract ideas have always been subversive of the social order. However, since the ability to be affected by concepts separately from their embodiment in tradition and life has been restricted historically to a small class of savants, the subversiveness of creative intellectuals has been limited to the instigation and support for those glacial movements of change that have avoided anarchy while civilizing mankind. Today, however, the lines of connection between intellectuals and the general public are far more open, people are attuned to the new, and it is of critical importance what chords they are hearing. Of course, the common man is entertained more than educated by television and reads little more than a parochial local paper. But the teachers of the reporters, writers, columnists, artists, and serial writers that feed the general public's desire for knowledge or stimulation act as a rapid transmission net for the fads and foibles of our cultural elite.

Insofar as the problems we have defined relate to the basic conceptions of man and civilization, the intellectuals of our time carry primary responsibility for both the intensification of our problems and their eventual solution. Intellectuals in the ancient world were generalists, both advisors to men of action and critics of the community. They knew more than their advisees both technically and generally. In our day, however, intellectuals as generalists should be distinguished from intellectual technicians. The technicians are men of science, engineering, or medicine. Immersed in a world of research, they are largely apolitical. Their political rancor is stirred primarily by denials of freedom or privilege that affect their professions. By contrast, the term *intellectual* should be used to refer to men of general ideas, a much smaller group of critics of the established order and promoters of new beliefs. They have a great deal of abstract knowledge and analytical ability, but they have little to contribute directly to the running of society. Every society needs intellectuals, and yet today the effects of their efforts through the press, the classroom, the theatre, or the art gallery are generally destructive and splintering. Too often they fall into the vulgar error of confusing criticism with opposition. While they have lost the ability to support the past, they are equally unable to establish a consensus for the future.

In his analysis of capitalism, Schumpeter (1950, pp. 145–155) points out that it was in the nature of capitalism to inflate the size of the intellectual class as it removed controls on the form and content of intellectual expression. Since intellectuals are by definition men of ideas, the society is thrown open to a barrage of ever more serious and widespread attacks against which it is powerless to defend itself. Indeed, Molnar (1974) sees liberalism as the foundation of totalitarianism, for the well-meaning liberal critique breaks down all institutions until only the state is left to fill the resulting vacuum. Even if the destructive ideas be those of anarchy, the state will always arise from the rubble as the institution of last resort. Then, to achieve order, the intellectuals will be muzzled.

Our analysis in Chapters Two and Three would suggest the complementary hypothesis that the intellectuals as a class will use their power over the pen and their control of education to press for an organization of society, including the form of government and economy, in which they would play a larger part than they do in pluralist or traditionalist states. In pursing the goals of what Gehlen (1969) calls their "antiaristocracy," intellectuals pursue their own interests like everyone else; their claims are just more global (see Hoffer, 1963, 1967). Should they succeed in establishing their hegemony, they would find that their critical interpretive role would be replaced by the dead hand of theocracy. A free intellectual cannot both operate the world and retain his distance. Yet as long as they are denied a positive role in our society that is based on a convincing doctrine that defines that role, intellectuals will strive to further undermine those shards of past doctrine by which we all live.

So far there is no revolution; our society persists. Its persistence becomes a proof of the gap that often exists between life and thought, with life much the stronger. Yet will there not come a time of economic pressure or warfare when the shallowness of this life will cause something to snap, the will to collapse, and the majority to reach out for a new solution, any solution—even the Weimar solution? As Gehlen (1969, p. 102) points out:

> The enlightenment is, in brief, the emancipation of the mind from institutions. . . . It destroys loyalty to non-national values; through criticism it brings our obligations into consciousness, where they are thought to death. It offers formulas that are useful in attack, but have no constructive force, as in talk of a "new humanity," or of the inhumanity of the rule of one over another. . . . Finally it leads to an extensive polarization that clears away the compromises, half-way measures and routine formulas of everyday life, and then there appears the aggression that has been hidden incognito in the ideal. The dove is a symbol of love and peace, but the biologist knows that it has not the least reluctance to kill its own species.

Contribution of Intellectuals to Crisis Resolution

Today many see the threat of breakdown dimly, and a few most clearly. Although solutions are offered, too often these are counsels of despair. Many, such as Schaeffer (1968), would have us go back, reaffirm the old beliefs, and put theology back into science. With a different emphasis, this is also the hope of Solzhenitsyn for the Russian people. Sorokin (1941) wants essentially the same thing, although he realizes the details of the old systems will never do. Others, such as Monod (1971), would have us grasp the nettle and promote the spiritualization of science. The desperate flailing to which the crisis leads even the most gifted is well illustrated by the fact that after a most reasonable exposition of the serious deterioration of our spiritual foundations, Monod proposes that the future can be based on a belief system in which knowledge itself becomes the ultimate cultural value. Monod does not mean it. First he knows that for most people knowledge fails to be sufficiently absorbing or infectious. Second, other values must have precedence, even for Monod. (Indeed, he suggests elsewhere in the same book (p. 153) that certain experiments on children must be ruled out on moral grounds, even though they would give us a valuable key to the nature of human consciousness.)

For most social scientists and planners, the solution is simply to make people happy in their cages, and the approach to this happiness becomes the major criterion. As Campbell (1972, p. 442) writes, "Ultimately, the quality of life must be in the eye of the beholder, and it is there that we seek ways to evaluate it." So Campbell (1972, 1976) must go on to poll people about their satisfaction with everything from food to self-actualization. This naive utilitarianism was refuted over seventy years ago by Moore (1903) in his criticism of what he called the *naturalistic fallacy*. No amount of polling or improvement in satisfaction indices can offer a substantial criterion for action, or else *Brave New World* was an eutopia and not the dystopia its orginator had imagined. Yet planners and social scientists such as Skinner (1960, 1971) continue to propose solutions to our spiritual malaise that vary only in details from Huxley's nightmare. More commonly, intellectual leaders deny that these are their goals, but close analysis will suggest that the identification of what is and what ought to be is at the unexamined heart of their approach.

To the planner, the problem of our time is inefficiency, particularly that inefficiency that results from dealing with crises only after they occur. As the futurist Lindamen said in an informal talk in 1974, we should replace "postcrisis politics" with "precrisis engineering." To many planners, the problem is also individualism. We must move, they say, from the primacy of the individual to the primacy of the individual in the group. This all sounds reasonable. Yet the past century has taught us to be suspicious of those who would do away with politics, who would engineer our lives, who would have us surrender individual to group purposes. In the long run, we always learn that groups do not actually have purposes and that, in the name of the people, individuals impose their special values and interests upon society.

In the 1960s, there reemerged another type of social thinker, with deep belief in a radical, community-forming ideology. Today, men with social ideologies may be socialists, Jainist "ecologues,"* or libertarians. However, it is in the marriage of certain aspects of socialism and of scientific progressivism that we find what is today the leading candidate for a new system of guiding ideas. This is a liberal socialism that struggles against the bureaucratic, technocratic, and totalitarian tendencies that afflict socialism in practice. At its best, as in the hands of the philosopher Rawls (1971), this system is open both to the accretion of new scientific knowledge and to rational, normative inquiry beyond the natural or social sciences. However, I do not believe that the resulting social utilitarianism is the answer on either account. Its relation to social science is too heavily influenced by the sociology of knowledge, its view of human values is restricted to an egalitarian modification of utilitarianism, its anti-individualism and statism remain unsupported by either science or a satisfactory ethics, and its academic pacifism lays a society based upon its doctrines open to eventual destruction, no matter what its internal virtues.

Pacifism has always tended to be as attractive to men of thought as it has been abhorrent to men of action. But in our present crisis, interest in pacifism is specifically related to turning inward, to

---

Ecologue is a personal coinage for those who make ecology into an ideology. Jainism is, of course, the Indian religion that rejects violence to all living creatures, including insects.

the voyages of self-discovery upon which so many in our society are now launched. Here is a desperate desire for wholeness, for an escape from the difficult and cold avenues of rational discovery. One futurist advises his audience to perceive the future with one's whole being, without intellectualizing and theorizing. The objective is to be both personal and social, yet dominated by personal feelings. The method seems most useful to individuals, or small, intimate groups of sharers. A population infected with such ideas is likely to save its individual souls and lose the world.

What Intellectuals Might Offer

We need to discover a more satisfactory and coherent basis for a doctrine that most rational persons can accept as a provisional guide for the future of mankind in this country and in the world or as a basis for progress toward more satisfactory answers in future generations. It must be a doctrine that offers a positive role to intellectuals, increasing their potential contribution to society without placing them in positions of inappropriate control. In this pursuit, failure awaits those who would abandon rationality and science. Practically, nonrationality results in untold suffering. Intellectually, it is dangerous to try to believe what one cannot believe. Nor can such a guiding doctrine be based on the currently fashionable theorizing about man or society. The scientific basis must be a theory of man and society that has met tests of both science and intuition over generations and still gives signs of future productivity. The doctrine should also not be based on beliefs about human values that deny large areas of what the best minds of the past have regarded as important possibilities or limitations, or that are so regarded by broad segments of the general populace. The past should broaden our human concern, but the details of our beliefs about those concerns cannot be based on what is past. The doctrine must be one that is generally acceptable to the best minds of the age. It must at the same time be conducive to quick and easy presentation to the normally intelligent and educated person (in America, the person with the equivalent of a college education) and have relevance to his problems. It must not only sell; it must be what I want for myself and humanity for as far as I can see.

By theory and example, the construction of this doctrine is a critical intellectual task for the next generation. If, in Sorokin's (1941) terms, the resolution of the crisis is to lead into an idealistic age, then we must develop a rational and humane idealism for that age.

The reader should carefully note that I have not attempted in this appendix to prove that a crisis exists or to sketch its real dimensions. To the doubting and to the optimists, offering such proof would be impossible. But I have tried to offer enough opinion and evidence to suggest the dimensions of the problem as many see it. Surely, there is a mythopoeic strain in the evidence, the hyperbole of Armageddon. Yet it is surely true that this myth represents the fact that for millions of people a crisis of meaning and understanding exists. Even if the crisis is not unique to our time, and even if failure to resolve it will not bring down civilization, the existence of the crisis in the minds of so many justifies serious attention.

The reader should also note that I have not tried to prove that the intellectual crisis is more important than others that worry our generation, such as the threat of nuclear destruction, famine, or resource depletion. Addressing these is beyond the scope attempted here. Yet clearly I feel that if we are to handle these other, more material problems satisfactorily, we must first deal with the spiritual crisis that besets so many of us.

References

ACKOFF, R., AND EMERY, F. *On Purposeful Systems.* Chicago: Aldine, 1972.

ADAMS, C. F. (Ed.) *Letters of John Adams Addressed to His Wife.* St. Clair Shores, Mich.: Scholarly Press, 1976. (Originally published 1841.)

ADELSON, J. "Psychological Research on a Profound Issue." *Science,* 1975, *4221,* 1288–1289.

AFL/CIO Free Trade Union News. "Andrei Sakharov Attacks Injustices, Lack of Freedom in the U.S.S.R." 1973, *28*(8), 4–5.

ALLAND, A., JR., AND MC KAY, B. "The Concept of Adaptation in Biological and Cultural Evolution." In J. Honigmann (Ed.), *Handbook of Social and Cultural Anthropology.* Chicago: Rand McNally, 1973.

ALLEN, F. R. *Socio-cultural Dynamics.* New York: Macmillan, 1971.

ALLISON, G. *Essence of Decision.* Boston: Little, Brown, 1971.

ALLPORT, G. *Personality: A Psychological Interpretation.* New York: Holt, Rinehart and Winston, 1937.

ALLWORTH, E. (Ed.) *The Nationality Question in Central Asia.* New York: Praeger, 1973.

ALMOND, G., AND VERBA, S. *Civic Culture.* Princeton: N.J.: Princeton University Press, 1963.

AMERICAN FRIENDS SERVICE COMMITTEE. *Uncommon Controversy: Fishing Rights of the Muckleshoot, Puyallup, and Nisqually Indians.* Seattle: University of Washington Press, 1970.

287

APPELBAUM, R. *Theories of Social Change.* Chicago: Markham, 1970.

ARGYRIS, C. *Integrating the Individual and the Organization.* New York: Wiley, 1964.

BAKER, R., AND ELLISTON, F. (Eds.) *Philosophy and Sex.* Buffalo, N.Y.: Prometheus Books, 1975.

BANFIELD, E. C. *The Moral Basis of a Backward Society.* Glencoe, Ill.: Free Press, 1958.

BARCLAY, W. *Ethics in a Permissive Society.* London: Collins, 1971.

BARNETT, H. *Innovation: The Basis of Cultural Change.* New York: McGraw-Hill, 1953.

BARRY, B. "John Rawls and the Priority of Liberty." *Philosophy and Public Affairs,* 1973, *2*(3), 274-290.

BATCHELDER, R. C. *The Irreversible Decision: 1930-1950.* Boston: Houghton Mifflin, 1961.

BAYLES, M. D. "Marriage, Love, and Procreation." In R. Baker and F. Elliston (Eds.), *Philosophy and Sex.* Buffalo, N.Y.: Prometheus Books, 1975.

BELL, D. "Toward the Great Instauration: Reflections on Culture and Religion in a Postindustrial Age." *Social Research,* 1975, *42,* 381-413.

BENNETT, C., AND LUMSDAINE, A. (Eds.) *Evaluation and Experiment.* New York: Academic Press, 1975.

BERELSON, B., AND STEINER, G. *Human Behavior: An Inventory of Scientific Findings.* New York: Harcourt Brace Jovanovich, 1964.

BERGER, P. *Pyramids of Sacrifice.* New York: Basic Books, 1974.

BERMANT, G. "Freedom and Determinism in Modern Psychology." Special report for Battelle Seattle Research Center, June 1970.

BERMANT, G. (Ed.), *Perspectives on Animal Behavior.* Glenview, Ill.: Scott, Foresman, 1973.

BERMANT, G., AND BROWN, P. *Evaluating Forensic Social Science Approaches to Problem Solving.* Columbus, Ohio: Academy for Contemporary Problems, 1976.

BERNDT, R., AND BERNDT, C. *Sexual Behavior in Western Arnhem Land.* Viking Fund Publications in Anthropology, No. 16. New York, 1951.

BLAU, P. *Exchange and Power in Social Life.* New York: Wiley, 1964.

BLOOMFIELD, L. *Language.* New York: Holt, Rinehart and Winston, 1933.

BLUMER, H. "Social Problems as Collective Behavior." *Social Problems,* 1971, *18,* 298-306.

BRACKER, M. "Warren Favors Profession to Give Advice on Ethics." *New York Times,* Nov. 12, 1962, p. 1.

BRADLEY, F. H. *Ethical Studies.* (2nd ed.) Oxford: Oxford University Press, 1927.

BRINTON, C. *The Anatomy of Revolution.* New York: Random House, 1965.

BRITTON, K. *Philosophy and the Meaning of Life.* Cambridge: Cambridge University Press, 1969.

BROWN, E. *A Literary History of Persia.* Vol. 1. Cambridge: Cambridge University Press, 1951.

BROWN, T. "Missile Accuracy and Strategic Lethality." *Survival,* 1976, *18*(2), 52–59.

BUGENTAL, J. F. T. *Challenges of Humanistic Psychology.* New York: McGraw-Hill, 1967.

BUHLER, C. "Human Life as a Whole as a Central Subject of Humanistic Psychology." In J. F. T. Bugental (Ed.), *Challenges of Humanistic Psychology.* New York: McGraw-Hill, 1967.

BUNZEL, J. *Anti-Politics in America.* New York: Knopf, 1967.

BURKE, E. *Works VII.* London: George Bell, 1885.

BURNS, A. L. "Ethics and Deterrence: Nuclear Policy Without Hostage Cities?" Adelphi Paper No. 69. London: International Institute for Strategic Studies, 1970.

BUTTINGER, J. *Vietnam: A Dragon Embattled.* New York: Praeger, 1967.

CAMPBELL, A. "Aspiration, Satisfaction, and Fulfillment." In A. Campbell and P. Converse (Eds.), *The Human Meaning of Social Change.* New York: Russell Sage, 1972.

CAMPBELL, A., CONVERSE, P., AND RODGERS, W. *The Quality of American Life.* New York: Russell Sage, 1976.

CANTWELL, R., *The Hidden Northwest.* Philadelphia: Lippincott, 1972.

CAUDILL, H. *Night Comes to the Cumberlands.* Boston: Little, Brown, 1962.

CHAGNON, N. "Yanomamo Social Organization and Warfare." In M. Fried, M. Harris, and R. Murphy (Eds.), *War: The Anthropology of Armed Conflict and Aggression.* Garden City, N.Y.: Natural History Press, 1967.

CHOMSKY, N. *Language and Mind.* New York: Harcourt Brace Jovanovich, 1972.

CHOPTIANY, L. "A Critique of John Rawls' Principle of Justice." *Ethics,* 1973, *83*(2), 146–150.

CHRISTENSEN, A. *L'Iran sous les Sassanides.* Copenhagen: Munksgaard, 1944.

CHURCHMAN, C. W. *Prediction and Optimal Decision.* Englewood Cliffs, N.J.: Prentice-Hall, 1961.

CICOUREL, A. *Method and Measurement in Sociology.* New York: Free Press, 1964.

CLECKLEY, H. "Psychopathic Personality." In D. Sills (Ed.), *International Encyclopedia of the Social Sciences.* Vol. 13. New York: Macmillan, 1968.

COBBAN, A. *National Self-Determination.* London: Oxford University Press, 1945.

COHN, E. *The Pacific Northwest and the Location Theory.* New York: King's Crown Press, 1954.

COHN, N. *The Pursuit of the Millenium.* (Rev. ed.) New York: Oxford University Press, 1970.

COLDEN, C. *The History of the Five Nations*. Ithaca, N.Y.: Cornell University Press, 1958.

COLSON, E. *The Makah Indians*. Minneapolis: University of Minnesota Press, 1953.

CONNOR, W., "Self-Determination: The New Phase." *World Politics*, 1967, *20*, 30–53.

DAHL, R. *After the Revolution*. New Haven, Conn.: Yale University Press, 1970.

DAHL, R. *Polyarchy*. New Haven, Conn.: Yale University Press, 1971.

DAHRENDORF, R. *Class and Conflict in Industrial Society*. Stanford, Calif.: Stanford University Press, 1959.

DAVIES, J. "Political Stability and Instability: Some Manifestations and Causes." *Journal of Conflict Resolution*, 1969, *13*, 1–17.

DE JOUVENAL, B. *The Ethics of Redistribution*. Cambridge, Mass.: Harvard University Press, 1951.

DEVLIN, P. *Too Proud to Fight: Woodrow Wilson's Neutrality*. London: Oxford University Press, 1975.

DE WOLF, R. "Myths of American Marriage." *Nation*, 1973, *216*(17), 527–529.

DIERKES, M. *Die Sozialbilanz*. Frankfurt: Herder, 1974.

DIGBY, J. "Precision-Guided Weapons." Adelphi Paper No. 118. London: International Institute for Strategic Studies, 1975.

DI PALMA, G., AND MC CLOSKY, H. "Personality and Conformity: The Learning of Political Attitudes." *American Political Science Review*, 1970, *64* (4), 1054–1073.

DORJAHN, V. "Fertility, Polygyny, and Their Interrelations in Temne Society." *American Anthropologist*, 1958, *60*, 838–860.

DURANT, W., AND DURANT, A. *The Lessons of History*. New York: Simon & Schuster, 1968.

DURKHEIM, E. *Suicide*. Translated by J. Spaulding and G. Simpson. Glencoe, Ill.: Free Press, 1958.

DWORKIN, G. (Ed.) *Determinism, Free Will, and Moral Responsibility*. Englewood Cliffs, N.J.: Prentice-Hall, 1970.

DYK, W. *Son of Old Man Hat*. New York: Harcourt Brace Jovanovich, 1938.

EHRLICH, I. "Participation in Illegitimate Activities: A Theoretical Empirical Investigation." *Journal of Political Economy*, 1973, *81*, 521–565.

EKVALL, R. "The Nomadic Pattern of Living Among the Tibetans as Preparation for War." *American Anthropologist*, 1961, *63*, 1250–1263.

ELAZAR, D. *Cities of the Prairie*. New York: Basic Books, 1970.

ELAZAR, D. *American Federalism*. (2nd ed.) New York: Crowell, 1972.

ELBING, A. O., AND ELBING, C. J. *The Value Issue of Business*. New York: McGraw-Hill, 1967.

ELLISTON, F. "In Defense of Promiscuity." In R. Baker and F. Elliston (Eds.), *Philosophy and Sex*. Buffalo, N.Y.: Prometheus Books, 1975.

EMERSON, R. *From Empire to Nation*. Cambridge, Mass.: Harvard University Press, 1960.

EMMET, D. *Rules, Roles and Relations.* New York: St. Martin's Press, 1966.

EPSTEIN, J. *Divorced in America: Marriage in an Age of Possibility.* New York: Dutton, 1974.

ETZIONI, A. *The Active Society.* New York: Free Press, 1968.

FAHEY, J. *The Flathead Indians.* Norman: University of Oklahoma Press, 1974.

FAIR, C. *The New Nonsense: The End of the Rational Consensus.* New York: Simon & Schuster, 1974.

FARBER, B. *Kinship and Class: A Midwestern Study.* New York: Basic Books, 1971.

FERMAN, L., KORNBLUH, J., AND HABER, A. (Eds.) *Poverty in America.* Ann Arbor: University of Michigan Press, 1965.

FESTINGER, L. *A Theory of Cognitive Dissonance.* New York: Harper & Row, 1957.

FINGARETTE, H. "Some Moral Aspects of Good Samaritanship." In J. M. Ratcliffe (Ed.), *The Good Samaritan and the Law.* Garden City, N.Y.: Doubleday, 1966.

FIRDOWSI, A. *The Shahnameh of Firdowsi.* Teheran: Khavar, 1931.

FLETCHER, J. *Situation Ethics.* Philadelphia: Westminster Press, 1966.

Fortune. "Fortune Directory of the 500 Largest U.S. Industrial Corporations." 1976, *93*(5), 316–338.

FRANKLAND, N. *Bomber Offensive: The Devastation of Europe.* New York: Ballantine, 1970.

FREESE, L. "Cumulative Sociological Knowledge." *American Sociological Review,* 1972, 37, 472–482.

FREUND, J. *The Sociology of Max Weber.* New York: Pantheon, 1968.

FRIEDRICHS, R. *A Sociology of Sociology.* New York: Free Press, 1970.

FRITZ, C. E. "Disaster." In R. K. Merton and R. A. Nisbet (Eds.), *Contemporary Social Problems.* New York: Harcourt Brace Jovanovich, 1961.

FULLINWIDER, R. "War and Innocence." *Philosophy and Public Affairs,* 1975, 5(1), 90–97.

GARDĪZĪ, A. S. *Ta'rīkh-e-Gardīzī.* Teheran, 1948.

GARFINKEL, H. *Studies in Ethnomethodology.* Englewood Cliffs, N.J.: Prentice-Hall, 1967.

GASTIL, R. D. "The Determinants of Human Behavior." *American Anthropologist,* 1961, *63,* 1281–1291.

GASTIL, R. D. "Civil Defense and Missile Defense." In J. Holst and W. Schneider (Eds.), *Why ABM?* New York: Pergamon Press, 1969a.

GASTIL, R. D. "Missile Defense and Strategic Doctrine." In J. Holst and W. Schneider (Eds.), *Why ABM?* New York: Pergamon Press, 1969b.

GASTIL, R. D. "Homicide and Regional Culture of Violence." *American Sociological Review,* 1971a, *36,* 412–427.

GASTIL, R. D. " 'Selling Out' and the Sociology of Knowledge." *Policy Sciences,* 1971b, 2, 271–277.

GASTIL, R. D. "U.S. Support for Democracy in Poor Countries." *Freedom-at-Issue,* 1971c, *10,* 7–14.

GASTIL, R. D. "A General Framework for Social Science." *Policy Sciences,* 1972, *3,* 385–403.

GASTIL, R. D. "Lower-Class Behavior: Cultural and Biosocial." *Human Organization,* 1973a, *32*(4), 349–362.

GASTIL, R. D. "The Pacific Northwest as a Cultural Region." *Pacific Northwest Quarterly,* 1973b, *64,* 147–162.

GASTIL, R. D. "The New Criteria of Freedeom." *Freedom-at-Issue,* 1973c, *17,* 2.

GASTIL, R. D. "Social Humanities." *Policy Sciences,* 1974a, *5,* 1–14.

GASTIL, R. D. "A Survey of Freedom." *Worldview,* 1974b, *17*(9), 47–52.

GASTIL, R. D. "Beyond a Theory of Justice." *Ethics,* 1975a, *85*(3), 183–194.

GASTIL, R. D. *Cultural Regions of the United States.* Seattle: University of Washington Press, 1975b.

GASTIL, R. D. "Kuhn's 'The Logic of Social Systems': The Rational First Approximation as Social Science." *Policy Sciences,* 1975c, *6,* 467–479.

GASTIL, R. D. "The Moral Right of the Majority to Restrict Pornography and Obscenity through Law." *Ethics,* 1976a, *86*(3), 231–240.

GASTIL, R. D. "Social Humanities." Paper presented at the annual convention of the American Psychological Association. Washington, D.C., Sept. 6, 1976b.

GASTIL, R. D. "Societal Limits on Majority Rights." *Journal of Social Philosophy,* 1976c, *7*(1), 8–12.

GASTIL, R. D. "Consideration of the Social Impact of Fusion Power." Seattle, Wash.: Battelle Memorial Institute, 1976d.

GASTIL, R. D. "The Comparative Survey of Freedom-VII." *Freedom-at-Issue,* 1977, *39,* 5–17.

GAZAWAY, R. *The Longest Mile.* Garden City, N.Y.: Doubleday, 1969.

GEHLEN, A. *Moral und Hypermoral: Eine pluralistische Ethik.* Frankfurt: Athenäum, 1969.

GLICK, P. C., AND NORTON, A. J. "Perspectives on the Recent Upturn in Divorce and Remarriage." *Demography,* 1973, *10*(3), 301–314.

GOOCH, G. P. *English Democratic Ideas in the Seventeenth Century.* New York: Harper & Row, 1959. (Originally published 1898.)

GOODE, W. J. (Ed.) *The Contemporary American Family.* New York: Quadrangle/New York Times Book Co., 1971.

GOODE, W. J. "Individual and Corporate Responsibility in Family Life." *American Behavioral Scientist,* 1972, *15*(3), 421–443.

GORER, G. *Himalayan Village.* (2nd ed.) London: Nelson, 1967.

GOULDNER, A. *The Coming Crisis in Western Sociology.* New York: Basic Books, 1970.

GRAUBARD, S. R. *Kissinger.* New York: Norton, 1973.

GRIFFITH, T. *The Waist-High Culture.* New York: Harper & Row, 1959.

GWERTZMAN, B. "Kissinger's Role in Tapes Explained to Senate Panel." *New York Times,* Sept. 11, 1973a, p. 1.

GWERTZMAN, B. "U.S. Science Body Bids Soviet End Harrassment of Sakharov." *New York Times,* Sept. 10, 1973b, p. 1.

HADDAD, G. M. *Revolutions and Military Rule in the Middle East: The Northern Tier.* New York: Spiller, 1965.

HAMMER, R. *One Morning in the War.* New York: Coward-McCann, 1970.

HAMPSHIRE, S. *Freedom of the Individual.* New York: Harper & Row, 1965.

HARDIN, G. "The Cybernetics of Competition: A Biologist's View of Society." In W. Buckley (Ed.), *Modern Systems Research for the Behavioral Scientist.* Chicago: Aldine, 1968a.

HARDIN, G. "The Tragedy of the Commons." *Science,* 1968b, *162,* 1243–1248.

HARMAN, W. "Key Choices for the Next Two Decades." In *A Look at Business in 1990: A Summary of the White House Conference on the Industrial World Ahead.* Washington, D.C.: Goverment Printing Office, 1972.

HARRIS, J. "The White Knife Shoshoni of Nevada." In R. Linton (Ed.), *Acculturation in Seven American Indian Tribes.* New York: Appleton-Century, 1940.

HART, C. W. "The Sons of Turimpi." *American Anthropologist,* 1954, *56,* 242–261.

HART, C. W. M., AND PILLING, A. R. *The Tiwi of North Australia.* New York: Holt, Rinehart and Winston, 1960.

HEILBRONER, R. *The Great Ascent.* New York: Harper & Row, 1963.

HEILBRONER, R. *An Inquiry into the Human Prospect.* New York: Norton, 1974.

HEXTER, J. H. *The History Primer.* New York: Basic Books, 1971.

HIRSCHMAN, A. O. *Exit, Voice, and Loyalty: Responses to Decline in Firms, Organizations, and States.* Cambridge, Mass.: Harvard University Press, 1970.

HOFFER, E. *The Ordeal of Change.* New York: Harper & Row, 1963.

HOFFER, E. *The Temper of Our Time.* New York: Harper & Row, 1967.

HOLMBERG, A. *Nomads of the Long Bow: The Siriono of Eastern Bolivia.* Garden City, N.Y.: Doubleday, 1969.

HOLST, J., AND SCHNEIDER, W. (Eds.) *Why ABM?* New York: Pergamon Press, 1969.

HOLSTI, O., AND NORTH, R. "The History of Human Conflict." In E. McNeil (Ed.), *The Nature of Conflict.* Englewood Cliffs, N.J.: Prentice-Hall, 1965.

HOMANS, G. *Social Behavior: Its Elementary Forms.* New York: Harcourt Brace Jovanovich, 1961.

HONIGMANN, J. J. (Ed.) *Handbook of Social and Cultural Anthropology.* Chicago: Rand McNally, 1973.

HOOK, E. B. "Behavioral Implications of the Human XYY Genotype." *Science,* 1973, *179,* 139–150.

HORGAN, P. "The Abdication of the Artist." *Proceedings of the American Philosophical Society,* 1965, *109,* 267–271.

HORTON, P. "Normality—Toward a Meaningful Construct." *Comprehensive Psychiatry,* 1971, *12,* 54–56.

HOWE, I. *The Decline of the New.* New York: Harcourt Brace Jovanovich, 1963.

HUIZINGA, J. H. *Rousseau, the Self-Made Saint.* New York: Grossman, 1976.

HUNTFORD, R. *The New Totalitarians.* New York: Stein and Day, 1972.

HUNTINGTON, S. *Political Order in Changing Societies.* New Haven, Conn.: Yale University Press, 1968.

IBN KHALDUN. "Prolegomena." In C. Issawi (Ed.), *An Arab Philosophy of History.* London: Murray, 1950.

IKLÉ, F. *Every War Must End.* New York: Columbia University Press, 1971.

IKLÉ, F. "Can Nuclear Deterrence Last Out the Century?" *Foreign Affairs,* 1973, *51*(2), 267–285.

IONESCO, E. "Fragments of a Journal." In B. Porter (Ed.), *Philosophy: A Literary and Conceptual Approach.* New York: Harcourt Brace Jovanovich, 1974.

IRVING, D. *The Destruction of Dresden.* London: Kimbar, 1963.

JACKSON, H. "First Human Détente." *New York Times,* Sept. 9, 1973, sec. E., p. 17.

JANIS, J. L. *Air War and Emotional Stress.* New York: McGraw-Hill, 1958.

JENNESS, D. *People of the Twilight.* Chicago: University of Chicago Press, 1959.

JENSEN, A. "How Much Can We Boost IQ and Scholastic Achievement?" *Harvard Educational Review,* 1969, *39*(1), 1–123.

JERVIS, R. "Easy Choices." *Polity,* 1970, *3*, 118–125.

JERVIS, R. *Perception and Misperception in International Politics.* Princeton, N.J.: Princeton University Press, 1976.

JOHNSTONE, H., JR. "The Nature of Philosophical Controversy." *Journal of Philosophy,* 1954, *51*, 294–300.

JONES, E. E., AND HARRIS, V. A. "The Attribution of Attitudes." *Journal of Experimental Social Psychology,* 1967, *3*, 1–24.

JOSEPHY, A., JR. *The Nez Perce Indians and the Opening of the Northwest.* New Haven, Conn.: Yale University Press, 1965.

KAGAN, J., AND OTHERS. "How Much Can We Boost IQ and Scholastic Achievement?" *Harvard Educational Review,* 1969, *39*(2), 273–347.

KAHN, H. *On Thermonuclear War.* (2nd ed.) Princeton, N.J.: Princeton University Press, 1961.

KAHN, H., AND WIENER, A. J. *The Year 2000.* New York: Macmillan, 1967.

KAPLAN, A. "On the Strategy of Social Planning." *Policy Sciences,* 1974, *4*, 41–62.

KECSKEMETI, P. *Strategic Surrender.* Stanford, Calif.: Stanford University Press, 1958.

KENNEDY, J. F. *Profiles in Courage.* New York: Harper & Row, 1955.

KEY, V. O. *The Responsible Electorate: Rationality in Presidential Voting 1936–1960.* Cambridge, Mass.: Harvard University Press, 1966.

KING, H. *The Box Man: A Professional Thief's Journey.* New York: Harper & Row, 1972.

KISSINGER, H. *The Necessity for Choice.* New York: Harper & Row, 1961.

KIZER, C. "Amusing Our Daughters." In R. S. Kelton (Ed.), *Five Poets of the Pacific Northwest.* Seattle: University of Washington Press, 1964.

KLUCKHOHN, C. "Universal Categories of Culture." In A. L. Kroeber (Ed.), *Anthropology Today*. Chicago: University of Chicago Press, 1953.

KLUCKHOHN, C., AND LEIGHTON, D. *The Navaho*. Cambridge, Mass.: Harvard University Press, 1946.

KNORR, K., AND READ, T. (Eds.) *Limited Strategic War*. New York: Praeger, 1962.

KOESTLER, A. *The Ghost in the Machine*. New York: Macmillan, 1967.

KOHLBERG, L. "A Cognitive Developmental Approach to Moral Education." *Humanist*, 1972, *32*, 13=16.

KOHLBERG, L., AND MAYER, R. "Development as the Aim of Education." *Harvard Educational Review*, 1972, *42*(11), 449–496.

KRAMER, H. "Where Are Today's Masters—and Tomorrow's?" *New York Times*, Aug. 29, 1976, sec. 2, p. 1.

KRISTOL, I. *On the Democratic Idea in America*. New York: Harper & Row, 1972a.

KRISTOL, I. "About Equality." *Commentary*, 1972b, *54*(5), 41–47.

KROEBER, A. L. *Cultural and Natural Areas of Native North America*. Vol. 38. Berkeley: University of California Publications in American Archaeology and Ethnography, 1939.

KROEBER, A. L., AND KLUCKHOHN, C. *Culture: A Critical Review of Concepts and Definitions*. Cambridge, Mass.: Peabody Museum, 1952.

KUHN, A. *The Logic of Social Systems: A Unified, Deductive, System-Based Approach to Social Science*. San Francisco: Jossey-Bass, 1974.

LEIGHTON, A. *My Name Is Legion*. New York: Basic Books, 1959.

LEONARD, J. "It May Not Be High Culture, But It Can Be Brilliant." *New York Times*, Aug. 29, 1976, sec. 2, p. 1.

LESLIE, G. *The Family in Social Context*. New York: Oxford University Press, 1967.

LEVINE, L. "Some Psychological Prerequisites for Peace." In J. F. T. Bugental (Ed.), *Challenges of Humanistic Psychology*. New York: McGraw-Hill, 1967.

LEVY, R. *The Social Structure of Islam*. (2nd ed.) Cambridge: Cambridge University Press, 1957.

LEWIN, M., AND KANE, M. "Impeachment of Nixon and the Risky Shift." *International Journal of Group Tensions*, 1975, *5*(3), 171–176.

LINTON, R. *Acculturation in Seven American Indian Tribes*. New York: Appleton-Century-Crofts, 1940.

LIPSET, S. M., TROW, M. A., AND COLEMAN, J. S. *Union Democracy*. New York: Free Press, 1956.

LIU, BEN-CHIEH. *The Quality of Life in the United States*. Kansas City, Mo.: Midwest Research Institute, 1973.

LIVINGSTONE, F. "The Effects of Warfare on the Biology of the Human Species." In M. Fried, M. Harris, and R. Murphy (Eds.), *War: The Anthropology of Armed Conflict and Aggression*. Garden City, N.Y.: Natural History Press, 1967.

LOEHLIN, J. C., LINDZEY, G., AND SPUHLER, J. N. *Race Differences in Intelligence*. San Francisco: W. H. Freeman, 1975.

LOFTIN, C., AND HILL, R. "Regional Subculture and Homicide: An Examination of the Gastil-Hackney Hypothesis." *American Sociological Review*, 1974, *39*, 714–724.

LOGAN, C. "Arrest Rates and Deterrence." *Social Science Quarterly*, 1975, *56* (3), 376–389.

LOGAN, F., AND WAGNER, A. *Reward and Punishment*. Boston: Allyn & Bacon, 1965.

LOH, R. *Escape from Red China*. New York: Coward-McCann, 1962.

LUCAS, P. "Edmund Burke's Doctrine of Prescription." *Historical Journal*, 1968, *11*(1), 35–63.

LUNDBERG, G. A. *Can Science Save Us?* London: Longmans, Green, 1947.

LURIE, N. "Menominee Termination: From Reservation to Colony." *Human Organization*, 1972, *31*(3), 257–270.

LURIE, N. "The Will-o'-the-Wisp of Indian Unity." *Indian Historian*, 1976, *9*, 19–24.

MC CLINTOCK, T. "Henderson Lewelling, Seth Lewelling and the Birth of the Pacific Coast Fruit Industry." *Oregon Historical Quarterly*, 1967a, *68*, 153–174.

MC CLINTOCK, T. "Seth Lewelling, William S. U'Ren and the Birth of the Oregon Progressive Movement." *Oregon Historical Quarterly*, 1967b, *68*, 197–220.

MACCOBY, E., AND JACKLIN, C. *The Psychology of Sex Differences*. Stanford, Calif.: Stanford University Press, 1974.

MC DONALD, D. *Against the American Grain*. New York: Random House, 1962.

MC MURTRY, J. "Monogamy: A Critique." In R. Baker and F. Elliston (Eds.), *Philosophy and Sex*. Buffalo, N.Y.: Prometheus Books, 1975.

MADDOX, B. "Neither Witch nor Good Fairy." *New York Times Magazine*, April 8, 1976, p. 16.

MAGRUDER, J. S. *An American Life: One Man's Road to Watergate*. New York: Atheneum, 1974.

MANIS, J. "The Concept of Social Problems: Vox Populi and Sociological Analysis." *Social Problems*, 1974, *21*, 305–315.

MARGULIES, R. Z., AND BLAU, P. M. "America's Leading Professional Schools." *Change*, Nov. 5, 1973, pp. 21–27.

MARNELL, W. *The Good Life of Western Man*. New York: Herder and Herder, 1971.

MASLOW, A. *Motivation and Personality*. New York: Harper & Row, 1954.

MATTHIESSEN, P. *Under the Mountain Wall*. New York: Viking Press, 1962.

MAVRODES, G. "Conventions and the Morality of War." *Philosophy and Public Affairs*, 1975, *4*(2), 117–131.

MEAD, M. "Alternatives to War." In M. Fried, M. Harris, and R. Murphy (Eds.), *War: The Anthropology of Armed Conflict and Aggression*. Garden City, N.Y.: Natural History Press, 1967.

MELDEN, A. I. *Rights and Right Conduct*. Oxford: Blackwell, 1959.

MERIAM, L. *The Problem of Indian Administration*. Washington, D.C.: Brookings Institution, 1928.

MILL, J. S. "Representative Government." In *Utilitarianism, Liberty, and Representative Government*. New York: Dutton, 1951.

MILLER, W. B. "Subculture, Social Reform and the Culture of Poverty." *Human Organization*, 1971, *30*(2), 111-125.

MILLS, C. W. *The Power Elite*. New York: Oxford University Press, 1956.

MITROFF, I. *The Subjective Side of Science*. Amsterdam: Elsevier, 1974.

MOLNAR, T. "Zur Gesellschaft der Zukunft." *Schweizer Monatshefte*, 1974, *54* (2), 97-104.

MONOD, J. *Chance and Necessity*. New York: Knopf, 1971.

MOORE, G. E. *Principia Ethica*. Cambridge: Cambridge University Press, 1903.

MOYNIHAN, D. P. *Maximum Feasible Misunderstanding*. New York: Free Press, 1969.

MURDOCK, G. P. *Social Structure*. New York: Macmillan, 1949.

MURPHY, J. M. "Psychiatric Labeling in Cross-Cultural Perspective." *Science*, 1976, *191*, 1019-1027.

MUSIL, R. *The Man Without Qualities*. New York: Coward-McCann, 1953.

NAGEL, T. "War and Massacre." In M. Cohen, T. Nagel, and T. Scanlon (Eds.), *War and Moral Responsibility*. Princeton, N.J.: Princeton University Press, 1974.

NATIONAL MERIT SCHOLARSHIP CORPORATION. *Annual Report 1970*. Evanston, Ill.

NATIONAL MERIT SCHOLARSHIP CORPORATION. *Semi-Finalist Booklet 1970-71*. Evanston, Ill.

NATIONAL RESEARCH COUNCIL/NATIONAL ACADEMY OF SCIENCES. *Long-Term Worldwide Effects of Multiple Nuclear Weapons Detonation*. Washington, D.C., 1975.

NEWHOUSE, J. *Cold Dawn: The Story of SALT*. New York: Holt, Rinehart and Winston, 1973.

New York Times. "Sakharov Warns on Dealing with Soviet." Aug. 22, 1973, p. 3.

NISBET, R. *Social Change and History*. New York: Oxford University Press, 1969.

NITZE, P. "Assuring Strategic Stability in an Era of Detente." *Foreign Affairs*, 1976, *54*(2), 207-232.

NORMAN, D. A. (Ed.) *Models of Human Memory*. New York: Academic Press, 1970.

NOVE, A. "Is There a Ruling Class in the U.S.S.R.?" *Soviet Studies*, 1975, *27* (4), 615-638.

NOZICK, R. *Anarchy, State, and Utopia*. New York: Basic Books, 1974.

NUTTIN, J., AND GREENWALD, A. *Reward and Punishment in Human Learning*. New York: Academic Press, 1968.

OBERDIECK, H. "A Theory of Justice." *New York University Law Review*, 1972, *47*(5), 1012-1028.

O'CONNELL, D. P. *International Law*. (2nd ed.) London: Stevens, 1970.

ODEN, T. "A Populist's View of Psychotherapeutic Deprofessionalization." *Journal of Humanistic Psychology*, 1974, *14*(2), 3–18.

OLSON, M., JR. "Rapid Growth as a Destabilizing Factor." *Journal of Economic History*, 1963, *23*(4), 529–558.

OLSON, M., JR. *The Logic of Collective Action: Public Goods and the Theory of Groups*. Cambridge, Mass.: Harvard University Press, 1965.

OSGOOD, R. E., AND TUCKER, R. W. *Force, Order, and Justice*. Baltimore: Johns Hopkins University Press, 1967.

OTTERBEIN, K. F. *The Evolution of War: A Cross-Cultural Study*. New Haven, Conn.: Human Relations Area File Press, 1970.

OTTERBEIN, K. F. "The Anthropology of War." In J. Honigmann (Ed.), *Handbook of Social and Cultural Anthropology*. Chicago: Rand McNally, 1973.

PACKENHAM, R. *Liberal America and the Third World*. Princeton, N.J.: Princeton University Press, 1973.

PADDOCK W., AND PADDOCK, P. *Hungry Nations*. Boston: Little, Brown, 1964.

PALMER, D. "The Consolation of the Wedded." In R. Baker and F. Elliston (Eds.), *Philosophy and Sex*. Buffalo, N.Y.: Prometheus Books, 1975.

PEARS, D. F. *Freedom and the Will*. London: Macmillan, 1963.

PECKMAN, J., AND TIMPANE, P. M. (Eds.) *Work Incentives and Income Guarantees*. Washington, D.C.: Brookings Institution, 1975.

PLESSNER, H. *Conditio Humana*. Pfüllingen, Federal Republic of Germany: Günther Neske, 1964.

POLAK, F. *The Images of the Future*. New York: American Elsevier, 1973.

POPE PAUL VI. *"Humanae Vitae."* In R. Baker and F. Elliston (Eds.), *Philosophy and Sex*. Buffalo, N.Y.: Prometheus Books, 1975.

POSTAL, P. "The Method of Universal Grammar." In P. Garvin (Ed.), *Method and Theory in Linguistics*. The Hague: Mouton, 1970.

POWERS, W. T. "Feedback: Beyond Behaviorism." *Science*, 1973, *179*, 351–356.

PURTILL, R. L. "On the Just War." In T. Beauchamp (Ed.), *Ethics and Public Policy*. Englewood Cliffs, N.J.: Prentice-Hall, 1975.

QUESTER, G. H. *Deterrence Before Hiroshima*. New York: Wiley, 1966.

RADIN, P. *Crashing Thunder: The Autobiography of an American Indian*. New York: Appleton-Century-Crofts, 1926.

RADIN, P. *The World of Primitive Man*. New York: Shuman, 1955.

RADIN, P. *Primitive Religion*. New York: Dover, 1957.

RAMEY, J. "Intimate Groups and Networks: Frequent Consequences of Sexually Open Marriage." *Family Coordinator*, 1975, *24*(4), 515–530.

RAMSEY, P. *Basic Christian Ethics*. New York: Scribner's, 1950.

RAMSEY, P. *The Just War: Force and Political Responsibility*. New York: Scribner's, 1968.

RASMUSSEN, K. "The Netsilik Eskimos." In C. Coon (Ed.), *A Reader in General Anthropology*. New York: Holt, Rinehart and Winston, 1948.

RAWLS, J. *A Theory of Justice.* Cambridge, Mass.: Harvard University Press, 1971.

RAYMOND, S. "State Sued in Second Phase of Fishing Dispute." *Seattle Times,* Sept. 12, 1976, sec. H, p. 11.

RICKMAN, H. P. *Meaning in History.* London: Allen & Irwin, 1961.

RIESMAN, D. *The Lonely Crowd.* New Haven, Conn.: Yale University Press, 1950.

RIESMAN, D. *Faces in the Crowd: Individual Studies in Character and Politics.* New Haven, Conn.: Yale University Press, 1952.

RIMM, D., AND MASTERS, J. *Behavior Therapy: Techniques and Findings.* New York: Academic Press, 1974.

ROGERS, C. *Client-Centered Therapy.* New York: Houghton Mifflin, 1951.

ROOSE, K., AND ANDERSEN, C. "A Rating of Graduate Programs." Washington, D.C.: American Council on Education, 1970.

ROSENBERG, A. *Der Mythus des Zwanzigsten Jahrhunderts.* Munich: Hoheneichen, 1930.

ROSENCRANCE, R. "Strategic Deterrence Reconsidered." Adelphi Paper No. 116. London: International Institute for Strategic Studies, 1975.

RUBIN, J., AND BROWN, B. *The Social Psychology of Bargaining and Negotiation.* New York: Academic Press, 1975.

RUSSETT, B. "Counter-Combatant Deterrence: A Proposal." *Survival,* 1974, *16* (3), 135–140.

SAMUELSON, P. *Economics.* (6th ed.) New York: McGraw-Hill, 1969.

SANTROCK, J. "Moral Structure: The Interrelations of Moral Behavior, Moral Judgment, and Moral Affects." *Journal of Genetic Psychology,* 1975, *127,* 201–213.

SAPIR, E. "The Heuristic Value of Rhyme." In D. Mandelbaum (Ed.), *Selected Writings of Edward Sapir in Language, Culture, and Personality.* Berkeley: University of California Press, 1949.

SAUR, K. *Publishers International Directory.* (4th ed.) New York: Bowker, 1969.

SCANLON, T., JR. "Rawls' Theory of Justice." *University of Pennsylvania Law Review,* 1973, *121,* 1029–1069.

SCHAEFFER, F. *Escape from Reason.* Downer's Grove, Ill: Intervarsity Press, 1968.

SCHUMPETER, J. *Capitalism, Socialism and Democracy.* (3rd ed.) New York: Harper & Row, 1950.

SCHWARTZ, A. "Moral Neutrality and Primary Goods." *Ethics,* 1973, *83*(4), 298–307.

SCHWEITZER, A. *Kultur und Ethik.* Munich: Beck, 1923.

SERVICE, E. R. "War and Our Contemporary Ancestors." In M. Fried, M. Harris, and R. Murphy (Eds.), *War: The Anthropology of Armed Conflict and Aggression.* Garden City, N.Y.: Natural History Press, 1967.

SHABAD, T. "Sakharov Accuses Soviet of Distorting His Views." *New York Times*, Sept. 9, 1973, sec. A, p. 3

SIMMONS, L. *Sun Chief*. New Haven, Conn.: Yale University Press, 1942.

SINGER, M. *Generalization in Ethics*. New York: Knopf, 1961.

SINGER, P. "Famine, Affluence and Morality." *Philosophy and Public Affairs*, 1973, 2(2), 229–243.

SKINNER, B. F. *Walden Two*. New York: Macmillan, 1960.

SKINNER, B. F. *Beyond Freedom and Dignity*. New York: Knopf, 1971.

SKOLNICK, J. *The Politics of Protest*. New York: Simon & Schuster, 1969.

SMELSER, N. *Theory of Collective Behavior*. New York: Free Press, 1962.

SMELSER, N. "The Social Dimensions of Nuclear Attack." In S. D. Vestermark (Ed.), *Vulnerabilities of Social Structure*. McLean, Va.: Human Sciences Research, 1966.

SMITH, D. M. *The Geography of Social Well-Being in the United States*. New York: McGraw-Hill, 1973.

SMITH, M. "The Puyallups of Washington." In R. Linton, *Acculturation in Seven American Indian Tribes*. New York: Appleton-Century-Crofts, 1940.

SMITH, P. *The Historian and History*. New York: Knopf, 1964.

SOLZHENITSYN, A. I. "Peace and Violence." *New York Times*, Sept. 15, 1973, sec. L, p. 31.

SORELL, W. *The Swiss*. New York: Bobbs-Merrill, 1972.

SOROKIN, P. A. *Social and Cultural Dynamics*. 4 vols. New York: American Book Company, 1937–1941.

SOROKIN, P. A. *The Crisis of Our Age*. New York: Dutton, 1941.

SOROKIN, P. A. *Sociocultural Causality, Space, Time*. Durham, N.C.: Duke University Press, 1943.

SOROKIN, P. A. *Society, Culture and Personality*. New York: Harper & Row, 1947.

SOROKIN, P. A. *Social Philosophies in an Age of Crisis*. Boston: Beacon Press, 1950.

SPENCER, B., AND GILLEN, F. J. *Arunta: A Study of a Stone Age People*. New York: Humanities Press, 1966. (Originally published 1927.)

SPENCER, R., JENNINGS, J. D., AND OTHERS. *The Native Americans*. New York: Harper & Row, 1965.

SPICER, E. H. *Perspectives in American Indian Culture Change*. Chicago: University of Chicago Press, 1961.

STARR, K. *Americans and the California Dream, 1850–1915*. New York: Oxford University Press, 1973.

STEFFENS, L. *The Upbuilders*. Seattle: University of Washington Press, 1968. (Originally published 1909.)

STEGNER, R. "The Psychology of Human Conflict." In E. McNeil (Ed.), *The Nature of Conflict*. Englewood Cliffs, N.J.: Prentice-Hall, 1965.

STEINER, G. *Business and Society*. New York: Random House, 1971.

STERN, T. *The Klamath Tribe*. Seattle: University of Washington Press, 1965.

SUREDA, A. R. *The Evolution of the Right of Self-Determination: A Study of United Nations Practice.* Leiden, The Netherlands: Sijthoff, 1973.

SWAN, J. *The Northwest Coast.* New York: Harper & Row, 1857.

TASK FORCE OF THE PRESIDENTIAL ADVISORY GROUP ON ANTICIPATED ADVANCES IN SCIENCE AND TECHNOLOGY. "The Science Court Experiment: An Interim Report." *Science,* 1976, *193,* 653–656.

TAYLOR, A. J. P. *The Origins of the Second World War.* Greenwich, Conn.: Fawcett, 1961.

TAYLOR, H. C., JR. "Aboriginal Populations of the Lower Columbia." *Pacific Northwest Quarterly,* 1963, *54*(4), 158–165.

THIBAUT, J., AND WALKER, L. *Procedural Justice.* Hilldale, N.J.: Erlbaum, 1975.

THOMAS, H. "An Existential Attitude in Working with Individuals and Groups." In J. F. T. Bugental (Ed.), *Challenges of Humanistic Psychology.* New York: McGraw-Hill, 1967.

TIGER, L., AND SEPHAR, J. *Women in the Kibbutz.* New York: Harcourt Brace Jovanovich, 1975.

TRIBE, L. "Policy Science: Analysis or Ideology?" *Philosophy and Public Affairs,* 1972, *2*(1), 66–110.

TROSPER, R. "Native American Boundary Maintenance: The Flathead Indian Reservation, Montana, 1860–1970." *Ethnicity,* 1976, *3,* 256–274.

TULLOCK, G. "Does Punishment Deter Crime?" *Public Interest,* 1974, *36,* 103–111.

TURNEY-HIGH, H. H. *Primitive War: Its Practice and Concepts.* (2nd ed.) Columbia: University of South Carolina Press, 1971.

TYLER, L. *Psychology of Human Differences.* (3rd ed.) New York: Appleton-Century-Crofts, 1965.

TYLER, L. *Individual Differences.* New York: Appleton-Century-Crofts, 1974.

ULICH, R. *The Human Career: A Philosophy of Self-Transcendence.* New York: Harper & Row, 1955.

UNGAR, R. *Law in Modern Society: Toward a Criticism of Social Theory.* New York: Free Press, 1976.

U.S. DEPARTMENT OF COMMERCE. *Statistical Abstract of the United States, 1972.* Washington, D.C., 1973.

U.S. DEPARTMENT OF LABOR. "A Study of Successful Persons from Seriously Disadvantaged Backgrounds." Final report prepared for Office of Special Manpower Programs. Washington, D.C., March 31, 1970.

VALENTINE, C. A. *Culture and Poverty.* Chicago: University of Chicago Press, 1968.

VALERY, P. "The Persian Letters." In P. Valery (Ed.), *History and Politics.* New York: Bollinger Foundation, 1962.

VAN GENNEP, A. *The Rites of Passage.* Chicago: University of Chicago Press, 1960.

VICKERS, G. "The Concept of Stress in Relation to the Disorganization of Behavior." In W. Buckley (Ed.), *Modern Systems Research for the Behavioral Scientist.* Chicago: Aldine, 1968a.

VICKERS, G. "Is Adaptability Enough?" In W. Buckley (Ed.), *Modern Systems Research for the Behavioral Scientist*. Chicago: Aldine, 1968b.

WALLACE, A. *Culture and Personality*. New York: Random House, 1961.

WALSTER, E., BERSCHIED, E., AND WALSTER, G. "New Directions in Equity Research." *Journal of Personality and Social Psychology*, 1973, *25*(2), 151–176.

WALZER, M. "Political Action: The Problem of Dirty Hands." In R. B. Brandt and others (Eds.), *War and Moral Responsibility*. Princeton, N.J.: Princeton University Press, 1974a.

WALZER, M. "World War II: Why Was This War Different?" In R. B. Brandt and others (Eds.), *War and Moral Responsibility*. Princeton, N.J.: Princeton University Press, 1974b.

WASSERSTROM, R. "Is Adultery Immoral?" In R. Baker and F. Elliston (Eds.), *Philosophy and Sex*. Buffalo, N.Y.: Prometheus Books, 1975.

WEBER, M. *The Protestant Ethic and the Spirit of Capitalism*. New York: Scribner's, 1958.

WEIGL, H. *Lern dieses Volk der Hirten Kennen*. Zurich: Artemis, 1962.

WEINBERG, A. M. "Science and Trans-Science." *Minerva*, 1972, *10*, 209–222.

WELLS, D. "How Much Can 'The Just War' Justify?" In T. Beauchamp (Ed.), *Ethics and Public Policy*. Englewood Cliffs, N.J.: Prentice-Hall, 1975.

WENNER, M. "The Politics of Equality Among European Linguistic Minorities." In R. P. Claude (Ed.), *Comparative Human Rights*. Baltimore: Johns Hopkins University Press, 1976.

WILLIAMS, D. *Trousered Apes*. London: Churchill Press, 1971.

WILLIAMS, R. *Biochemical Individuality*. Austin: University of Texas Press, 1969.

WILSON, E. O. *Sociobiology: The New Synthesis*. Cambridge, Mass.: Harvard University Press, 1975.

WILSON, J. Q. *Thinking About Crime*. New York: Basic Books, 1975.

WINCH, P. *The Idea of a Social Science*. London: Routledge, 1958.

WITKIN, H. A., AND OTHERS. "Criminality in XYY and XXY Men." *Science*, 1976, *193*, 547–555.

WOLF, E. *Peasant Wars of the Twentieth Century*. New York: Harper & Row, 1969.

WOODWARD, R. "W. S. U'Ren and the Single Tax in Oregon." *Oregon Historical Quarterly*, 1960, *61*, 46–63.

WYNNE-EDWARDS, V. C. "Ecology and the Evaluation of Social Ethics." In J. W. S. Pringle (Ed.), *Biology and the Human Sciences*. Oxford: Oxford University Press, 1972.

ZIMAN, J. M. *Public Knowledge*. Cambridge: Cambridge University Press, 1968.

ZIPF, G. K. *Human Behavior and the Principle of Least Effort*. Cambridge, Mass.: Addison-Wesley, 1949.

ZOSIMUS. *Zosimus: Historia Nova*. San Antonio, Tex.: Trinity University Press, 1967.

Index

A

Aaland Islands, 209
Abnormality, definition of, 41
Aborigines, Australian, 152-155, 204
Acculturation, Indian/white, 199-204
Ackoff, R., and Emery, F., 6, 39
Action: control balanced with, 256-259; in humanistic framework, 111-112; as individual capacity, 30; responsibility and, 256
Adams, C. F., 122-123
Adams, J., 122-123
Adelson, J., 37
Adversary procedure, 19
Affiliation, rational source of, 53-55
AFL/CIO Free Trade Union News, 170
Aggression, sex differences in, 88-89
Alcohol, Indian use of, 200
Alcoholics Anonymous, 177
Alcoholism, humanistic analysis of, 177-178
Alland, A., and McKay, B., 12

Allen, F. R., 27
Allison, G., 87, 219, 233
Allport, G., 9, 48
Allworth, E., 204
Almond, G., and Verba, S., 133
Alter egos, 100-101, 250
Alter ideals, 85
Altruism, 89
American Friends Service Committee, 209n
Amish, 213, 215
Analysis, in humanistic evaluation, 176-178
Antiaristocracy, 282
Apache, White Mountain, 214
Appelbaum, R., 26
Aquinas, T., 275
Argyris, C., 163
Aristotle, 24, 42
Arts: in California, 158; crisis in the, 277-278; in Switzerland and the Northwest, 160-161
Arunta, 152-155
Ashland, Oregon, theatre in, 161